DRAMA WITH CHILDREN

DRAMA
WITH
CHILDREN

Geraldine Brain Siks

University of Washington

Harper & Row, Publishers
New York / Hagerstown / San Francisco / London

Sponsoring Editor: Larry Sifford
Project Editor: Richard T. Viggiano
Designer: Emily Harste
Production Supervisor: Kewal K. Sharma
Compositor: Maryland Linotype Composition Co., Inc.
Printer and Binder: Halliday Lithograph Corporation
Art Studio: Danmark & Michaels Inc.

DRAMA WITH CHILDREN

Library of Congress Cataloging in Publication Data

Siks, Geraldine Brain.
    Drama with children.

    Bibliography: p.
    Includes index.
        1. Drama in education.   I.   Title.
PN3171.S535   371.33'2   76-43301
ISBN 0-06-046151-9

*To all children,
my students, colleagues, teachers, friends, and
my family, especially Charlie.*

Contents

APPENDIXES

Foreword

Geraldine Brain Siks begins *Drama With Children* with the image of all children arriving at school naturally endowed with dramatic imagination, all capable of delighting and learning by "allowing the imprisoned glory to escape" (Browning) through meaningful dramatic action.

To emphasize the belief that every child is so endowed, she concludes her book with a poem by a teacher of handicapped children, who invites a deaf child to join in the drama. And why not? For as the poet/teacher points out to the child of silence (in Taras B. Denis's poem in Chapter 14):

rivers run,
insects crawl,
flowers climb,
snowflakes fall—
each
without a shout.

Geraldine Siks places drama at the core. of the school's language arts program, which is to say at the heart of education itself, and gives to the classroom teacher the tools that in skilled and loving hands could effect a simultaneous happening—the education of children *through* drama and *in* drama.

A significant new book in children's drama by a longtime friend and gifted teaching colleague is in itself an occasion for celebration. The 1977 publication date of *Drama with Children,* following so close upon the Bicentennial celebration, infuses its appearance with a special sense of occasion. The philosophy basic to this book is in tune with the spirit of 1776, underscoring as it does the dignity and value and creative powers of each human being and in particular the power of the dramatic imagination.

Our nation was founded on an image—the image of all men being equal in the sight of God and before the law, born with inalienable rights to life and freedom and the pursuit of happiness. A unique form of government was imagined and eventually brought into being to protect those human rights. That for 200 years the realities of our national life have not mirrored perfectly the ideal does not make any less valid the original image.

At the heart of realizing more fully that ideal is our capacity to imagine. What a powerful gift—imagining. In *Alexander Dogun's Story: An American in the Gulag*, Dogun describes his seven years and eight months in a Russian prison. Dragged from his black cell to be interrogated hourly, with little food as well as little sleep, he was saved from madness by his memory and his imagination. To keep vivid his dream of returning to America he would walk from one end of his cell to the other, counting each measured step as he imagined himself walking out of prison across Moscow, Poland, Germany, and France, on the floor of the Atlantic, to the United States. His dream became reality in 1971 when he arrived in New York.

To keep alive and channel this glorious imagination is the province of the arts. In drama children use their imaginations in very physical and active ways. As *playmakers*, they imagine characters in an action; as *players* they imagine themselves as characters interacting in an action in action; and as *audience* they enjoy and appreciate their own imagined action and that of others. It is an individual and a social *act*, as well as an individual and a social *art*.

Geraldine Siks examines the concepts and processes involved in each role: playmaker, player, audience. She draws upon her own long, continual experiences, explorings, and findings to present very practical ways the classroom teacher can master the art of guiding children in developing further their natural dramatic impulses and imaginations. In the process she answers one of her own questions: "How may a child's education help him to live his life in dignity with individual purpose and *joi de vivre?*"

She writes as she teaches, with skill and with love. Others who have been motivated by her teaching or by one of her many previous publications to explore the use of drama in special areas and with special children have also been invited to share their experiences in this book.

The author of *Drama With Children* modestly remarked on the eve of its publication that it is not a finished product but a work in progress. We might also say that of the revolution we celebrate this Bicentennial year; it too is a work in progress. Hurrah for works in progress!

AGNES HAAGA
Professor of Drama
University of Washington

Preface

Drama with Children grew out of my classes with college students, children, and teachers. It is intended to serve as a guide for those persons concerned with drama as an art in children's basic education.

This book should be of use to teachers and children's leaders in many ways. It may be referred to for information about drama processes, concepts, structure, goals, and learning experiences. It may be used as a handbook for quick reference for drama activities that can be used occasionally with children. The material, however, is organized to contribute to an understanding of the art of drama as it relates to child development and learning. The book presents a structured approach to drama as an art and provides a wide range of representative learning experiences for children.

Drama with Children is divided into three parts. Part 1 provides a philosophical basis for drama in education; examines the process-concept structural approach as it relates to child development; and investigates the teaching-learning process. Part 2 deals with teaching. It organizes the art of drama into its structural components: player, playmaker, and audience. It identifies elements, concepts, and goals for each component; and provides learning experiences for each of the goals. Part 3 includes the experiences of ten teachers and leaders in the field to illustrate the use of drama as a method of teaching and to show the extensive use of drama with all children. Included in the appendixes are a selective bibliography, three plays and a scenario for use with children, and suggestions for audiovisual and instructional materials.

This book also offers material help for graduate students doing research in drama as an art. The formulation of this structure of drama from a process-concept view is based on fifteen years of research and experimentation by myself and many others. It appears also that this approach will undergo further development.

The approach to drama described in *Drama with Children* grew out of two kinds of persistent questions. First were those posed by teachers and students who asked me what to do when children did not respond to the dramatization of stories and to procedures I had suggested in my book *Creative Dramatics: An Art for Children*. The other probing questions were asked over a decade ago by Jack Morrison and Irving Brown, who were then Consultants in Theatre and Dance, Arts and Humanities Branch, U.S. Office of Education. Their questions, addressed to the Children's Theatre Association of America (CTAA) of the American Theatre Association (ATA), asked whether drama was being taught as an art in childhood education.

These persistent questions led to a desire to investigate drama as an art in education in other countries. During the academic year 1965–1966, pursuant to a contract with the U.S. Office of Education, I researched the field in seventeen European countries. Through the assistance of Gerald Tyler in England, founder-chairman of ASSITEJ (international association of theatre for children and youth), I studied philosophies and procedures employed by Peter Slade, Brian Way, and other teachers of drama and movement throughout England. In Norway, Ingrid Bowman Björn-Hansen and Halfdan Skanland arranged visits to leading schools and theatre centers. In Sweden, Elsa Olenius, Founder of the Stockholm Childrens' and Youth Theatre assisted in my research. In Czechoslovakia, I observed the Jiri Wolker Theatre and consulted with Vladimir Adamek and Jana Milenova. Throughout the countries of Denmark, Belgium, France, Austria, West Germany, Spain, and Portugal I found fewer answers in my pursuit of how to include drama as an art in childhood education.

In 1967 two significant occasions occurred that influenced my thought. First was the International Conference on Theatre Education in Washington, D.C., sponsored by ATA. I participated as a delegate from the United States, and with delegates from twenty-four countries there too, the same persistent questions were pursued. Next, for six weeks that summer I was a member of a research task force of 25 artists and educators who worked at the Central Atlantic Regional Educational Laboratory at Airlie House, Warrenton, Virginia. The teams were charged with the task of investigating the basic processes and elements of the arts in order to write performance objectives for young children. In the drama team the questions took a sharper focus as researchers aimed to identify the basic processes and concepts of this art.

Hoping for a breakthrough in this inquiry, the Washington Association of Theatre Artists (WATA) selected a drama committee to work with the staff of the Curriculum and Instruction Division of the Office of State Superintendent of Public Instruction. The committee, chaired by

Gregory Falls, and of which I was a member, was charged to prepare criteria to improve and increase public school education in the art of drama in the state of Washington. During a three-year period the concept of a structural approach to drama evolved and resulted in the publication of *Drama Education Guidelines* in 1973.

This concept was further developed by a Washington State Drama Committee appointed in 1973 by Charles Blondino, State Supervisor of Language Arts, Office of the Superintendent of Public Instruction. Serving as a member of this committee with three classroom teachers and Mr. Blondino, I proceeded to identify concepts and goals and to write learning activities. This work resulted in the publication of *Spotlight on Drama: K-6* in May 1975.

A careful analysis and revision of committee developments were made. Research was continued by graduate students and with exploration in classes with children. Thus the approach evolved. The time had come for the idea to be put into a new book and to be explored, developed, tested, and refined.

In addition to all the persons mentioned, many others have helped with this book. It is not possible to name the many students, colleagues, friends, and children who have contributed in various, helpful ways. To each I am grateful. My thanks go to each one who wrote an essay in response to my request, and to Masayuki Sano for "a magic hood."

For specific acknowledgment I am indebted to my own teacher Winifred Ward for her loyal friendship and inspiration for nearly forty years. I express my appreciation to four Executive Directors of the School of Drama at our university who have been patient with my research and teaching during this period: Gregory Falls, Jack Sydow, James R. Crider, and Paul Hostetler. To Agnes Haaga, Director of Children's Drama in our department, I especially thank for her foreword to this book and for her encouragement. Other members of our department to whom I am grateful are Aurora Valentinetti, Warren C. Lounsbury, Eve Roberts, and Marion Carey.

Special gratitude goes to Eloise Hayes, University of Hawaii and her outstanding students Nobue, Thelma, Frances, and Toki, who were enthusiastically responsive to the exploration of the creative processes of drama in the summer of 1966. I thank many colleagues in CTAA particularly Barbara McIntyre, Anne Thurman, Emily Gillies, Moses Goldberg, and Bernard Rosenblatt of CEMREL.

It is a pleasure to thank those persons who helped with the manuscript: Les Elliott, whose advice on writing books has been helpful for twenty-five years; Mary Wheeler, who cheerfully typed the manuscript under a time bind; and Sheri Liberman, who assisted with the appendixes.

Everyone who has written a book knows there are persons who make such a creative endeavor possible. It is my uncommon family that I thank: my mother, my sisters Hazel and Phyllis, my brothers George and Gene, my two sons Jan and Mark, and my husband Charles—each encouraging in a particular way.

August, 1976   G.B.S.

Part 1

DRAMA IN EDUCATION

Overview and Rationale
for the Art of Drama
with Children

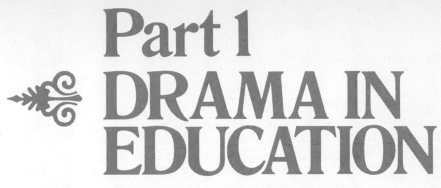

If you give a boy a fish, you sustain him for a day;
If you teach a boy to fish, you sustain him for a lifetime.

NORSE PROVERB

Introduction

Drama comes in the door of the school with every child.

WINIFRED WARD

Drama *does* come to school with children, but they don't know or even care that it is called "drama." What children care about is the opportunity to express their feelings, thoughts, and imaginings in satisfying dramatic experiences. The importance of such expression for the development of a child has been recognized during the past decade by more and more elementary school teachers. These teachers want to learn how to teach drama as an art. In order to do so they must know what it means: "Drama comes in the door of the school with every child." They must ask themselves what, especially, is the nature of drama, and what does drama have to offer to a child's education that is unique.

A FIRST LOOK AT THE PROCESS-CONCEPT STRUCTURE APPROACH TO DRAMA

The nature of drama in education may best be understood by examining a new experimental method for teaching drama to children, the process-concept structure approach. This approach, based on experimental research and teaching during the last fifteen years of my long teaching career, reflects the input of many educators and artists both here and in other countries.

The term "process-concept structure" refers to the conceptual framework on which a drama program is based. This framework exists primarily for the teacher or leader and provides a guide for designing drama

3

activities and involving children in the dramatic process. This dramatic process includes the creative processes by which children originate and form drama, such as perceiving, responding, imagining, creating (improvising and forming), communicating, and evaluating. The concepts of the framework are based on drama principles that are fundamental to learning the skills of the related roles of player, playmaker, and audience.

As this approach was evolving, we found that the most effective way to communicate its philosophy and procedure was to invite persons to observe the children in a workshop situation. We then had a reference point for discussion. The same procedure will be followed throughout this book. Descriptions and analyses of seven children's classes will be given in the first four chapters, and different ways that other teachers have applied the approach will be described in Chapters 13 and 14. These descriptions are intended to illuminate the philosophy and to serve as teaching guides.

Drama Workshop with Nine- and Ten-Year-Olds

Fourteen nine- and ten-year-olds (eight girls and six boys) met for the first time in an after-school drama class.[1] Most of the children were not well acquainted with each other, although several had come to the class in car pools. As the children gathered to get acquainted with each other and the teacher, they discussed their reasons for joining the workshop. It was evident that most of them wanted to "be in a play" or "make up plays."

Alert to the children's motivations, the teacher suggested that they get started by unwinding and waking up their bodies and imaginations. Then they would make up short plays in pairs or in small groups. The children seemed responsive to the plan, although many appeared self-conscious in the presence of several student observers. (The student observers were then asked to participate rather than to observe.)

Everyone was asked to move into the open space of the room to find their own personal space, and to remove their shoes if they wished, which most everyone did. Tense feelings were discussed briefly, and then the children and adults were involved in an activity called "Up Tight." They were guided to breathe deeply, tighten up muscles in their fingers, hands, arms, shoulders, neck, face, back, toes, feet, knees, legs, and stomach, and hold their tightened positions until a signal was given to relax by releasing the tenseness with a big, long sigh. After trying this twice from a standing position and twice from a sitting position, and

[1] Composite account from university students' observation reports, and instructor's plan, evaluation, and taped recording of a laboratory drama class for children, School of Drama, University of Washington, Seattle, WA, October, 1973.

breathing and sighing deeply, most of the children appeared to relax. Laughter, which generally eases tensions, came easily as they started to interact with each other and the teacher.

Next, the children were guided to explore their individual resources for expression through body movement. They were asked to discover how the joints and muscles of their bodies worked together by seeing how many ways they could *bend, stretch,* and *shake* different body parts. While children were exploring the movement of shaking, they were asked to think of objects that shake naturally. Several objects were named, including: my dog Shadow when he gets out of water, a salt shaker, jell-o, our washing machine when it finishes the spinning cycle, and me when I turn on the cold water in the shower.

To activate the process of imagining, children were asked to think about objects by concentrating first on a dog and how it shakes after it gets out of water: "Here is the problem: What will you do to show the water, first when the dog gets into it, and next when the dog shakes it from its coat? Imagine for yourself *where* the dog is in relation to the water. Is it near a pond, stream, lake, ocean, creek, or where? Ask yourself *where* the water is, *where* the dog is, and what kind of dog it is. Picture in your mind what the dog does to get in the water. Is it after a bird or stick or something else, or is it thirsty or hot? Picture in your mind *what the dog does* when it gets out to shake the water from its coat. Each one of you should work this out in your own way at the same time and nobody should just watch—the observers should work on it too."

Working simultaneously and individually, the children became involved to varying degrees in improvising actions. All of the children worked on the floor on their hands and knees except for four who remained standing. Individuals concentrated on hand, leg, head, and whole-body movement to show imagined water by splashing, jumping, swimming, running, and shaking, depending on their interpretations of the dog. Some children used barking sounds. When everyone was finished they were asked to discuss this experience with a person near them. Guided in a similar way, the children created actions of other shaking objects that they had named.

Exploration of body movement in relation to opening and closing the body then followed. Children stretched to open their bodies to a horizontal and then to a vertical position. They closed their bodies by bending to make themselves as small as possible. Next they improvised the actions of objects named by the children that open and close. These included: water faucet, knife blade, elevator door, morning-glory blossom, and the door to the classroom being opened and shut.

The use of senses was explored next by concentrating on the sense of sight. Children were asked to close their eyes and recall different lines and shapes that they had seen in the room. They identified and named straight lines (in doors, heating vents, and ceiling tiles); curved lines (in the floor and lamps); and angular lines (in corners of doors, ceiling tiles, and wooden blocks). The children next identified a variety of shapes, including round, square, rectangular, spherical, and irregular shapes found in chairs, tables, scenic blocks, a drum, and a toy car model that belonged to one of the boys.

The children were guided to combine the concepts of line and shape with movement in an activity called "Lining." Each child was asked to see if he or she could make a straight line in space by using only a finger, then a hand, an arm, two arms, one foot, one foot and leg, and finally the entire body. This activity was continued by focusing the children's thinking on the use of body parts to make curved and angular lines, and then on the use of their entire bodies to make a variety of shapes, and then on the use of their entire bodies to make a variety of shapes such as those they had "found" in the room.

In a new activity called "Shaping" children worked in pairs to discover how two people working together could spontaneously form different shapes in action. The children responded in rapid succession as the teacher called out the names of the same objects as in "Lining." These objects shown in action included: a rocking chair, a table moving, a drum beating, a Volkswagen backing up, and lights turning on and off.

Again much laughter resulted as youngsters found genuine pleasure in interacting in the problem-solving activities. Several children asked if they might see how others did the shapings. The teacher explained that it was important for each one to learn to concentrate and to adapt quickly to the actions of the other person so that their actions would be believable. The teacher assured the children that once they learned to keep their attention focused on what they were doing, they would be ready to share their creations with each other.

Continuing with the sense of sight and the concept of shape, the teacher asked the children to watch the changing shapes of a single sheet of newspaper she was holding. As the teacher folded, twisted, opened, and closed the newspaper she imagined each emerging shape to be a particular object by creating an action in relation to that object. For example, when the folded newspaper took on the shape of a small hand mirror, the teacher improvised the action of brushing her hair in front of the mirror. When the newspaper was twisted and looked like a baseball bat, the teacher improvised the actions of batting an imaginary ball.

Each child was then asked to take a sheet of newspaper and bend, twist, open, close, and shake it in the same way that they had explored body movement. The children were asked to watch the newspaper each was manipulating to see how many different imagined objects could be seen emerging from the changing newspaper shapes. Responses came quickly, with the variety of imagined objects including: sword, necklace, baby, flowers, bullfighter's cape, horns of a bull, and the steering wheel of a Datsun 240 Z.

A new problem was then presented. The children were asked to imagine a place, a person, and an action. "Using your newspaper object to help you get started, imagine that you are *someone* different from yourself doing something with the object. Next, imagine *where* this person is. Then, ask yourself *what* the person is doing with the object. When you have a clear picture try to make it come alive in actions."

After a first try and a brief discussion about how individual children approached this problem, each child was asked to find the partner he or she had worked with previously, and to share *who* their imagined persons were and *what* their objects were used for.

Continuing with the problem and extending it , the teacher introduced a new challenge. "The next problem is difficult, but from the way each of you has been concentrating, I think you will enjoy working on this, too. Now that you and your partner know *who* each of you imagined yourselves to be and *what* each object is, imagine a place *where* these two persons might be together. It may be the place one of you imagined or it may be a different place that you agree upon. Decide next *what* the persons *do* with their objects in relation to each other. Ask yourselves what their relationship is. Maybe it is friendly, in which case one person simply meets and greets the other. It may be a relationship in which these two persons are strangers and one asks the other for information. Or, it may be a relationship in which the persons are in danger, angry, happy, or fearful. Keep your actions simple so you can show clearly by using the objects where you are and what you do in relationship to each other. Discuss it and agree upon a plan. Next, arrange the space and bring your imagined experience to life by using the objects to show *where* you are and *what* you do."

An improvisation of an airplane pilot and an Indian scout grew out of this problem. It was created by two of the older boys who were so absorbed in their playing that their concentration on the imagined experience was outstanding. Following this, the boys asked if they could share their "play" with the others. They were ready and eager and it meant much to them. The teacher had to make a quick decision. If she permitted the boys to show their creation their affective needs and incentives would be satisfied but other children might want to share their "plays" too. It was clear to the teacher that most of the children needed more experience before they would be secure and skillful enough to communicate to others. On the other hand the boys' sharing could benefit all the children as an aesthetic and learning experience.

The teacher inquired whether any of the others felt they were ready to show their "plays." Several said they wanted to tell but didn't want to show. The teacher explained that with more experience everyone would probably learn skills that would help them feel confident and be ready to show. The teacher suggested that everyone become an audience to watch the boys create their "play."

Hugh, imagining himself to be the pilot, had transformed a large sheet of newspaper into two objects, a paper plane and a parachute. Kenny, his partner, had created a hunting knife. Together they decided the place was "a pine forest east of the mountains with the open sky above." They explained that their relationship "started as if they were enemies and it ended up as friends." Hugh began by creating sound effects for the plane, which he held outward in his right hand. As he ran through the room, he propelled the plane higher by lifting his hand upward. Suddenly, with appropriate vocal sounds matching his movements, he made the plane jump and move irregularly. Sailing the plane upward, he let it go, pulled the other piece of paper from under his sweater, and maneuvered it over his head to form a parachute. Moving gradually from a high level in the open space of the room to a lower level, he dodged imagined trees, suddenly landed face down, and remained sprawled on the floor, perfectly still and silent.

Kenny, the Indian scout, watching the action from behind a large wooden block, an imagined pine tree, held his paper knife poised as he moved cautiously to put an end to the "white meteor or a machine from the sky." After looking over the situation, the scout jabbed his hunting knife into the chute several times and then into the pilot's shoulder. The scout was stunned by the pilot's piercing cry and writhing movements, followed by sudden silence and stillness. Amazed at injuring a living being, the scout covered the bleeding wound with a leaf hastily yet carefully selected from a nearby bush. Slowly the scout turned the pilot's body over so that he could apply artificial respiration. After considerable effort on the part of the scout, the pilot opened his eyes. Startled and relieved, the scout rose quickly to his feet and opened his arms widely, asking silently and humbly for the pilot's pardon. The pilot, too weak to stand, lifted himself with great effort to a sitting position and extended his hand to the scout in a friendly gesture.

After the improvisation was completed Kenny explained, "We planned it a little different from the way it came out. We planned for the scout to start to kill the pilot 'cause he was on the Indian's reservation, but the pilot would beg for his life and promise to give the scout something. But when he screamed in pain and seemed to be dying from my knife our plans changed, 'cause then I had to do what the Indian would do. They only kill for meat or in self-defense, and I wasn't having to defend myself. That leaf I put on him is a leaf Indians use for powerful medicine to stop bleeding."

Following this experience the children commented on their feelings of sympathy with both the scout and the pilot. When encouraged to ask questions, the children wondered about when this experience had occurred, where the Indian reservation was located, what kind of plane and parachute the pilot had, and the nature of the custom of using the leaf for medicine.

This was an unusual experience for beginners. Not only had the boys succeeded in forming dramatic action, but they had unconsciously taken a human truth and formed it into a brief moment of drama that aroused a gamut of feelings for everyone present. The other imagined relationships were also satisfying to the children. Although most of them were unable to create clear physical actions, they were able to reveal a wide range of interests and emotional content in their imagined human relationships. Included were: a mother wearing a hat as she and her daughter put flowers on a grave; a bullfighter fighting a bull in an arena; and a nurse taking a baby to a mother sitting up in a hospital bed.

Chief Features of the Process-Concept Structure

The workshop described above indicates that, given the proper approach, children can learn the skills and concepts needed to originate and form drama. The three fundamental aspects of this approach are the conceptual framework, the learning experiences, and the strategies and procedures used by the teacher. The framework centrally places the child as the learner in the three related roles, which are the fundamental components of drama: the player, the playmaker, and the audience. The elements of each of these components are then reduced to concepts. Learning experiences are designed to guide children to explore and eventually learn to apply the concepts. Teaching strategies and procedures are used to guide children to explore a concept or a cluster of concepts while children experience one or more of the creative processes of drama.

In the workshop the children primarily explored concepts found in the role of the player. These included: (1) relaxation, (2) body movement (nonlocomotor, shape, relationships), (3) the sense of sight, and (4) imagining and improvising action in a relationship between two persons in an imagined environment. The children participated as well in the role of audience for the "play" created by the two boys. The creative processes experienced by the children were those of perceiving, responding, imagining, and creating. The content of the experiences was drawn from the children's perceptions and imaginations. However, the content was stimulated by the children's responses to the problem-solving nature of the activities and the kind of teaching strategies and procedures used. The structure will be discussed in more detail in Chapter 3.

PHILOSOPHICAL BASIS OF DRAMA IN EDUCATION

Purpose of Drama in Education

The ultimate purpose of drama in education is to open children's minds, stimulate their imaginations and language abilities, and spark their enthusiasm for continued personal development and discovery. In other words, drama should help the child learn about himself or herself and the world around and grow accordingly.

Drama can also serve a related purpose as a teaching tool. It may be used to help children explore factual knowledge and concepts in other subject areas and "try on" social experiences they are likely to encounter in real life.

Regardless of the purpose to which drama is put in a given situation, the experience can only succeed for a child when the child has acquired some basic drama skills and has learned how to use the dramatic process with confidence and understanding. This conviction is supported by Brian Way, who affirms that "drama is a useful tool for teaching other subjects . . . but only after drama exists within its own right. We cannot use number to solve interesting problems until we have experienced and to some extent mastered number itself: no more can we use drama to understand or experience history or bible stories or literature until we have experienced and mastered certain basic aspects of drama itself. Ultimately, drama is a valuable tool, but first the tool itself must be fashioned."[2] The child must master such skills as concentration, relaxation, and self-control of the body and emotions for expression through improvised action and speech.

Rationale for Drama in the Language Arts Curriculum

The process-concept structure approach to drama is integral to the language arts curriculum of the elementary school. Its use is based on a thesis proposed and advanced by James Moffett. He contends that "drama and speech are central to a language curriculum, not peripheral. They are base and essence, not specialities. I see drama as the matrix of all language activities, subsuming speech and engendering the varieties of writing and reading."[3] This thesis rests on the assumption that dramatic interaction—doing things verbally in situations with other people—is the primary vehicle for developing thought and language.

The approach presented here recognizes the importance of language as a means of ordering reality in thinking, talking, listening, reading, and writing. Through the creative language processes used to explore, share, and communicate experience in drama, children develop abilities to use language independently and creatively.

Primary Aim of the Process-Concept Structure Approach

The primary aim of the process-concept structure approach is the same as the ultimate goal of drama in education, namely, to foster each child's

[2] Brian Way, *Development Through Drama* (Education Today Series) (London: Longman and Atlantic Highlands, NJ: Humanities Press, 1967), p. 7.

[3] James Moffett, *Teaching the Universe of Discourse* (Boston: Houghton Mifflin, 1968), pp. 60–61.

self-development and learning. A prime consideration in working toward this goal is the nature of the drama program. In an effective program, the developing child becomes involved with the many elements, processes, and forms of drama. It is questionable whether the major educational goals for drama can be achieved if drama activities are shared occasionally without regard for structure or fundamental processes and concepts. The process-concept structure is intended to make the entire teaching-learning process in drama more certain, more efficient, and more predictable in fostering each child's self-development and learning.

Learning experiences in drama, as in any other subject, must be thoughtfully planned, structured, and guided. They must be cumulative in effect so that through them children gain the necessary skills and attitudes to express and communicate in a variety of drama forms. The process-concept structure approach does not, however, attempt to teach children to become professional actors and actresses, any more than mathematics and science classes in elementary schools train professional mathematicians or scientists.

Values of Drama in Education

The value of drama lies in its unique power to stir human emotions through its sensory qualities—content formed in action. The greatest single value of drama in education is that each child can experience this unique power.

Perhaps this uniqueness can be better understood by referring again to the boys' spontaneous creation of the pilot and scout. This dramatic moment touched a universal chord for all who experienced it because of its synthesis of content and form. The scout asked the pilot to forgive his impulsive actions. This experience is felt by the very young child who has had to say to another, "I'm sorry." And it is felt by all persons who have ever said, in effect, "Give me your pardon, sir, I've done you wrong." If drama and the related arts become central in children's basic education, they should serve to advance aesthetic, cultural, and moral values for the citizens of our country.

Thesis of this Book

This book, organized in three parts, is concerned with teacher education in drama as it relates to the education of children in the elementary school. The thesis is that since the teacher is the person to include drama as an art in the school curriculum the teacher must have a good understanding of child development and learning and of drama as an art. The present volume offers a philosophical basis for a structured approach to drama in the elementary school, along with representative learning experiences and teaching procedures.

Part I focuses on the philosophical background; Part II on learning experiences; and Part III on practical application of drama in the basic education of children. Throughout, "elementary school" refers to kindergarten through sixth grade; "preschool," to children from two through four years of age; "kindergarten," to five-years-olds; "primary," to first, second, and third grades; and "intermediate," to fourth, fifth, and sixth grades.

IMPLICATION OF THE ARTS IN EDUCATION

Why are the arts basic to the education of children? Imagine, if you will, that you are in New York City at United Nations headquarters. In the lobby of the General Assembly Building two objects catch your attention. One is the facsimile of Sputnik, a gift from the USSR., with a statement that this spacecraft represents the greatest scientific development of the twentieth century. The other is the Foucault Pendulum, a gift from the Netherlands. It swings ceaselessly a hundred feet or more above the marble floor. The pendulum's 200-pound shining sphere, suspended by a single steel wire, shifts its plane-of-swing slowly in relation to the rotation of the earth. Inscribed on the sphere is a message to all people from Queen Juliana of the Netherlands: "It is a privilege to live this day and tomorrow."

The United Nations concept and these gifts reflect the human condition of the world community in the waning years of the twentieth century. Sputnik signals an age of space exploration, of scientific and technological advance, of nuclear power—an age of rapid change. The ever-moving pendulum reminds us of universal constants and raises questions concerning humanity. Is it indeed a privilege for all children and youth to live this day? Is it a privilege for them to dream of tomorrow when they will inherit a civilization of awesome complexity? What is life and its unique privilege? What enhances the quality of life for the individual, for society, for the world? What matters? What doesn't? How may children's educations help them to live their lives in dignity with individual purpose and joi de vivre?

Scholars have long pondered these questions, and today scholars continue to formulate answers that will lead to a new perception of human beings and the purpose of life. The search for knowledge during the past several decades has produced an intellectual revolution. This has led to a demand for change in many aspects of living, particularly in education. In our country, in no area of education is this demand more justifiable than in the arts and humanities. Our country is caught up in a major revolution to incorporate in basic education the aesthetic, humanistic, and moral development of children and youth in consonance with their cognitive and affective development.

Perceptive educators today view the active learning processes of the arts as essential in a child's total educative process. Harry S. Broudy, an advocate of aesthetic education, questions why imagination or its development or use has been discussed so little in educational philosophy. Believing the ability to imagine to be peculiar to the human species, Broudy points out: "The world of actuality, insofar as that world is the work of the human mind and hand, is imagination's legacy. Out of this legacy each individual and each generation can by imagination create possibilities which, if actualized, change the world and enlarge the legacy for future generations."[4]

In our society, aided by vast knowledge and research, the educational challenge remains. It is essential that we have teachers who know how to satisfy children's individual developmental needs. Learning experiences in school are needed that will cause every child to wake up to each new morning knowing and feeling that "it is a privilege to live this day and tomorrow."

SUGGESTED ACTIVITIES FOR ADULT STUDENTS

1. Discuss the children's workshop from the following viewpoints:
   a. Your immediate spontaneous response;
   b. Children's exploration of specified drama concepts in the learning role of the player;
   c. The teacher's guidance.
2. With a small group of peers discuss two of the following:
   a. What is meant by "drama comes in the door of the school with every child"?
   b. With the children's workshop as a frame of reference, what does drama have to offer to children's education that is unique?
   c. Why do you believe the arts should be included in the basic education of all children?
   d. Consider the implications of Harry S. Broudy's statement concerning imagination.
3. Arrange to work with a small group of children for a fifteen-minute period. Guide them to explore the same concepts (relaxation, body movement, and the sense of sight) with the same learning experiences used with the children in the workshop. Following your guidance identify the differences between the children's responses and perceptions in the two groups.
4. Arrange to work with a group of your peers. Guide them to explore the "imagining concept" used in the children's workshop with the same learning experience (manipulation of the newspapers). Then discuss with your peers their responses, perceptions, and creations. Identify differences between the peers' and children's responses. Identify and discuss other easily available materials that can be used as the newspapers were to involve children in further exploration of this same concept. Test out the materials with peers to determine their effectiveness for use with children in this particular learning experience.

[4] Harry S. Broudy, *Enlightened Cherishing: An Essay on Aesthetic Education* (Urbana: University of Illinois Press, 1972), p. 13.

2
Considering Child Development and Learning

The art of the child is the art of a human being with perceptions and emotions, reactions and fantasies, which differ in nature from the perceptions and emotions, reactions and fantasies of the adult.

SIR HERBERT READ
The Grass Roots of Art[1]

By nature children are inclined to turn the experiences of their inner and outer worlds into play. A term used to describe this natural imaginary or symbolic play activity is "dramatic play." In this kind of play the child identifies with a person or thing and in the process impersonates by imitating the remembered characteristics. For example, a child may imitate the actions and sounds of a firefighter and a fire engine, or the unique rhythmic walk and manner of talking of a parent or teacher. Frequently, the child uses objects such as blocks or toys as symbols to represent persons or things.

What is the content and nature of dramatic play? Why does two-year-old Sean, who watches hydroplanes racing with their white rooster tails flying, run around his house later that day shaking a piece of white wrapping paper and making vocal motor sounds as he charges through open space? Why do eight-year-old Angela and several of her classmates who have read *Where The Wild Things Are* play after school that they are "wild things" creating their own exciting "rumpuses"?[2] Why does ten-year-old Kris organize and lead several of his friends as they "play war" in a vacant lot for nearly three hours on a Saturday afternoon?

[1] Herbert Read, *The Grass Roots of Art* (New York: Wittenborn, 1955), p. 102.
[2] Maurice Sendak, *Where The Wild Things Are* (New York: Harper & Row, 1963).

14

Answers to these questions concerning the content and nature of children's dramatic play lie in an understanding of child development.

IDENTIFYING DEVELOPMENTAL CHARACTERISTICS AND NEEDS OF FIVE- AND SIX-YEAR-OLDS IN A DRAMA WORKSHOP

As ten children enter a large room the teacher greets each one by name.[3] A frolicsome, novel musical recording, "Dueling Banjos," is playing.[4] Quickly the children pile coats and sweaters on a side table, and some remove their shoes and begin to slide around the smooth floor. Others hop, jump, or twirl to the jaunty rhythm.

These five- and six-year-olds reflect basic behavior patterns characteristic of their ages. For most of the children this is the eighteenth meeting. The relationship between the children and the teacher is comfortably casual. There is mutual trust. The children are physically and mentally active and are beginning to develop a genuine social awareness of each other, resulting in cooperative and gregarious patterns of playing. However, they still have relatively short attention spans for they shift rapidly from one area of interest to another.

Lowering the volume gradually until the music fades, the teacher invites the children to sit on the oversized blanket beside her to share their feelings and ideas. Many are eager to respond and vie to be heard. Each seems to want personal recognition. This age group needs help in channeling impulses, so here they are learning when to speak and when to listen.

"Let's all try to hear *Steve* tell us what he was imagining when he turned around and around with his arms going stiffly up and down." The teacher encourages the children to explain their *purposeful, rhythmical activity.* She continues to focus attention on specific bodily actions as youngsters discuss how the music made them feel and act.

When each has had an opportunity to talk, a suitcase is opened. It contains ten pairs of bright yellow and green oversized cotton work gloves. The children don them, and the teacher guides the group to create actions of imaginary persons wearing these gloves. "Who might wear *these* gloves? What would you *do* if you were that person? When you are ready, move to a place where you can do what your imaginary character might do."

Immediately some of the children jump up and begin to wave their gloved hands in random movements. Again, the instructor comments upon

[3] By permission of Eleanor DeVito Owen, Associate, School of Drama; composite account from university students' observation reports, and instructor's guidance plan and evaluation of a laboratory drama class for children, School of Drama, University of Washington, Seattle, WA, 1973.

[4] "Dueling Banjos" by Eric Weisberg and Steve Mandell, Warner Brothers label.

purposeful, involved actions. Soon one child becomes a clown, another a boxer. Yet another makes himself fat by holding his imaginary stomach and says, "Look! I'm Laurel and Hardy."

The teacher guides by moving among the children, giving verbal directions and noting concentrated effort and tendencies toward clear actions and strong characteristics of imagined persons. By using a large drum she introduces new rhythms and moods. She prods image making with comments such as, "What *else* would your character do? If very, very tired, how would he or she act? If someone came up behind you and suddenly tapped your character on the shoulder, what might your character do?"

A child begins to use the gloves to shovel snow. One youngster, who has been making heavy lifting actions, develops an exaggerated backache. A child catches something which he later describes as "eels." A little girl waves to "someone in a parade."

After several minutes of involved activity, the drum beat ceases and the teacher beckons the children back to the blanket. Again, she encourages individuals to verbalize their feelings. Two of the five-year-olds are reluctant to join the group. They choose to talk and play separately. The teacher guides by asking them to open the remaining suitcase together. Curiosity unites them into a focused group activity.

When the suitcase is opened the children see an array of colors. The suitcase contains ten lengths of different textured fabrics: some light, some heavy; some rough, some smooth; some patterned, some plain. Quickly each child grabs for a piece of cloth. After much snatching and bargaining each child is finally satisfied with his or her final selection. A careful observer might note one or two frustrated or envious "selectors." Almost immediately the children wrap, drape, and knot the material. Some require help in arranging the cloth to their satisfaction. Others struggle through alone. Snap clothespins function as clasps.

As the children arrange and rearrange the pieces of cloth their images grow larger and clearer. Soon their fantasies emerge into moving, talking characters. There is Superman, Underdog, Queen, Princess, Drunkman "who is really a thief," Ghost, Nurse, and Bartender. Two children settle for simple capes. They become observers of the more actively involved players. As the children move about creating their imaginary settings the teacher comments on what she sees. She focuses upon particular actions or demonstrated feelings as expressed by the imaginary character. For example, she might say, "It looks like a robber is trying to escape with something, hiding it under his coat. . . . I wonder if somewhere in the room it is very dark for I notice a character feeling his way around and squinting very hard to see what is in front of him."

By reenforcing the action of the character, the teacher tangentially encourages continued action and deeper characterization. If she were to praise a youngster by his or her given name, several negative interferences would occur: (1) the child's involvement and concentration would be greatly weakened; (2) other children would be swift to check out this activity to determine why it gained personal recognition and might be tempted to imitate the praised youngster; and (3) whatever mood might have been established would be intruded upon, thus weakening the essential drama quality.

When the children return to the blanket they discuss their playing. During the somewhat noisy period the Bartender and Drunkman had dominated with their dialogue. The elevated noise threshold had been permitted—the teacher even encouraged it—to satisfy idiosyncratic modes of expression which result in spontaneous actions and interactions that are frequently incorporated into a story play.

The children are now prepared to make up a story for their play. They first must decide where the story begins and how their characters fit in. Almost automatically they establish the first scene in the bar with Bartender "cleaning the counters." The children, guided by the teacher, continue to plan the story sequences; some youngsters jump up to arrange scenic blocks and a wooden crate for the various scenes. When the story is completed, the teacher guides a summary discussion so each child knows: (1) how the story begins, (2) what the sequences are, and (3) how the story ends. Each Character goes to his or her beginning place. There is a pause. The teacher flicks the light and waits until all are ready to begin. The two children wearing capes and the teacher sit together as the audience.

The drama unfolds. Drunkman comes into the bar and orders a beer. When Ghost floats in to scare him, a chase ensues. Drunkman hits Ghost and then runs away. Superman and Underdog hurry in to help Ghost by bringing him to the Ghost Hospital to "let him be repaired" by a very friendly Nurse. Underdog and Superman then search for and find "Ghost's attacker" and discover that he is a "jewel thief." Drunkman, feigning limpness, is bodily dragged to the Queen who together with the Princess is holding court enthroned on a double tier of blocks. The Queen and Princess proclaim that he should "go to jail and be sent to sea." Underdog and Superman accept both verdicts. After a brief stint in jail, Drunkman is put into the boat (crate). It topples over and "the bad thief drowns in the water." Despite the seemingly dire consequences, the children are exuberant over their accomplishment, and even the revived antihero Drunkman is satisfied with the outcome.

Back on the blanket and before replaying, the audience responds to the newly created drama. The players, audience, and teacher make suggestions focusing on strengthening the plot and characterizations by adding to, modifying, or deleting from the original presentation.

Developmentally, these children are determining moral and social as well as physical boundaries. The child who played Drunkman, especially, had regularly challenged the teacher's tolerance for socially unacceptable behavior. By taking this orientation seriously and by incorporating his character into the play, the teacher encouraged the external expression of his fantasy. Further, it allowed all the children the opportunity to wrestle with the possible consequences of drunkenness. Acceptance of the denouement—nobody saved the thief—reflects the group's moral convictions. For this age group justice is swift. Right is right and wrong is wrong; there is no in-between. In an interesting postscript this particular child introduced no more strongly antisocial characters in the six remaining sessions.

Summary of Workshop Goals and Procedures

This workshop was guided by an experienced teacher who enjoys and understands children and drama.[5] She is consciously aware of how to involve children in creative language processes. Her goals and guidance procedures can be summarized as follows.

DEVELOPMENTAL GOALS

(1) To encourage group interaction and cooperation through the acceptance of ideas and actions of others; (2) to stimulate and reenforce divergent thinking and behavior within a structured framework.

SPECIFIC DRAMA GOALS

(1) To introduce fabric materials as visual and tactile stimulation for the children's creation of personalized costumes to enhance the identification with self-generated imagined characters; (2) to strengthen and channel individual abilities through improvised actions and dialogues; (3) to foster externalization of perceptions and fantasies through the use of blocks as physical markers in the imagined setting; (4) to foster the development of a more conscious awareness of dramatic action through the creation of plot sequences and character relationships; and (5) to synthesize spontaneously expressed content into a "play," thereby enabling the children to mirror and explore the prevailing social and moral values of their homes, neighborhoods, and society.

GUIDANCE PROCEDURES

The guiding framework for the age group is to have repeated shifts from spontaneous action to impulse-controlled thought and dialogue. Structurally, the session is organized into a series of flexible units: (1) warm-up, (2) character invention and identification, (3) story construction, (4) story improvisation, (5) story evaluation and revision, and (6) replaying with substitutions, modifications, and additions or deletions of plot sequences and characterizations.

[5] By permission of Eleanor DeVito Owen.

Initially, the teacher's task is to unify and focus the mood of the group. This is best accomplished by establishing an environment that is related to a planned theme by the use of selected physical objects (blocks and crate) and music to foster spontaneous group interaction. This initial stimulus assists each child in making the transition from the varied school and car-pool activities to a unified focus on drama. During story construction the teacher guides the development of an idea through the logical interactions of the imaginary characters. Stress is placed upon clarification of the beginning and ending actions and of the major conflict. During group evaluation emphasis is on the belief in the characterization, concentration, and adherence to the agreed upon story line. Replaying provides for shifts in roles. It encourages social growth through the creation and playing of alternative solutions to the dramatic conflict.

EXAMINING ASPECTS OF CHILD DEVELOPMENT AND LEARNING

As observed in this workshop, children come to a group experience, whether in or out of school, with a variety of individual behaviors, needs, capabilities, motivations, and at different stages of individual development. The teacher must have a good understanding of the leading theories of child development, language development, and learning. Considerable literature is available. *The Developing Child* by Helen Bee is an excellent source for students, parents, and teachers.[6]

Implications of Personality Development Through Drama

According to Freud, Erik Erikson, and others, a child's social and emotional experiences are of central importance in his or her personality development. The child's ego develops as the child resolves emotional problems experienced during relationships with other children as well as with adults. To assist the development of children's personalities several basic factors need to be considered in planning drama activities and in guidance.

First, the child needs to acquire a sense of self-trust and trust in others whenever he or she enters a new group experience. Regardless of the child's age, it is necessary to alleviate the embarrassment he or she feels when asked to express individually until he or she feels self-confident in relation to the others.

Second, the child's ego needs to be strengthened through successful individual and group experiences so the child gradually develops a sense of self-esteem and individual worth in relation to the group.

Third, the child's emotional development evolves through sequential

[6] Helen Bee, *The Developing Child* (New York: Harper & Row, 1975).

phases that influence the child's pattern of behavior. A teacher needs to identify and respect each child's phase of emotional development and guide accordingly. Within a group one child may need to satisfy natural drives for initiative and industry through leadership in group projects. Another child in the same group may need to interact with peers and gain peer approval by contributing with far less responsibility.

Fourth, children need to deal with a variety of content as they imagine characters and create dramatic action and plays. Their development depends on the capacities of their egos to deal with conflict, to adapt, to encounter frustration, and to find solutions that bring harmony between inner needs and outer reality.

CONTENT OF DRAMA FOR YOUNGER CHILDREN

As observed in the workshop with five- and six-year-olds, drama for younger children deals with imagined characters based on reality and on fantasy. Children's deep unconscious drives are expressed overtly through their imaginings of characters in action in a variety of circumstances. The content and action of their spontaneous drama allow children to create an imaginary set of circumstances in which they attempt to give vent to feelings and to solve problems which they are unable to do in reality.

Because the roots of identification go deep into early childhood children need opportunities to identify with parental and capable work-oriented adult roles. These may include the roles of police officer, doctor, firefighter, cowboy, store clerk, and bus driver. A little girl cannot *be* her mother but she can *be like* or act *as if* she were her mother. The same is true of a little boy who needs opportunities to explore and discover for himself the satisfaction of masculine values. Because they have inner, unconscious drives for self-preservation, power, and mastery of circumstances, children need to center their drama in fantasies that satisfy these drives. They must make believe that they are powerful fantasy creatures such as capable giants, witches, monsters, robots, and machines. Magic appears to be needed for it enters frequently into a child's imaginings, drawings, personal dramatic play, and vocabulary. Children also respond to stories concerned with family experiences, holidays, and nonsense.

CONTENT OF DRAMA FOR OLDER CHILDREN

During the intermediate school years from approximately nine to eleven years of age the child incorporates real-life situations into the content of drama activities. The content deals for the most part with circumstances where there is a sense of struggle, excitement, and adventure. Children seem to want and need to imagine themselves as persons who experiment with power, courage, and loyalty, and who solve difficult problems. Their unconscious drives tend to lead them into drama that allows them to struggle heroically for survival. Heroes hold particular appeal for both girls and boys, particularly heroes who have risen from "underdog" status. Heroes in Greek and Roman mythology appeal to many children. Content that centers in achievement and idealism holds strong appeal for most ten- and eleven-year-olds whereas many nine-year-olds continue to be interested in fantasy.

In *Childhood and Adolescence* the authors emphasize that one "of the most striking characteristics of the middle years in our own and many other societies is that children have a special, separate subculture with traditions, games, values, loyalties, and rules of its own. . . . It is handed down by word of mouth, it includes many rituals and magical formulas whose original meanings have been lost, it is hidebound and resistant to alien influence and to change. . . . This culture is seen in the group codes of solidarity, stoicism, prowess, conformity, and the like, but shows forth perhaps most vividly in the ancient tribal rituals."[7] When children are guided to work in small groups to originate and form plays, the content often includes ritualistic celebrations and ceremonies. Because children value peer relationships during these years such imaginings are best accomplished in small groups. For the most part there is a strong division between the sexes. Boys prefer to work with boys and girls with girls.

Implications of Intellectual Development Through Drama

For more than half a century Jean Piaget has researched the development of intelligence in children and contributed greatly to the understanding of a child's intellectual development and concept learning.[8] Explained most simply, Piaget believes that a child's mental development results from the child's interaction with and learning from his or her physical and social environments.

In *Piaget's Theory of Intellectual Development: An Introduction,* the authors, Herbert Ginsburg and Sylvia Opper, point out, as others have done, that "Piaget's theory divides intellectual development into four major periods: sensorimotor (birth to two years); preoperational (two years to seven years); concrete operational (seven years to eleven years); and formal operational (eleven years and above)."[9] From these they have extracted a number of general guiding principles with implications for educational practice. These authors identify and describe these principles in detail.[10] They are stated here in summary form.

[7] L. Joseph Stone and Joseph Church, *Childhood and Adolescence: A Psychology of the Growing Person,* 3rd ed. (New York: Random House, 1973), pp. 354–356.

[8] Jean Piaget, *The Language and Thought of the Child* (New York: Harcourt Brace Jovanovich, 1926).

[9] Herbert Ginsburg and Sylvia Opper, *Piaget's Theory of Intellectual Development: An Introduction* (Englewood Cliffs, NJ: Prentice-Hall, Inc., 1969), p. 26.

[10] Ibid., pp. 218–231.

The first of these is that the child's language and thought are different from the adult's. The teacher must be cognizant of this and must therefore attempt to observe children very closely in an attempt to discover their unique perspectives.

Second, children need to manipulate things in order to learn. . . . The child must physically act on his environment. . . .

Third, children are most interested and learn best when experience is moderately novel. When a new event is both familiar enough so that it may be assimilated without distortion into current cognitive structure, and novel enough so that it produces some degree of conflict, then interest and learning are promoted. . . . Children should work individually, with freedom, at tasks of their own choosing.

Fourth, the child's thought progresses through a series of stages, each of which contains distinctive strengths and weaknesses. Teachers should respect both of these. . . . In order to accomplish this, the teacher . . . must perceive each individual child's inadequacies and strengths. He must circumvent the former and exploit the latter.

Fifth, children should talk in school, should argue and debate. Social interaction, particularly when it is centered about relevant physical experience, promotes intellectual growth.[11]

These major principles of Piaget's theories are particularly relevant to educational procedures for drama with children. By its nature drama activity involves children in social and physical activities where they are required to think, talk, manipulate concrete materials, and to share viewpoints in order to arrive at decisions. Implementation of these principles in innovative ways calls for an attitude on the part of the teacher to be willing to learn from each child. This requires the teacher to observe the child carefully to gain an insight into the child's current level of functioning and then to provide learning experiences to meet the child's needs.

Psychomotor Development Through Drama

A detailed discussion of learning experiences designed to foster a child's motor development through drama is included in Chapter 6. As the child is guided to explore his or her physical resources for expression through body movement the child's psychomotor development is fostered. To do this effectively, the teacher needs to have an understanding of the body mechanism and fundamental body actions, and must know how to help a child execute a movement skill properly. Among many good sources are Evelyn L. Schurr's *Movement Experiences for Children*[12] and Geraldine Dimondstein's *Children Dance in the Classroom*.[13]

[11] Ibid., pp. 230–231.

[12] Evelyn L. Schurr, *Movement Experiences for Children* (New York: Appleton-Century-Crofts, 1967).

[13] Geraldine Dimondstein, *Children Dance in the Classroom* (New York: Macmillan, 1971).

Implications of Behavioral Development Through Drama

Learning theorists, for the most part, view children's behavior as being governed by laws of learning and view development as a consequence of learning. These theorists take the position that the child is changing continually as learning occurs. Stone and Church affirm that the child's ability to imitate the actions of other people, real and imagined, is a way that *learning influences development.* Persons whom the child observes, hears about, or imagines provide models for behavior. These authors support the significance of drama and dramatic play in child development. They state: "However trivial or specious role playing may seem, it gives the individual a chance to try on styles of life and the values they contain, and thereby to discover those modes of being that he or she finds most congenial and meaningful."[14]

Factors in a child's behavior that need to be considered in educational practices in drama include the following: First, learning experiences need to be appropriate to the individual's capabilities and be motivated by the child's interests and expectations. This means that the teacher needs to provide for individual differences with a variety of environments, stimulation, teaching procedures, and alternative learning experiences. Second, the child needs to know the goal toward which he or she is working. That goal needs to be presented as part of a whole so that the child grasps the notion and purpose of what he or she is doing and why. Third, the child's attempts should be re-enforced with a variety of encouragements to satisfy individual needs in relation to each child's capabilities and values. Fourth, the child needs to explore a variety of roles and points of view, and to perceive the chief characteristics and behavior of each role.

LANGUAGE DEVELOPMENT THROUGH DRAMA

When drama is taught as an art it stimulates and integrates children's learning in the language arts. John Stewig, in *Spontaneous Drama,* makes a strong case for the inclusion of drama in the language arts curriculum of the elementary school.[15]

It has been shown how children in the drama workshops become involved in the language processes of thinking, talking, listening, speaking, responding, and communicating with each other as they interact to plan, create, and respond to their own spontaneous creations and to those of their peers. These kinds of continuous experiences provide children with opportunities to use language and to communicate in a variety of different ways that appeal to children. In the process-concept structure

---

[14] Stone and Church, op. cit., p. 168.
[15] John W. Stewig, *Spontaneous Drama, A Language Art* (Columbus, Ohio: Charles E. Merrill Publishing Co., 1973).

drama experiences are designed as well to integrate a child's language in each of the related learning roles of player, playmaker, and audience.

Language Development in the Role of the Player

As players, children become involved in language experience in the ways already pointed out, and they explore language in other fundamental ways. These include nonverbal and verbal expression.

NONVERBAL EXPRESSION

When children explore body movement to discover how they may express themselves in action with their entire bodies or with body parts they also discover how body actions "speak" without words. Once children gain skills and learn how to control their expressive body movement, they are then ready to use these abilities as they think and communicate the meanings and feelings of imagined characters.

VERBAL EXPRESSION

Speech activities are designed to encourage each child to improvise words and dialogue for imagined characters in a variety of circumstances. Activities are designed so that a child can perceive how he or she may use language to communicate meaning through the use of pitch and projection.

In expressing verbally in drama children become involved with words and vocabulary in two basic ways. These include the vocabularies related to the art of drama and to the content of each activity. Vocabulary related to drama includes words concerned with drama elements, concepts, and processes in the related drama components. Vocabulary related to the content changes with each drama activity. Because of children's active and direct involvement with the vocabulary of imagined characters children associate words with meanings. For example, in the drama workshop with the five- and six-year-olds the vocabulary related to the experiences of Ghost, Drunkman, and Superman had vivid meaning for these particular children. Drama activities may focus directly on an exploration of words to identify their meanings through action. Verbs and adverbs, adjectives and nouns, and metaphors and similes are explored through action.

Language Development in the Role of Playmaker

As playmakers, children explore language and gain skills in oral composition and oral interpretation, and they are motivated to apply reading and writing skills in a variety of playmaking activities.

ORAL COMPOSITION

In exploring the elements of plot and character children originate and improvise dialogue and action spontaneously to create a set of circumstances for imagined characters. In the process of constructing a dramatic plot, children create by composing orally as they imagine characters and think on their feet to improvise action, words, and dialogue as they advance the plot incidents.

ORAL INTERPRETATION OF LITERATURE

In the activities of story dramatization, Story Theatre, and Reader's Theatre children interpret literature through spontaneous and extemporaneous improvisation. Story dramatization is the activity in which children are guided to create an informal drama from a story extemporaneously. After hearing or reading the story children are guided to improvise character action and dialogue, unit by unit, in each of the main plot incidents. Children are guided to interpret theme and mood when they put the incidents together to create the informal play.

Story Theatre is the activity in which children act out a story spontaneously as it is told or read by the storyteller (teacher or a child). Children participate simultaneously in the roles of audience, players, and playmakers. Audience children sit in a semicircular formation with a large playing space in front of them. In the role of player and playmaker, children interpret the story by volunteering spontaneously to improvise the action of the characters to correspond to the storyteller's narration. The players return to the audience as soon as the characters they are interpreting are no longer present in the incident being told. Players are required to think and cooperate instantly whenever they volunteer for characters in order to improvise and communicate the action simultaneously with the narration. If several players volunteer simultaneously to be the same character the players are required to decide instantly who is to be the character. As playmakers children are guided also, to improvise sounds spontaneously to interpret story action and mood. In the audience role children listen, observe, and enjoy the interpretations so they are prepared to respond with evaluations after the story is finished.

Reader's Theatre is the activity in which a group of children read, interpret, and improvise the action of a scripted play to communicate the play to an audience of peers. The players, cast as the play's characters, read from the scripts as they work together to interpret the play extemporaneously. Guidance procedures for each of these playmaking forms are described in Chapter 11.

READING

In the satisfying activities of playmaking children are motivated to read for several reasons. Frequently they read stories, plays, and poetry to seek a particular kind of experience to dramatize or to use for Story Theatre. During story dramatization children may read a story several times to seek particular information needed in the process of dramatization. That information may include identification of: the purpose underlying the action of a particular character; the series of plot incidents that build the character's struggle; the different sounds needed to build the mood and "music" of the story; and the different places of action required in the story.

The extremely simple form of Reader's Theatre requires children to read a play four times in order to participate in this satisfying experience.

WRITING

A playmaking experience can motivate children to write when it has stimulated enthusiastic involvement and the children want to extend the experience. They may be encouraged to write, among other things, a different ending or beginning for the play, or a letter to or from the leading character. They may want to describe what happened to the leading character ten years later. "What if" stories appeal to children when they have had an enjoyable experience. For example, they may write about "What if" this story happened in a different place, or time; or "what if" the leading character had avoided the problem.

Language Development in the Role of Audience

As children alternate learning roles and become an audience they acquire a new perspective. They strengthen their listening skills, their powers of observation, their appreciation for the efforts and concentration of others, and their appreciation of literature as it is brought to life through a variety of drama activities. Chapter 12 describes the audience role more fully.

SUGGESTED ACTIVITIES FOR ADULT STUDENTS

1. With a group of peers discuss the children's workshop, first in view of Herbert Read's statement that opens this chapter, and then from the assumption that drama experience fosters child development.
2. Locate a child between the ages of five and ten years of age and obtain permission to observe the child four different times during the child's different school activities. While observing be as unobtrusive as possible and do not invite any kind of contact or interaction with the child or any of the children. Observe the child's behavior accurately without attempting to interpret it. Write down what the child does, says, and how the child interacts with others and the environment. When you complete the observation organize your findings to identify some of the child's developmental characteristics, needs, and interests.
3. In a school or public library examine several children's books that are

recognized as being the most popular with children of a given age level. Examine the content, text, and illustrations to identify factors that probably contribute to the book's appeal.

4. Read again the children's workshops at the beginning of this chapter and of Chapter 1. With a group of peers identify teaching procedures and instructional materials that appear to be based on principles of Piaget's major theories of intellectual development, personality, and behavioral development.

3
Drama: An Art and a Language Art

The drama arose out of fundamental human needs in the dawn of civilization and has continued to express them for thousands of years.

JOHN GASSNER
Masters of the Drama[1]

Art, language, and learning lie within the child. It is the teacher's task to guide children to express these experiences in a way that will be significant to each child and to the group. How does a teacher accomplish this?

The purpose of this chapter is to consider this question. Beginning with a description of a drama workshop with a group of seven- and eight-year-olds, the chapter will then turn to a more comprehensive look at the process-concept structure approach to drama as an art.

DRAMA WORKSHOP WITH SEVEN- AND EIGHT-YEAR-OLDS

Tiffany, Tracey, Mark, and Bobby are seven- and eight-year-old partici-pants in an after-school drama workshop with ten other children of the same age.[2] It is the twelfth time that most of the children have worked together. For the first eight hours they participated as players. The children are now involved in playmaking, exploring concepts of how to build a plot with beginning, middle, and ending incidents in which there

---

[1] John Gassner, *Masters of the Drama*, 3rd rev. ed. (New York: Dover, 1953), p. xix.

[2] Composite account from university students' observation reports, and instructor's plan, evaluation, and taped recording of a laboratory drama class for children, School of Drama, University of Washington, Seattle, WA, February 1973.

are conflict and resolution. This is the children's fourth exploration of these concepts.

On this day these four children arrive ahead of the others. As they enter the room they are immediately attracted to an assortment of empty packing cartons of varying sizes and shapes which have been placed in the open space of the room. The children are invited to play with the cartons, to make believe they are particular things in particular places. After several minutes of enjoyment, each child is asked to select one carton and all are to work together using the four cartons and as much space as they need to make one particular place for a play to happen. After several trials with various arrangements, the children report that they have made a "one-room apartment." Tiffany shows how two boxes have become two beds, and Tracey shows that one box is a television set and the other a door leading out of the apartment. Mark explains that the two chairs he has arranged together as far from the "apartment" as space permits are "a big tree in a thick forest," and Bobby, standing in an open aisle, describes that space as a police station. The teacher asks if the children have decided who is going to be in the play, and the children explain that they planned on that when they made the "places."

Emphasizing the concept of plot construction, the teacher asks, "Have you decided who causes the trouble in the beginning of the story? Have you figured out what each person will do in the middle of the story because of the trouble he or she is in? Have you thought about how the story people will bring an end to their trouble, or will you let them work that out?"

The children talk together briefly. Tiffany asks if they can act out their play to show their plot to the other children who have now arrived. Because the players are highly motivated and confident, they are soon involved in creating their play with their peers as audience.

Tracey and Tiffany imagine themselves to be a Mother and her Daughter living in the apartment watching television at night. Not finding a good program, Mother decides it is time for them to go to sleep, and each stretches out on a bed. Almost at once Mother gets up to lock the outside door and asks Daughter to say her prayers. Soon both seem to be asleep. Mark, imagining himself to be a Kidnapper, walks cautiously to the apartment door. Finding it closed, he "picks the lock," enters the apartment slowly, sprays "some sleeping spray" on Daughter, wakes her up, and tells her not to scream "because I mean it." He tells her to stand up even though she is sleepy; this she does. Taking her by the shoulder he guides her through the door and out to his imaginary car. He tells her to get in, and they drive around the space of the room twice before stopping by the big tree. After ordering Daughter to get out of the car, Kidnapper ties her to the tree with imaginary ropes and tells her to "stay in this thick forest and be quiet." He tells her he is going to find a telephone to call her Mother to get "one hundred dollars," and when he has the money he will let her go.

When the telephone rings Mother wakes up and finds her Daughter missing. She tells Kidnapper she doesn't have one hundred dollars but will give him all the money she has in her purse. He tells her to throw the purse out the window, then to close the window and turn off all the lights, and not to watch "because I'm dangerous." As soon as Kidnapper finishes talking, Mother calls Police Officer. He asks where she lives, what Daughter's name is, and what she is wearing. Police Officer tells Mother not to throw her purse out the window but to lock the apartment door and wait until he gets there. Police Officer jumps on an imaginary motorcycle and, with realistic motor sounds, circles the room three times looking for Kidnapper. In the forest Daughter tries to wiggle herself free from the imaginary ropes. Kidnapper drives past the apartment looking for the purse but, not finding it, he returns to the forest. By this time Daughter has worked herself free and starts running, but Police Officer sees her and takes her home on the motorcycle.

The happy Mother embraces Daughter and at the same time thanks Police Officer. Daughter, apparently relieved to be safe at home, stretches out on the bed. Mother tells Daughter she will cook their "favorite late dinner of chicken souffle and punch." Before Police Officer leaves, he asks Daughter where Kidnapper is and she tells him Kidnapper must be in the "thick forest." Police Officer leaves, gets on his motorcycle, circles the room until he catches sight of Kidnapper hiding behind the big tree. Kidnapper, seeing Police Officer approach, jumps into his car. There is a fast chase around the room until Police Officer, using his finger and thumb for an imagined gun, shoots the tires on the car, catches Kidnapper, puts handcuffs on him, and tells him to get on the motorcycle, which he does. Policeman takes Kidnapper to jail, locks him in, and says, "You have to stay there fifty years to think about what you did."

When the play ends the children in the audience laugh and clap and cheer. Not unlike drama audiences throughout the centuries, the children have been a part of a ritualistic experience. For most of these young children this appears to be satisfying emotionally since their feelings of fear and sympathy are strong. They identify with the characters. They have experienced an ancient theme of love and hope in a struggle in which good triumphs over evil.

The teacher asks the two groups to sit together on the floor so they might talk about the play. Several youngsters comment on what they saw and heard that made the play "exciting and fun." The children are then guided to discuss the plot concepts. They decide the beginning showed the kidnapping problem quickly, the middle incidents showed how Mother, Police Officer, and Daughter worked to get Daughter back home, and the ending was "the way it should end because Kidnapper did an awful bad thing and needed just what the Police gave him." A child suggests that they could make the ending longer "if we had a trial for Kidnapper." This is discussed in relation to both plot construction and legal values.

Being guided to reflect on the content of the play, the children talk about a kidnapper. This brings strong verbal responses from all except two children since this is a subject they all feel strongly about. Several children volunteer suggestions and generalizations about what to do "so a kidnapper won't get you." The children talk about not talking to strangers. One child explains that you should never take candy or toys from strangers. Another says that you should never get into a stranger's car. Yet another insists that you need to put both chains and locks on the doors to your house. Several children remind the others that you should "mind your parents." They talk about police officers, jails, and punishment. It is apparent that for all of them this has been a meaningful experience from the point of view of feelings and from the satisfaction of realizing that they are learning "how to make a good play."

EXAMINING THE CHILDREN'S WORKSHOP AS AN ART, A LANGUAGE ART, AND A LEARNING EXPERIENCE

An Art Experience

To observe these children originating and forming a play for an audience of peers is to witness a mircocosm of the art of drama. The experience shows how all of the children became involved in structuring drama by relating the basic components of the player, the playmaker, and the audience. It illustrates how four of the children were stimulated by the manipulation of packing cartons and their arrangement in space to imagine the basic circumstances of a plot. As the children interacted to exchange their ideas, their plot began to take the form of a story. Within a general plan they were able to form a play from their feelings and perceptions. They were able to improvise believable actions and dialogue for their imagined characters, and to bring the action to a climax and an ending that grew out of the struggle. They were able to communicate their play to an audience of peers.

It is important to consider the cumulative drama activities these children experienced during their eleven hours together. For the first eight hours they participated in the role of players to explore fundamental concepts. When most of the children had learned to concentrate to apply some of the basic concepts the children progressed to the role of playmakers in their ninth class meeting. For three consecutive hours the children explored plot concepts. Important, too, from the viewpoint of drama as an art is the realization that each of the children's experiences were guided.

A Language Art

The entire workshop experience illustrates how drama is central to a child's language processes. Essentially, the children were involved in the processes of thinking, abstracting, interacting, talking, speaking, listening, and communicating in a drama experience that was "exciting and fun" for everyone.

Beginning with the manipulation of packing boxes and cartons, the children as players and playmakers were stimulated to perceive, imagine, recall, and select from memory their forming concepts of kidnapper, mother, police Officer, law, and punishment. The initial stimulation motivated them to interact verbally to exchange ideas, and to organize and reorganize their thoughts about plot incidents. With a general plan they proceeded to create a plot, characters, and dialogue by improvising actions and words. Creation led to the involvement of all of the children in the experience.

The children in the role of the audience received the communication of the players and playmakers by listening to words and sounds, and by observing actions, character relationships, and feeling. They responded by clapping, laughing, and cheering. Following the play they expressed their reactions verbally to the playmakers, commenting on particular actions, sounds, dialogue, and character. Several children asked questions and offered suggestions for replaying the play.

A Learning Experience

From the view point of learning, the workshop experience reveals children's efforts and desires to organize and master their visible and invisible worlds through drama. It shows how children explain perceived feelings and preconceptions of law and morality to themselves.

The experience illustrates how developmental needs are met through drama. The experience described above provided a strong release for physical and emotional energies. It encouraged interaction in the small group of four and in the larger audience group. It provided many opportunities for problem solving and provided the four children in the small group with a most satisfying experience from the viewpoint of nurturing egos and building each child's self-confidence. In the feedback discussion that resulted from the play the children probably learned some safety precautions from each other that they will remember.

A SECOND, MORE COMPREHENSIVE LOOK AT THE PROCESS-CONCEPT STRUCTURE APPROACH TO DRAMA AS AN ART

Principles of Art

What gives a work of art its capacity to arouse human feeling and thought? A human being—the imager, the creator—one might say. That is true, but it would also appear that every work of art that conveys feeling and thought to others does so because of two essential factors: content and form.

These two factors are expressed by Sir Herbert Read as two fundamental principles governing all art. He describes them as "a *principle of form,* derived, in my opinion, from the organic world, and the universal objective aspect of all works of art; and a *principle of origination* peculiar to the mind of man, and impelling him to create (and appreciate the creation of) symbols, phantasies, myths which take on a universally valid objective existence only in virtue of the principle of form. Form is a function of *perception;* origination is a function of *imagination.* These two mental activities exhaust, in their dialectical counter play, all the psychic aspects of aesthetic experience."[3]

Read's principles govern the process-concept structure approach to drama with children. By nature children originate and express what is deepest in their feelings and in their unconscious drives. Children need to learn, however, how to *perceive* and *form* drama in its many varied forms.

Nature of the Art of Drama

The word "drama" comes from the Greek *drao* meaning "I *do,* I *struggle.*" Drama essentially is human action—the imagining of characters in action. It is a form of art that tells a story of conflict through the action and speech of the characters. The story is acted out by players who impersonate the characters by imagining and making believe they are the story characters. Most drama is acted out by players for the enjoyment of an audience.

In drama the story content comes from feelings caused by a conflict that reflects human experience. Such a conflict may be caused by forces in the physical environment, by another person or persons, by an idea or belief, or by an inner conflict of the individual.

The origins of the art of drama are uncertain. Most civilizations have had some form of drama. Among the many theories of origin offered, it has been suggested that the source of drama lies in *mimesis* since mimicry is as old as the human race and is evident in primitive religious ceremonies, games, and tribal events. In such rituals tribal priests who believed in sympathetic magic imitated the actions and sounds of animals or supernatural beings to appeal to the gods. It has also been suggested that drama began with religious ceremonies in which hymns were sung at the tombs of dead heroes. While the chorus chanted the hymns of praise a member of the chorus or a person as an actor was introduced to depict events from the life of the dead hero; thus drama is thought to

[3] Herbert Read, *Education Through Art,* 3rd rev. ed. (London: Faber and Faber, 1958), p. 33.

have begun. Others have suggested that drama originated from the enactment of stories of real life events. These included struggles and victories resulting from events such as battles and animal hunts.

All of these theories reveal essential characteristics of drama: action, impersonation, feeling, *mimesis,* imagination, and the creation of events and of a story told in action and words. All have a common structure.

Structure of the Art of Drama

What is the basic structure of the art of drama? Or, what distinctive parts interrelate to give structure to the art when it reaches the play form and is communicated to an audience? The most basic parts, as indicated previously, include the players, playmakers, and audience. This structure was evident in the children's improvised play of the Kidnapper-Daughter-Police Officer. It was evident in the five- and six-year-olds' improvised play of Ghost-Drunkman-Superman. It was present in the boys' improvisation of the Pilot and Indian Scout. Although there is a difference in the aesthetic quality and form of each of these experiences, the basic structure of each is the same. Each drama was formed through the interrelationship of the creative processes of the players, playmakers, and audience.

Nature of the Art of Drama with Children

"Drama with Children" is an inclusive term. It designates all group activities designed, structured, and guided by a teacher or leader to involve children in the processes of discovering, creating, and experiencing drama as an art and a learning experience.

The art of drama is a process of originating and giving form to action, language, characters, a story, and a play. Children create drama in the related roles of players and playmakers. As players, they imagine, impersonate, and form the action of characters. When children progress in their skills and abilities as players they experience the processes of playmaking. When children become able to concentrate enough to imagine, impersonate, and communicate the character action of the play to an audience, drama then becomes theatre. The audience may be alternate participants or peers invited from another classroom.

Drama is formed into theatre *only* as a step in children's progress of discovering how to improvise and form a play, not as theatre in the strict sense. Its purpose is educational, not professional, and it has no director. A play is presented to an audience of peers so that the players and playmakers may tell a story of their own improvisation and communicate it to others. The source of the story will depend upon the level of experience and skill the children have. Advanced students may be able to originate and form a play from their own imaginings. Plays may also be *improvised* and *formed* from many different sources, such as written stories, poems, legends, a series of sounds or a musical composition, paintings, cartoons, episodes from history, experiences from real life, or play scripts.

Identification of Drama Elements

The elements of drama are the essential parts inherent in each of the related roles of the player, playmaker, and audience.

ROLE OF THE PLAYER

Basic elements include: (1) relaxation, trust, and concentration; (2) body movement; (3) the five senses; (4) imagination; (5) language, voice, and speech; and (6) characterization (Figure 1).

ROLE OF THE PLAYMAKER

Basic elements include: (1) plot; (2) character; (3) theme; (4) dialogue; (5) melody-sound; and (6) spectacle (Figure 1).

ROLE OF THE AUDIENCE

Basic elements center in the roles of: (1) perceiver; (2) responder; and (3) evaluator (Figure 1).

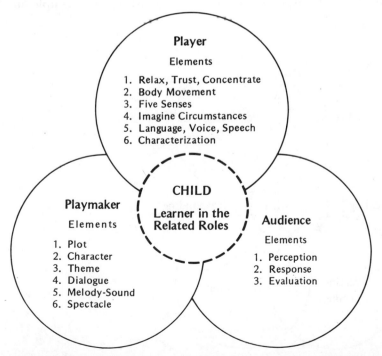

Figure 1 Conceptual Design—Structural Components and Elements.

To enable a child to explore and discover the basic skills and concepts of each role, these elements are broken down into concepts.

EXAMINING FUNDAMENTAL DRAMA PROCESSES

The creative processes used in drama can be identified as learning processes in education. Although each person creates and learns in an individual way, there are processes common to players, playmakers, and the audience. Most fundamentally these include: (1) perceiving; (2) responding; (3) imagining; (4) creating or forming; (5) communicating; and (6) evaluating (Figure 2).

In drama these processes are interdependent. The child is guided to explore the processes through each of the learning roles. Learning experiences are applied to each of the basic elements to enable the child to acquire skills, concepts, and enjoyment in creating and receiving drama. Exploration of concepts through learning processes is cumulative and, in part, sequential. This means that one process does not necessarily precede or follow another in the sequence listed here. On the one hand, there are instances when processes need to be explored sequentially as listed here, particularly when children have reached a level of learning in which they are ready to create and present a play for their peers. On the other hand, when children are first being introduced to drama concepts, processes may be experienced singly or in clusters. For example, in

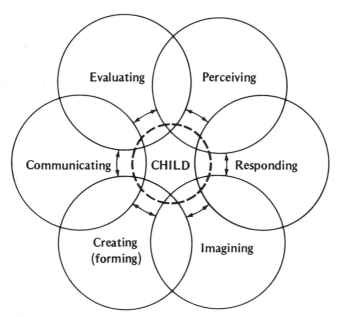

Figure 2 Conceptual Design—Drama Processes.

exploring the concepts of tension and release in relaxation, children will only use the processes of responding and perceiving.

Perceiving

Perception is the process by which children use their senses or sensory perceptions to extract information from the physical environment. The child matches what is sensed to frames of reference stored in the memory. Through this process the child is able to discriminate among sensory stimuli and identify sensory properties such as a color, a range of colors, shapes, objects, sounds, textures, odors, and tastes. The child is also able to *interpret* the meaning of sensory perceptions and thus provide a link between *sensing*, on the one hand, and *behaving*, on the other. This process is not directly observable and can only be understood by observing behavioral responses made to stimuli. In the comprehensive exploration of drama concepts the child learns to perceive sensory qualities and properties that give distinctive form and meaning to an action, characterization, and a play.

In drama perceiving may be as simple as identifying the color of a fabric. It also may be as complex as observing, responding to, and interpreting a character by improvising action in relation to the action of another person who is also an imagined character.

Responding

The natural human process of responding is basic to learning and living. It pervades the total creative process of forming drama. Learned responses must be acquired in a specific sense, or they will not appear. To encourage personal response a few basic points need to be emphasized. First, a stimulus must be distinctive enough for a child to attach a response to it. Second, the child must be induced to attend or receive the stimulus. Next, the response expected must be within the child's capabilities. For example, if a child is expected to respond to other children constructing a dramatic plot, he or she must know basic concepts of plot construction.

Because of a human need to be accepted by his or her peers, and to feel competent and have a sense of achievement, effective motivation and behavioral reenforcement in the learning of drama can be provided by a positive response from peers. Response may be nonverbal, a single statement, interaction, or participation in any number of different ways. It may be as complex as seeking a solution to a difficult problem, or offering evaluation based on the comprehension of governing principles.

Imagining

Imagination is a birthright that comes into the world with every child. It is as mysterious and as wonderful as a child's heartbeat. It is powerful for it springs from a rhythmic, vital source. It is delicate for it roots in sensitivity. It is original because it comes from within the child's mind. In some unexplainable way a child has a flash of inner vision. It seeks fulfillment.

Imagining is the process by which a human being forms a mental picture of what is not physically present, or of what has never been actually experienced. Or it may be a process of combining images from previous experiences. In exploring and creating drama a child imagines in order to originate solutions for a broad range of artistic problems. Imagining is at the core of the creative process in drama.

Creating (Forming)

By nature children are inclined to create. They paint, speak, sing, dance, make sounds, and make believe with joyous abandon. They create in an almost reckless way. They are crude and confident in their freshness. They are expressive. This does not mean that every child will grow up to be an artist. It does mean that children arrive in the world with the potential for developing dramatic imagination and with the desire to create.

Creating pervades the entire range of processes required to form drama. Children use improvisation almost exclusively. (By improvisation is meant the process used to make up dialogue and actions and other drama forms spontaneously or extemporaneously.) Even when they use a play script children create the play by improvising character, action, and dialogue in each related unit of the play. Occasionally, but rarely, children may memorize the lines of a play after it has been developed improvisationally.

Although creation is an individual, subjective process in drama, the act of creation often requires collaboration between two or more persons. Children learn to cooperate with others to create and synthesize individual processes that result in an artistic whole.

Communicating

Communication is a process by which a person interacts with another person or persons to impart "something" as partakers in the experience. The act of communication usually implies that something immaterial is to be imparted through language to convey thought, feeling, an attitude, or a particular meaning. In drama children learn to communicate through language processes that are, as pointed out, both verbal and nonverbal. As the child participates in the different learning roles of drama, the child acquires flexibility through active participation in verbal communication processes.

The child learns to communicate nonverbally through action, expressive body movement, and through a variety of symbols unique to the art of drama. These symbols include light, sound, color, shape, and space, and evolve from the playmaking elements of spectacle and sound.

Evaluating

The process of evaluation influences and attends the entire scope of the creative learning process in drama. The child learns to appraise personal efforts when he or she is player or playmaker, and the efforts of others when part of the audience. Evaluation pertains to the degree to which each child pauses to consider and assess the quality and decisions surrounding individual and eventually group effort and achievements. Decision making is inherent in the formation of drama. A child must continually respond to stimuli. He or she must select impulses, images, objects, colors, shapes, and sounds, and interact with and respond to others and to meaning. As the child acquires skills and concepts, the child is able to consciously evaluate dramatic forms on the basis of learned aesthetic criteria.

SUGGESTED ACTIVITIES FOR ADULT STUDENTS

1. With a group of peers discuss each of the following:
   a. John Gassner's statement that opens this chapter;
   b. Herbert Read's statement concerning the two fundamental principles that govern all art;
   c. The children's workshop from the viewpoint of satisfying developmental needs and of fostering language development;
   d. The process-concept structure from the viewpoints of concepts, processes, and the interrelationship of the two.
2. With a group of peers attend a theatre production. At a later time, discuss the production from the following viewpoints:
   a. Structure;
   b. Content and form;
   c. Elements of the play;
   d. Audience response.
3. Assume that you are a classroom teacher at the fourth grade level in an elementary school. You have introduced the process-concept structure approach to drama as an integral art in the language arts curriculum. You are enthusiastic about the children's response to the learning activities. You have been asked to explain this approach at a faculty meeting by responding to the following questions asked by teachers:
   a. What is meant *exactly* by the terms "process," "concept," and "structure"?
   b. How are the processes and concepts interrelated?
   c. Give two or three examples of how the child experiences the processes through the exploration of specific concepts.

d. What are the distinctive features of a drama learning experience?
e. If there is a goal for each learning experience, what is the ultimate goal for the child, the final goal of all the learning experiences?
f. What criteria do you use to evaluate the child's achievement of a goal or several goals?

4
The Teaching-Learning Process

Children have two visions, the inner and the outer. Of the two the inner vision is brighter.

SYLVIA ASHTON-WARNER
Teacher[1]

To teach children is both a privilege and a challenge. The teacher is the person responsible for providing the essential requirements of a successful drama program for children. This chapter investigates the teacher's responsibilities by looking at the relationships between what the teacher does and what the children do that appear to influence development and learning. The investigation is organized in four parts.

First, it shows how the teacher uses the process-concept structure in a single workshop and in several workshop experiences, and it examines teaching strategies, procedures, and learning experiences. Second, it considers a learning environment. Third, it looks into evaluation. It concludes by examining some aspects of drama curriculum planning.

DRAMA WORKSHOPS WITH NINE-, TEN-, AND ELEVEN-YEAR-OLDS

Twenty-First Workshop: Introducing Concepts of Sound

Fifteen children (eleven girls and four boys) are ready to begin a new experience in playmaking.[2] Most of the children have participated

[1] Sylvia Ashton-Warner, *Teacher* (New York: Simon & Schuster, 1963), p. 32.
[2] Composite account from university students' observation reports, and instructor's plan, evaluation, and taped recording of laboratory drama classes for children, School of Drama, University of Washington, Seattle, WA, May 1973.

together for twenty class meetings. During the first ten hours the children explored concepts in the role of the player. In the next ten hours they applied these concepts to playmaking. They have experienced concepts in each of the playmaking elements except in the elements of melody (sound) and theme.

The children are asked to organize into four groups. The four boys form one group, three girls another, and two groups organize with four girls in each. The workshop begins with the teacher guiding the children to recall plot concepts and then to discuss sound. Next they are asked to listen to a two-minute recording, "Underwater Adventure," from *Listen, Move and Dance*, Volume 1.[3] The recording uses a variety of instrumental and electronic sounds to depict water bubbles, a struggle on the ocean floor and, finally, the return to the surface. From the viewpoint of plot the music forms a beginning, an introduction of tension which rises to a climax, and a resolution.

The children are not given the title or a description of the recording. Rather they are asked to listen, to imagine basic circumstances and a plot with beginning, middle, and ending incidents in which a character struggles to overcome a problem. Following this the players exchange ideas to agree on a story in which they can tell the plot in three sentences. The recording is then played again, serving as a soundtrack, while players imagine the plot action in relation to the sound. Next the students are asked to decide who will be each of the characters in their play. With this accomplished, they listen to the recording again with each player imagining what their characters want and do in the story.

Attention is next focused on the element of spectacle. Children have previously explored this element through scenic and costume design on a simplified level by focusing on concepts of shape, line, color, and texture. Each group, working in a different corner of the room, is asked to select no more than four scenic objects (blocks, chairs, stools, benches). They are to arrange the objects in space to create the requirements for their play's setting. When this is done the students are guided to consider their characters in relation to a costume. They are to use a single piece of fabric only if it will heighten the image of their character or character's action.

After about five minutes on these problems the groups are ready to improvise the actions to the recorded music to share their plays with each other. Prior to each sharing, a player in each group describes the play's setting. The goal for the audience is to identify the characters and plot of each play through its actions.

The first group imagines a "forest clearing in front of a cave." Their

---

[3] *Listen, Move and Dance*, vol. 1, recording arranged and directed by Vera Gray, Capitol Records, Inc. (H 21006).

plot begins with three Witches, each wearing a black cloth over her shoulders, mixing an evil brew over an imagined fire. Their large Cat prowls nearby keeping watch. Suddenly the Cat gives a warning meow. The Witches are alarmed. From their actions and the soundtrack it appears as if a rainstorm is breaking. The Witches hurry to put out the fire to save their brew and themselves by moving everything inside the cave. As the storm reaches its height (recording) and then subsides, the Witches and Cat watch from their cave.

The second group imagines a "goldsmith's dungeon with a door to the outside and a door to the inside." The plot begins with the Goldsmith melting an imaginary golden statue (large piece of golden colored satin fabric). As the Goldsmith stirs the bubbling gold with a long imaginary poker, a Stranger sneaks in. When the Goldsmith starts to pour the gold into a mold, the Stranger picks up the poker and demands gold. The Goldsmith gives a sharp whistle. Immediately, two huge barking Dogs appear from the inside door and start after the Stranger who defends himself with the poker. A fight develops. Finally the Stranger drops the poker and pleads with the Goldsmith for mercy. The Goldsmith orders the Dogs to stop their attack, and to guard the Stranger. The Goldsmith uses his hand to give a command to one of the Dogs who runs out the door. Apparently the dog is going for help. While the other Dog guards the Stranger, the Goldsmith examines the gold.

The boys' group imagines their setting to be "the deck of a small ship with the ocean below." The plot begins when the Captain helps two Divers make their descent into the ocean. Suddenly one Diver is attacked by a Shark. (At this moment the boy pulls a small, bright red scarf from under his navy blue sweater to give the effect of blood.) The other Diver swims to the rescue and uses a tranquilizer gun to ward off the Shark, who soon quiets down and swims away. The Captain instructs the Divers to surface, and they return to the ship.

The last group imagines their setting to be "a swamp in the jungle near a large tree on the edge of a stream in the days of the cave man." The plot begins with a Lioness and her young Cub drinking from the stream, after which they stretch out to sleep under the tree. A Cave Man searching for water is surprised by the suddenly awakened Lioness, who attacks him. He defends himself with an imaginary club. After a vigorous struggle, the wounded Cave Man climbs a tree and the injured Lioness, nudging her Cub, goes growling off into the jungle.

After each improvisation the audience responds by identifying characters and plot and asking questions when actions are not clear. Participants offer feedback by discussing imaginative ways in which individuals and groups used the element of spectacle to create settings and costumes. The teacher commends each group for its inclusion of conflict and resolution incidents in the plot, and for the way they listened to the same music to imagine and create different original plots.

Continuing with the element of sound, the teacher stimulates a short discussion about the use of sound to heighten both the action and mood of a play. The players are guided to explore their *vocal* abilities by constructing a variety of sounds and moods including: rain, outboard motor, friendly lion, angry lion, barking watchdogs, and water bubbling in a kettle. Next, the players explore the use of objects to improvise sound. The objects are: tin cans each partially filled with seeds or grains, small cardboard tubes of various lengths, and several sheets of newspapers. The sounds include: gentle rain changing to heavy rain; gentle wind building to a strong, haunting wind; and a small crackling fire changing to a raging forest fire.

The participants are introduced to two new problems concerned with sound. First, they are to improvise dialogue that the players can use to communicate the plot and characters. Second, a sound crew is to construct appropriate sounds to communicate the action and changing moods of the play. Working in the same groups as previously, each group is assigned to serve, also, as a sound crew for another group. The sound recording is to be used only if the sound crew believes it is needed.

To solve these problems, the first group improvises dialogue in which each Witch tells the others who she is going to hex at the midnight hour. When the storm breaks, the Witches give sharp, hasty orders to each other, for each wants to save herself, but wants the others to save the brew. The sound crew has one student use a plastic straw to blow into a milk carton filled with water to suggest the sound of the bubbling brew. Another person uses two drums to make sudden thunderclaps. The other two use their voices and tap their hands on the floor to create the sound of rain and wind. Following each improvisation, the audience comments on ways in which the sounds and dialogue caused the play to be better understood and "felt."

Twenty-Second Workshop: Introducing Concepts of Spectacle

This workshop focuses on the dramatic element of spectacle, emphasizing concepts of lighting. A discussion points out that lighting is used for visibility, to help an audience see the action clearly; to establish physical conditions such as time and weather; and to create the changing moods of a play. Simple lighting equipment is introduced. This includes the light switches in the room, room lights, electrical outlets, a single spotlight mounted on a standard, several colored gelatins in frames to use over the spotlight, and several small flashlights. The teacher demonstrates different ways in which visibility, physical conditions, and moods can be achieved with this simple equipment.

After learning to manipulate the equipment, the children organize in the same groups as for the twenty-first workshop. Each group is given a lighting problem to solve by using no more than three pieces of equipment. Problems include the construction of: (1) firelight for a fire to melt gold; (2) lightning to follow thunderclaps; (3) a jungle sunrise changing slowly to daylight; and (4) visibility underwater with flashlights for divers. With enthusiasm and interaction each group works to solve its problem. After their first trials, they experiment further with new solutions offered during evaluation.

A new problem is presented. The children are asked to see if, as four groups, they can create one play by working together. One group is to be the players, another the audience, the third the light crew, and the fourth the sound crew. Challenged by this problem, the children discuss together which group is to be responsible for each task. The "witches" group agrees to be first to create their play. They arrange the space by using a ladder for the cave's entrance, a scenic block for a rock next to the fire, and two chairs for trees. The second group, who previously constructed sound, is in charge of lighting. The third group, who has not worked on this play, becomes the sound crew, and the fourth group is the audience. The players and playmakers work together to communicate the play to the audience. After this first experience in collaboration the children ask if they may do this the next time with the other plays.

Twenty-Third Workshop: Introducing the Concept of Theme

After the "warm-up" and a spirited discussion of the previous session, the concept of theme is introduced. The teacher points out that each of their original plays deals with a need to survive. In three plays the characters are up against forces in the physical environment. The Witches are up against the storm, the Divers against the Shark, and the Cave Man against the Lioness. In the Goldsmith and Stranger play each person is up against the other. It is explained that a play, like a story, joke, cartoon, or painting, always *has something particular to say* about human beings. After some discussion the teacher says, "Think about these kinds of questions: What message to do you want your play to convey, what feelings do you want it to arouse in the audience? Is your play saying that to survive takes courage or quick thinking? See if you can agree on a theme and express it for yourselves in a clear statement of action."

Each group discusses its theme. When they are ready the teacher, following the children's requests, explains that they are to continue in the same way as they worked in the last meeting. The teacher clarifies the problem.

Although the children's attempts to weave a theme into their improvised plays are serious, the results for the first trials are only fair. However, the students are able to give the notion of a theme for each play, and they seem pleased with their efforts.

A heated discussion occurs about the theme of the last play, "The Cave Man and the Lioness." Concern centers on whether only the Cave Man or only the Lioness should survive, rather than both of them winning out. Several children take the viewpoint of the Cave Man and feel that he should kill the Lioness because, as one child says, "In history the Cave Man had to kill wild animals to keep from *being* killed." Others, strong to defend their viewpoints, feel that the Cave Man should not kill the wild animals but should always be prepared to save himself. By the time the class ends, almost every child has expressed an opinion. However, the two girls who had imagined themselves to be the Lioness and the Cub feel strongly that humans should never kill animals. These two girls, who are neighbors, continue to discuss this burning issue as they leave for home.

Twenty-Fourth Workshop: Synthesizing Playmaking Elements

At the final meeting of the year, some children have invited their parents to attend. The procedure used at previous sessions is followed. However, a new problem is introduced. Children, working in the same groups, are assigned new responsibilities as playmaking crews. A crew is to create light or sound for a play that they have not lighted or created sound for previously. Each playmaking unit is to work to see how they can communicate the play's theme by strengthening the plot and characters with dialogue, sound, light, and color. This new challenge appears to recharge the students' energies. With enjoyment and confidence each group works to "put all that we've learned together." Final efforts are satisfying.

After the last play, the two girls who developed the characters of the Lioness and the Cub say they have "something to share." They explain that they have thought about their play all week and they have written a song about it that shows the theme. They want to sing it for the others. This is their song, which they sing in two-part harmony.

SWEET ANIMALS

Animals are vanishing from this earth.
Men with stupidity don't know their worth.
They've killed them off with rifle and knife.
Soon there won't be any more animal life.
(Refrain to animals)
Animals, sweet animals,
My heart is with you.
Animals, sweet animals,
You're crammed in a zoo.
Animals, sweet animals,
My heart is with you
Animals, sweet animals,
Soon there'll be few.[4]

[4] By permission of Barbara Chateaubriand and Crystal McConnell.

EMPLOYING STRATEGIES AND PROCEDURES

A teacher uses different techniques to involve children in different kinds of learning experiences. These techniques evolve from two basic methods: strategies and procedures. A *strategy* is applied in a basically stable form covering a wide range of teachers, teaching situations, students, and grade levels. A *procedure* is intended to be adapted to meet the particular circumstances of the teaching-learning situation. Such circumstances include the teacher's individual teaching style; the experience, age, and developmental needs of the students; and the content and nature of the learning experiences.

Major Strategies

CONCEPT LEARNING

This strategy, as illustrated in the drama workshops, evolves directly from the process-concept structure and forms the stable framework for the drama program. It aims to involve the student in experiencing and learning basic concepts of the drama elements. It provides a firm basis for the teacher's guidance and cumulative learning experiences for the students.

PROCESS INVOLVEMENT

The major processes used to explore and create drama are interrelated with the concepts in the learning experiences. This strategy aims to establish within each student a firm basis for involvement in the total creative process. In this strategy the processes of perceiving, responding, imagining, and creating pervade all learning experiences by being included as an integral part of the goal and experience.

Processes of communicating and evaluating are included whenever a teacher determines that the group is ready. On the one hand, these two processes pervade most of the learning experiences indirectly. On the other hand, a teacher puts direct emphasis on these processes whenever the teacher recognizes that individuals and an entire group are ready to explore these higher levels of learning.

Major Procedures

WORKSHOP PROCEDURES

A workshop procedure means that experiences are designed to involve children in *working* to solve problems or to reach a goal or goals. It is an active-participation procedure. Within a basic workshop pattern several different kinds of related procedures are used. These include: (1) directed; (2) problem-solving; (3) exploratory; and (4) competency-based.

DIRECTED PROCEDURE

In this procedure the teacher gives children directions to follow. The children are encouraged to try to do what the teacher directs them to do with each child being encouraged to respond in his or her own honest way. Used most frequently in introductory drama experiences, this procedure supplies the child with directions that explain what the child is to do, but do not tell or show the child how to do it. For example, a teacher gives directions in movement exploration by stating, "Walk on the outside of your feet . . . the inside of your feet . . . your toes . . . your heels." Each student responds by concentrating on the movements or on figuring out how to do them.

PROBLEM-SOLVING PROCEDURE

This procedure is used whenever a teacher senses that individuals have gained a sense of trust in themselves and others and are ready to solve drama problems. To use this procedure the teacher introduces a concept and then presents a problem in terms of the task to be accomplished. For example, in the twenty-first workshop, the teacher presented a problem based on the concept of plot: "a plot is built with beginning, middle, and ending incidents in which a character struggles to overcome a problem." The children were presented with the problem by the following statement: "Listen to the recording to imagine *where* the story takes place, *who* is in it, and *what* happens to show the problem, the struggle, and how the problem is overcome."

While allowing freedom for experimentation this procedure requires a child to imagine, concentrate, problem-solve, and cooperate with others. To use this procedure effectively a teacher needs to learn to design learning experiences in the nature of problems.

EXPLORATORY PROCEDURE

This is a procedure about halfway between the directed and problem-solving procedures in relation to a child's thought processes. It allows the child to explore independently to discover concepts and to improve skills. For example, a teacher focusing on the concept of the nonlocomotor movement of bending may say to the participants, "In your own personal space, see how many different ways you can discover to bend the finger joints in one of your hands."

During the exploration of the task, the teacher moves among the children helping a child if needed, or asking questions to cause the child to better perceive the task or ways to achieve it. After all of the children have had time to explore, individuals who volunteer are encouraged to show others how they achieved the task. Following this, the children are encouraged to continue to explore for a short time to try new or different explorations. This procedure appeals to preschool and kindergarten children and to older children who are being introduced to drama.

COMPETENCY-BASED PROCEDURE

This procedure motivates self-directed learning. For example, a child who has learned several playmaking concepts may be ready to work independently in a number of different ways including the following: constructing a dramatic plot, taking photographs of particular environments to be used to stimulate the imagining of basic circumstances, or planning a drama activity based on a concept of the child's choosing. Whenever the child is ready, the work is presented to the teacher for evaluation. If the work is successful in relation to established criteria, the child proceeds to a higher level of learning, or uses the particular project to involve other children in a drama experience. Teachers who have used this procedure have been pleased with the way a highly motivated child succeeds in involving other children in learning.

FACILITATING THE TEACHING-LEARNING PROCESS

The task of teaching is complex. It cannot be guided by a single set of rules or principles that apply to all teaching-learning situations in drama. However, a teacher may perform certain functions to bring about necessary conditions for learning. Two essential functions include planning the drama lesson, and teaching in a broadly sequential and flexible pattern.

Planning a Lesson

A teacher plans a single lesson within the context of a unit of learning. Guidelines for planning a single lesson include: (1) assess the developmental needs and interests of individuals in the group; (2) list concepts and processes to be introduced or reenforced; (3) state goals in terms of expected learner outcomes; (4) list instructional materials and arrangements of the physical environment; (5) design and describe briefly the learning experiences in order of presentation, including organization of the students and of the time; and (6) list evaluation procedures.

Sequential Flexible Teaching Pattern

A teacher's way of teaching must remain flexible. It is governed in part by personality, teaching style, experience, and knowledge. The teacher aims to influence the conditions of learning by using a flexible teaching pattern that evolves in four broadly sequential steps. These include: (1) orientation, (2) presentation, (3) guidance, and (4) evaluation.

ORIENTATION

In the orientation step, a teacher aims to establish a friendly atmosphere. As individuals enter the classroom the teacher greets them individually, listens to them, and encourages interaction to foster individual response. The teacher is alert to children's behavior and interests to determine the kind of experiences needed to meet individual and group needs. Using a direct procedure, the teacher guides the children into a "warm-up" activity aimed to foster relaxation.

The teacher then generally proceeds to activities related to movement exploration. This kind of orientation serves to involve the child's entire self—physical, intellectual, social, and emotional. (Orientation procedures are described in some detail in the first three chapters.)

An alert teacher forms the habit of silently wondering, while observing children's behavior, "What's going on here? What does this child need? What does this group need from the viewpoint of activities to meet developmental needs?" A teacher needs always to adapt experiences to the particular needs of each child and the group of children.

PRESENTATION

The presentation procedure includes the different means a teacher uses to present the activities. It includes the stimulation used to focus children's attention. Primary considerations in presenting learning experiences are clarity and variety. Clarity is essential. To work on a problem, or to follow directions to achieve a goal, the child needs to know *what to do*. A teacher aims to present goals clearly so every child in the situation—players, playmakers, audience—knows *what to do*. Likewise, the teacher asks open-ended questions to stimulate the children's recall of concepts and previously learned capabilities that are applicable to the learning experience at hand.

Variety refers to the various means a teacher uses to present stimuli, including problems and goals. Verbal communication is essential but should not be used exclusively. Children respond to novelty. The teacher seeks to use a variety of sensory stimuli. For example, these may include: audiovisual materials, concrete material which children may manipulate, literature, games, riddles, cartoons, first-hand experiences, and interviews with appropriate persons. A presentation is used that seems most appropriate in relation to the students and the particular learning experience.

GUIDANCE TO EVOKE STUDENT RESPONSE

A teacher uses different techniques to encourage student participation. The teacher observes as the students respond or fail to respond to the presentation of an activity. On the one hand, if several students appear confused as to what to do, the teacher either questions the group to determine the reason or the teacher clarifies the presentation. The goal may need to be restated in a different way. Key concept words may need to be emphasized. These words may be repeated until students perceive the task and proceed on their own. On the other hand, if only one or two students need help the teacher assists them individually. In introductory experiences a teacher may participate actively with the students to encourage everyone to respond. Or the teacher may move among a group of students who are reluctant to begin and encourage them through active participation. Or, the teacher may serve as a partner for a child who has no partner when others are working in pairs.

A teacher may guide in a character role related to the imagined circumstances for several different purposes. Among these are: to pose questions to deepen the belief and involvement in the unfolding drama; to introduce a new problem or challenge in the plot or circumstances; to assist the players in coping with a problem that arises out of the evolving dramatic action; to involve the players in action that causes them to realize the theme of the drama; or, to assist individuals in meeting developmental needs through the playmaking experience.

EVALUATION

In the evaluation step, the teacher guides students to discuss the outcomes of their activity trials, and to draw conclusions at the end of each session. Feedback after each experience should be brief and to the point, and guided in relation to the needs and abilities of the children. The focus of the evaluation is always on the activity as it relates to the goal—the problem the students set out to solve. Evaluation is never of the child. Rather it is of what the child does. Whenever an audience is included the teacher first asks the audience to offer responses by asking, "Did the players solve the problem?" For example, in the twenty-second workshop the players were given the following problem: "Construct firelight for the fire to melt gold by using no more than three pieces of lighting equipment." In response to the question the audience and the teacher determine whether the participants solved the problem through at least one aspect of it. "Did they use three pieces of equipment? Did they try? Did they succeed in making others imagine and believe that a fire was burning?"

The teacher uses care in questioning during the evaluation to allow for variations in each child's way of solving problems or reaching a goal. Evaluation is particularly important to encourage further trials and to foster the self-esteem and ego development of each child.

To encourage self-evaluation a teacher frequently asks students to assess their own progress or to discuss with a partner by answering such questions as these: "How did you do? Did you have any trouble? What questions do you have?" Evaluation by participants, by peers, and by the teacher are critical factors in helping students develop clearer expectations for themselves and know what constitutes achievement.

Evaluations at the end of the session provide opportunities for students to make generalizations concerning their progress and concerning the *content* of the experience.

ESTABLISHING A LEARNING ENVIRONMENT

School is a planned environment. The teacher is the key person responsible for planning and establishing a learning environment for drama experiencing. An environment is governed by many factors including primarily the physical and social characteristics of the classroom.

Characteristics of the Physical Environment

Certain physical characteristics of the environment influence student response in relation to active participation in learning. These include: room temperature, lighting, sound level, humidity, oxygen content, arrangement of desks or chairs, and location of activity centers in relation to doors and windows. Other factors are the size, shape, and color of the room, and the kind of floor covering.

SPACE

Space is an influencing environmental factor. If an area is either too large or too small it affects both individual response and social interaction. A teacher considers ways to organize a room to facilitate social interaction and to make the best physical use of available space. Generally a large spatial area needs to be limited by boundaries to facilitate children's concentration. A small area generally needs to be enlarged, if possible, by rearranging movable furniture. What is most often needed is an open area of space where twenty or more children have room to move individually to explore concepts of body movement without being restricted; and an open area that can be arranged and rearranged when needed by children to explore a variety of drama concepts. Space that permits flexible arrangements to provide needed working areas for players and playmakers, and room for an audience, is ideal. However, the open space of a basement room or a large corridor has worked effectively for innovative teachers.

Young children in preschool and kindergarten seem to concentrate on drama activity better if they remain in the security of their own classrooms. Children in primary and intermediate grades respond enthusiastically to opportunities to work in specialized physical environments such as a school auditorium, multipurpose room, or occasionally an outdoor environment.

INSTRUCTIONAL EQUIPMENT

Equipment and materials should be selected from the viewpoints of safety and flexibility in their use.

EQUIPMENT FOR USE IN EXPLORING CONCEPTS
IN THE ROLE OF THE PLAYER

To facilitate children's exploration of concepts the most basic equipment needed includes: (1) a record player adaptable to different speeds with a variety of selected recordings, and (2) a hand drum or cymbal. Not essential but useful are a tape recorder with microphones and a supply of tapes or cassettes.

LIGHTING EQUIPMENT FOR USE IN PLAYMAKING

Lighting equipment should be portable rather than permanently mounted. The minimum needed are the lights within the room. However, a few pieces of basic equipment stimulate children's interest in exploring qualities of light. These include: (1) one or two "light trees," each equipped with one or two movable spotlight lamps, 150 or 200 watts each, prefocused with swivel base and clips to hold color frames (Figure 3); (2) a selection of stage cables, cable connectors, and color gelatins in a variety of colors in frames to fit the lamps; and (3) several flashlights with batteries.

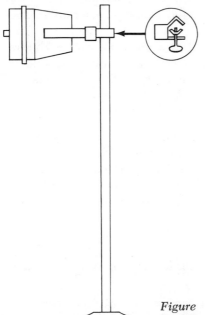

Figure 3 "Light-Tree" (Courtesy Warren C. Lounsbury).

The illustration of a display light called an "accentlight" shows the detail of the C-clamps used to fasten the U-shaped yoke to the standard.[5] Local lighting fixtures companies may be able to furnish display light for use as "light trees." The standard shown is also commercially manufactured but could be easily made by mounting a flange on a Christmas-tree-like X-base and screwing a 4' to 6' length of pipe into it. Use either ¾" or 1" pipe and flange. Cable should be heavy-duty plastic or rubber-covered wire that will withstand the abuse normally accorded portable equipment.[6]

INSTRUCTIONAL MATERIALS

Some scenic, costume, and sound materials are needed.

SCENIC MATERIALS

Suggested but not necessary materials include: (1) three or four 3' or 5' wooden ladders, (2) two or three small tables of different sizes and shapes, (3) several folding chairs, (4) several two- or three-fold open-framework screens (useful but not necessary), and (5) eight or ten wooden blocks, both cube and L-shaped (Figure 4). Blocks should be constructed in 16" cubes and 16" x 32" L-shapes from ½" plywood that may be painted and repainted in different colors.

COSTUME MATERIALS

Suggested minimum materials include a selection of fabrics in different colors and textures in varying widths and lengths from one foot to two or three yards. Other useful but not necessary materials include: (1) an assortment of discarded sheets, towels, and drapery materials cleaned or laundered and dyed in a variety of colors; (2) a supply of snap clothespins and masking tape to be used as a quick means for children to fasten fabrics together; and (3) an assortment of different kinds of hats, caps, gloves, headdresses, and several discarded and laundered medical or dental laboratory coats.

SOUND EXPLORATION MATERIALS

The following materials are useful but not necessary: (1) a tambourine, (2) two maracas, (3) two musical whistles for simulating sounds of sirens and bird calls, and (4) an assortment of discarded materials from which children may improvise sounds. These include such objects as hub caps, spikes suspended on strings, sandpaper, coconut shells, a large sheet of tin, cardboard tubes of varying lengths and diameters, plastic straws, and several empty cans with plastic lids into which a variety of objects may be placed.

Physical materials to be used as "properties" and as stimuli for imag-

[5] "Accentlight" available through Lighting Services, Inc., 77 Park Avenue, New York, NY 10016.

[6] Information courtesy of Warren C. Lounsbury, Associate Professor Emeritus and Technical Director, School of Drama, University of Washington, Seattle, WA.

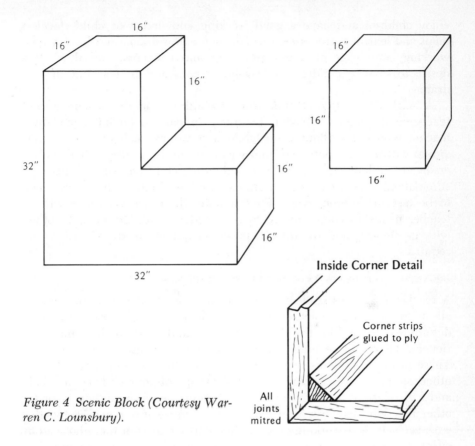

Figure 4 Scenic Block (Courtesy Warren C. Lounsbury).

ining may be collected by the children and the teacher. For example, such objects may include: a piece of driftwood, a small chest, a watch on a chain, a police badge, a lantern, a microscope, and binoculars.

Characteristics of the Social Environment

The social environment in a drama workshop stimulates the social processes of interaction and communication. The teacher is primarily responsible for setting up and controlling external conditions to influence social interaction. Such conditions include classroom organization and management, keeping order, managing discipline, and establishing an enthusiastic attitude toward drama. An effective social environment requires gaining attention, presenting appropriate stimuli, communicating effectively, and guiding in relation to individual needs and to the objectives of the learning situation.

TEACHER QUALIFICATIONS AND ATTITUDES

Teachers who succeed in establishing and controlling such conditions appear to have three essential characteristics in common. First, they enjoy children and have a good working knowledge of child development and learning processes; second, they enjoy drama and have a good working knowledge of drama processes and concepts; and third, they desire to involve children in learning drama and in learning through drama.

A teacher's positive attitude toward children and drama affects both teacher and student behavior. Learning appears to be influenced by a teacher who cares about every child and values each one as an individual with unique potential, idiosyncracies, and one life to live. Teachers need to adapt their guidance to individual children. All students need stimulation, guidance, encouragement, and evaluation, but these need to be met in different ways. For example, there are occasions when a teacher needs to communicate to one student with firmness, to others with gentleness, and to still others with cajoling, as the situation may require.

ORGANIZING STUDENTS INTO DIFFERENT GROUPINGS

A teacher organizes students into a variety of smaller working units to allow for social interaction and individual learning. Organization is determined largely by the drama concepts and kinds of learning experiences. There are several patterns a teacher may use for organization. These include: students work simultaneously but independently of each other; students work in pairs, in small groups of four or five, in a half-and-half relationship with half of the students being an audience for the other half who explores a problem; or an entire group works together with each student working on an individual part within the whole group effort. Groups in each of these patterns may be set up according to abilities, sex, ages, and heights by using a numbering-off system, or by encouraging students to organize themselves into a particular group pattern.

Students may be guided to organize themselves into groups in different ways. These may include: selecting colors or numbers from a box or hat, electing leaders who then take turns to choose group members, and electing leaders with each student then joining the leader of his or her choice.

KEEPING ORDER TO FOSTER SELF-CONTROL

Most children need to be helped to develop concentration and self-control. Whenever a large group of children interact in active participation there is generally considerable talking and laughing. This kind of interaction is natural and should be allowed to continue for several moments. Often children's spontaneous interaction gives way to concentration as children begin to work on the given activity.

In instances where children do not start to concentrate on their own, it is necessary for the teacher to assist them. The teacher can do this by establishing order. The teacher explains that the starting signal for the activity will be given when everyone is quiet and concentrating on the problem or the directions. Their quiet concentration will show that they are ready for the beginning signal. The teacher explains that he or she will receive an action (behavior) cue from the group that will show that they are concentrating or ready to begin.

A beginning signal for an activity may be given by a sound made by a drum, cymbal, or bell. One beat on the drum signals the children to start. Two beats on the drum signals them to stop the activity. To stop means that the child should stop talking and moving and "freeze" in whatever position the child is in at the moment the signal sounds. The novelty of "freezing" appeals to most children. This is an effective means to help a child to develop self-control. However, it is only effective if it is enforced. Children perceive quickly whether a teacher is firm or lax about keeping order and they respond accordingly.

EVALUATING PROGRESS OF STUDENTS AND PROGRAM

Evaluation is a continuing process used by the teacher to measure changes that occur in students, in the group, and in the program as a result of the teaching-learning process. Because the child is the focal point of the educative process, evaluation focuses first on each child's participation. Next it focuses on each child's progress in acquiring skills, applying concepts, and using drama processes. To employ evaluation a teacher uses the criteria stated in each goal and concept that the child explores during a given experience. In this structural approach to drama both objective and subjective measurements are used to evaluate student progress.

Objective performance tests may be devised by the teacher whenever a group completes a unit of learning. These are designed in the same way as the learning experiences but focus on students' abilities to apply a cluster of concepts. Tests aim to determine the approximate level of the process-concept competency of a student. Is the student able to perform with others as a part of a whole class experience? As a distinct character among others? With a partner in an imagined circumstance? Is the student able to identify plot incidents? Can the student construct a dramatic plot with others, or independently?

Subjective measurements are made by close observation of each child's individual response and participation. Observations are recorded on performance charts, anecdotal records, tape recordings, and by occasional photographs or kinescopes of students in action.

Results of objective tests and subjective observations are used to assess strengths and weaknesses of individual progress and of the program; to serve as motivating forces for individuals and the group; and to provide reports for individuals and parents. If letter grades are needed they should reflect the individual's growth in relation to the individual's capabilities. The emphasis must be to build on that which each individual can do, and to encourage a continuing desire to participate. A student will succeed naturally if appropriate goals are based on the student's capabilities.

The program is evaluated yearly in terms of physical facilities, equipment, and instructional and consumable materials. An evaluation of these factors serves as the basis for budget requests to insure continuance and maintenance of the program.

A teacher's self-evaluation is a key factor toward continuous improvement of a program. This should be done at the end of each learning unit or at four- or six-week intervals. A teacher evaluates self-progress in relation to the progress of the students. A further consideration in self-evaluation is professional growth. This is probably reflected most clearly by a teacher's participation and interaction with other persons at drama and educational conferences, and in-service courses.

CONSIDERATIONS IN DRAMA CURRICULUM PLANNING

The drama curriculum is a planned sequence of learning experiences structured in relation to the components of the player, playmaker, and audience.

Using the Drama Structure

The child, at the center of each learning experience, is introduced to drama through the component of the player. Because the player-audience relationship forms the core of the structure, the audience is introduced whenever the teacher recognizes that a sense of trust has been established. Playmaking elements are generally introduced after children have explored many concepts in the role of the player and have gained some essential skills needed by the player to participate in the role of playmaker.

INTRODUCING CONCEPTS IN THE ROLE OF THE PLAYER

The teacher has two chief options for introducing children to these concepts. The first is to provide learning experiences that are clearly sequential growing out of each of the elements in the role of the player. The second is to provide learning experiences that are cumulative but not particularly sequential. (The reader is referred to the first chapter of the book to identify one way in which player concepts were structured.) A sound guideline is for the teacher to select or design learning experiences based on concepts that meet the developmental needs of individuals and the group.

Playmaking concepts are introduced whenever a teacher recognizes that most of the children have gained player skills needed in the play-making process. When students progress to playmaking, many teachers continue to provide player-concept activities at the beginning of each playmaking workshop. These activities serve as an organic "warm-up" for the students. They also provide continuing exploration and improvement in the skills and concepts needed by the player.

Division of Allotted Time for Drama Experiences

Assuming that the drama curriculum is an integral part of the language arts curriculum there will be an allotted time for drama every day or every week. Suggested time blocks are: fifteen-minute periods daily, thirty-minute periods three days a week, or an hour period once or twice a week.

FIFTEEN-MINUTE PERIODS DAILY

Teachers prefer this time allotment when children explore the concepts of the player, for children seem to learn player skills in short, concentrated experiences. However, when children progress to playmaking longer periods are needed for exploration of player, playmaker, and audience concepts.

In introductory experiences a fifteen-minute period daily focuses generally on a different player element each period. Some teachers prefer to use five minutes of each period for movement exploration, and the following ten minutes for exploration of a different player element each day.

THIRTY-MINUTE PERIODS THREE TIMES A WEEK

Patterns similar to those described for the fifteen-minute period are used. However, a longer period provides more time for the exploration of the concepts in each of the elements. With more time each week children learn necessary skills and progress more quickly to playmaking experiences.

ONE-HOUR PERIOD WEEKLY OR BIWEEKLY

An hour period needs to be divided into three or four smaller time periods. Learning experiences are organized to allow for exploration of the concepts in each of the player elements. However, as children progress time should be organized to allow the children to explore learning in the role of the audience as well.

Teachers who have used an hour period find that in introductory experiences children seem to want to spend more time on movement exploration and less time on speech and the other related player elements. However, as the children progress the emphasis in the time blocks shifts. The reader is referred again to the description of children's workshops to identify different ways in which an hour time period was organized.

SUGGESTED ACTIVITIES FOR ADULT STUDENTS

1. With a small group of peers, discuss the four drama workshops described at the beginning of the chapter from the following viewpoints:
    a. Children's involvement and enjoyment;
    b. Children's interaction in language experiences;
    c. Children's involvement in drama processes and concepts;
    d. The teacher's role in guiding.
2. Arrange to work with a group of children in a classroom or recreational program for one hour, or for two thirty-minute periods.
    a. Design a plan including the learning experiences by following the guidelines suggested for Planning a Lesson. Aim to introduce the children to three different concepts in the role of the player.
    b. Guide the children according to your plan and by using the four steps suggested in a Sequential Flexible Teaching Pattern.
    c. Evaluate your guidance in relationship to the children's responses to the goals and learning experiences. Identify both strengths and ways to strengthen your planning and guidance. Identify what you consider the chief problem, and discuss with your peers possible ways to resolve it.
3. Visit a classroom where there is limited physical space. Consider innovative ways in which the physical environment may be improved by providing for more space.
4. Assume that you plan to include drama as an integral part of the language arts curriculum at a given grade level.
    a. Develop a list of selected physical materials to provide limited yet adequate equipment and instructional materials.
    b. Design a curriculum guide to be used for the first month (four weeks) for a class that meets twice each week for thirty-minute periods. Emphasize children's learning in the role of the player. Identify and state the specific elements and concepts you will guide the children to explore during each of the four weeks.

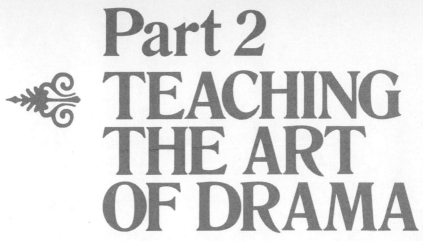

Part 2
TEACHING THE ART OF DRAMA
Children Learn Drama by Experiencing Its Processes and Exploring and Applying Its Concepts

The lion's skin lies close by, near the fire. Suddenly the leader jumps to his feet. "I killed the lion! I did it! I followed him! He sprang at me! I struck at him with my spear! He fell down! He lay still!"

He is telling us. We listen. But all at once an idea comes to his dim brain. "I know a better way to tell you. See! It was like this! Let me show you!"

In that instant drama is born.

ROBERT EDMOND JONES
The Dramatic Imagination[1]

[1] Robert Edmond Jones, *The Dramatic Imagination* (New York: Theatre Arts Books, 1941), p. 46.

5
Relaxing, Trusting, and Concentrating in the Role of the Player

Relax and the senses take wing.

AN ANCIENT PROVERB

Children use their bodies and voices to express themselves spontaneously. They need, however, to learn to draw upon their inner resources to develop the skills that are needed to consciously create actions and words for imagined characters. A child's inner resources include all the child's faculties, abilities, and totality of experience. Through learning experiences centered in drama processes and concepts children teach themselves to draw upon their inner resources. Through cumulative experience focused on these particular drama goals children learn how to relax and concentrate as they gradually learn to trust themselves and others.

The most essential concepts that children need to explore and apply are fundamental in the role of the player. These include: (1) relaxation, concentration, and trust; (2) body movement; (3) use of the five senses; (4) imagination; (5) language, voice, and speech; and (6) characterization (Figure 5).

The general purpose of this and the next six chapters is threefold. First, it is to identify the concepts essential in the role of the player. Second, it is to show how goals are formulated for each concept and stated in terms of what the child as learner does and will be able to do. Third, it is to provide learning experiences for each concept. (In statements of the goals and learning experiences the child is referred to as the student.)

The specific purpose of this chapter is to identify concepts and pro-

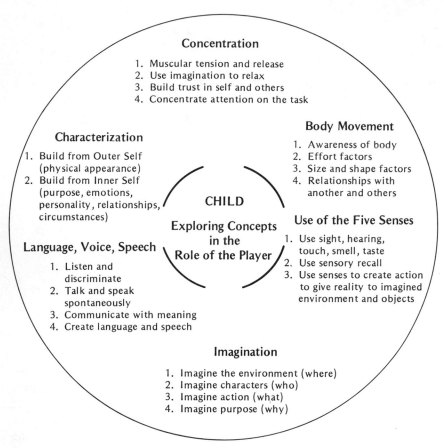

Figure 5 Conceptual Design—Structural Framework for Exploration of Concepts in the Role of the Player.

vide learning experiences designed to guide the child to consciously relax, trust, and concentrate. Very little learning or enjoyment is likely to occur if a child is tense, self-conscious, and afraid to participate and interact with others. A teacher who is alert to the developmental needs of children will recognize that indirect and direct activities are effective and will need to know how to design and present them.

An indirect activity is one in which children become involved but are not given a reason for the activity. Activities of this nature include active physical games that cause children to concentrate, trust, and relax without their conscious realization of why the game is used. Such games have several distinctive features. They are quickly and easily organized, include all the children as players, depend on a few simple rules and little or no equipment, and require players to concentrate on playing the game by running and fleeing to avoid being tagged by a person who is designated as It. Games meeting these requirements include "Red Light," "Charlie Over the Water," "Old Mother Witch," and "Loose Caboose."[2] Tag games are effective and enjoyed by children, particularly squat tag for younger children and chain tag for older children.

CONSIDERING RELAXATION, CONCENTRATION, AND TRUST

Relaxation

In the role of the player, a child needs to use images and impulses to imagine, believe, improvise, and adapt to the actions of others. If the child is tense and more conscious of self than of the task at hand, the flow of images and impulses is hampered. Relaxation is an ability to release tension in muscles in specific parts of the body, and to free the whole body from an "uptight" state of feeling. Imagery often assists children to learn to relax.

GOAL AND LEARNING EXPERIENCES FOR RELAXING, CONCENTRATING, AND BUILDING TRUST

· Goal

The student is able to consciously relax and demonstrates an ability to trust self and others through concentrating and participating in activities.

· LEARNING EXPERIENCE PROBLEM

To identify a need to learn to relax, to trust self and others, and to concentrate on solving problems.

1. The students sit together on the floor in a large circular formation. Using two string puppets the teacher places one puppet in a totally collapsed position in the center of the circle. The other is used to gain the children's attention with statements similar to the following: "Hi, have you noticed my friend lying there on the floor? He is totally relaxed. I am comfortably relaxed while I talk to you. What does it mean to be totally relaxed? . . . comfortably relaxed? Why do you think all people need to learn how to relax and stay comfortably relaxed?" The teacher summarizes the children's responses to point out the reasons for relaxation.

2. The students' attention is focused on a puppet who follows a natural impulse perhaps to sing, dance, whistle, or converse with the students for a minute or two. When the puppet retires the teacher explains: "This puppet is very trusting. It trusts itself. It trusts me. It trusts

² Evelyn L. Schurr, *Movement Experiences For Children* (Englewood, NJ: Prentice-Hall, 1967), pp. 327–339.

you. What does it mean to trust others? . . . to trust yourself? Why do you think persons need to learn to count on themselves and everyone in the group when they do activities or make up plays?" The teacher summarizes the discussion by using the children's responses to point out the reasons for learning to trust oneself and others.

3. The students' attention is focused on a string puppet who walks in and then collapses on the floor. The teacher asks the children to watch to see how the puppet concentrates. The teacher, working with the strings, asks the puppet to raise one arm, to wave to the children, and to lower its arm again. The puppet concentrates on the actions. The teacher then asks the puppet to raise and lower its other arm, to lift its head and back so it can sit up, and then to raise and wave both arms. The puppet concentrates as the teacher repeats each of the actions. Following this the teacher asks the puppet to relax totally, and it collapses.

The teacher asks the children if the puppet concentrated, and continues with the following questions: What does it mean to concentrate? Why do you need to learn to concentrate? The teacher summarizes the discussion to point out reasons for learning to concentrate.

· LEARNING EXPERIENCE PROBLEM (RELAXING)

To explore contraction and relaxation of muscles with body parts and with the whole body.

1. The teacher guides the students to organize in a circular formation and sit on the floor. The teacher directs the students to place their arms at their sides, their hands on the floor, their legs and feet outward straight in front of their bodies, and their heads upward. Observing their positions, the teacher guides the students to sit up straighter, lift heads higher, place hands firmly on floor, and keep legs straight to increase tension in all the muscles. The students are then guided to relax slowly by letting the tension go in each body part until the student is in a comfortable sitting position using no unnecessary tension. The students discuss with a partner the differences between the tense and relaxed feelings. The students are guided to stand slowly and walk back to their chairs using no unnecessary tension.

2. The students are guided to move by hopping on one leg and letting the other leg and the arms hang limp, free from unnecessary tension. They are guided to find personal space where each is to stand in a comfortable position with no unnecessary tension. Each student is guided to tense the muscles in each part of his or her body and to hold the tightened muscles until a signal is given to relax. The students discuss with a person near them the differences in the feelings of being tense and relaxed.

3. The students are guided to sit on the floor in a relaxed position and then to slowly lie down in a totally relaxed position. They then are to breathe deeply and hold their breath while they tense up muscles as

each body part is named by the teacher. They are then to relax and exhale with a loud, long sigh as the tension is released in all the muscles.
This is repeated three times. The students are guided to tense and relax
the muscles in each body part for him- or herself, and to breathe easily.

· LEARNING EXPERIENCE PROBLEM (RELAXING)

To explore relaxation by using imagery as a stimulus and to identify
imagery as a means for relaxation.

1. The students are guided to listen and respond to the following
directions: "Imagine you are a cat settling down to get ready to sleep in
a sunny, warm place; stretch each muscle the way a cat does; as you
slowly exhale let every muscle become loose and sink down to the floor
to enjoy a short cat nap." After one or two minutes of relaxation, the
students discuss the use of their imaginations to help them relax.

2. The students are shown a dandelion puff. They are asked to concentrate on what happens to a single seed when the puff is blown upon.
After watching a seed float through space and alight somewhere in the
room, the students are guided to organize into groups of five and form
a large dandelion puff. Each is to imagine he or she is a dandelion seed.
At a given signal they are to imagine that they are blown by a strong
wind into the sky, where each floats lightly through space until it slowly
falls to rest. The students pair off and discuss whether their imaginations
helped them to relax tense feelings.

3. The students work in pairs. One student imagines he or she is lying
on a warm sandy beach completely relaxed, facing upward with eyes
closed, arms outstretched with palms upward, legs outstretched sinking
into the imagined sand. The relaxed student must keep the muscles and
entire body free from tension and trust the partner. The partner must see
whether the student is relaxed in such a trustful way that the student
remains relaxed. The partner lifts slowly the student's arms, hands, and
head, and moves each body part gently to see if the muscles are free
from tension. The roles are then reversed. The students discuss to see if
their concentration on the imagined environment was strong enough for
them to remain relaxed. They also discuss mutual trust.

Trust

Children need to learn to trust themselves and others in their peer group.
All children need to gain self-confidence. They need to count on themselves by learning to trust their own images and impulses, and by taking
personal risks to explore problems and activities with others. Individual
and group trust is acquired generally through satisfying, enjoyable experiences over a period of time. However, experiences should be provided
to establish an attitude of trust at the first few class meetings, and to
help the children count on the respect and cooperation of each other.

· LEARNING EXPERIENCE PROBLEM (BUILDING TRUST)

To explore the ability to trust oneself and others by taking personal risks and depending on self and others.

1. The students choose partners to see if they can trust each other as each, in turn, takes the other on a trust walk. One partner pretends to be blind and is blindfolded by the seeing partner. The seeing student then takes the blind student for a walk inside the room and helps him or her *see* one particular object by using other appropriate senses. The blind student depends on the partner for safe guidance and to describe any changes in directions, pathways, or levels. At the end, the seeing student removes the blindfold, and the partners discuss the walk by talking about feelings they experienced, about their trust or lack of trust in each other, and about the particular objects. The experience may be continued by guiding the students to take a one-minute outdoor walk from a given place in the outdoor environment.

2. The students organize into small groups of five. Each group forms a circle by holding hands and stretching arms to full length. The students drop hands and number off from one to five. The first four students work together to see if they can form a statue. The fifth student watches to see the statue forming and to give it a name when it is completed. The students begin with student number one moving backward for several steps outside the circle, then running and jumping into the center of the circle to "freeze" into the body position he or she takes on stopping. Student number two repeats the action by stopping close to number one to relate without touching. Each student, according to number, repeats the action to relate to another student. Students "hold" the statue while the fifth student walks around it to observe it from different angles and identify it by name. The experience is repeated until each student has had an opportunity to observe and name the statue.

This experience may be expanded and varied. For example, the statue may turn into a mobile that moves at different speeds when it is completed without changing its original shape. Or the students may build a statue that can move to a different place in the room without the statue form being broken.

Concentration

When children concentrate they focus their attention, thoughts, and efforts on the task of the activity. Without concentration children cannot imagine, interact, and control their natural and impulsive actions as they improvise words and actions appropriate to a given activity. There will be little involvement and thus little enjoyment and learning. As explained in the previous chapter, one of the most effective ways to help children form the habit of concentration and self-control is to assist them with an outside control.

Another effective means used to foster concentration is a technique in which children are guided to close their eyes and concentrate on a particular task before they start an activity. To guide the children to start from a quiet, still position appears to improve both their concentration and imagination. Because of the individual nature of the creative processes, however, this technique needs to be used in relation to the needs of children. For example, if a small group of children starts spontaneously to concentrate and create, it seems important to allow them to continue.

· LEARNING EXPERIENCE PROBLEM (CONCENTRATING)

To explore the ability to concentrate by trusting oneself to work with another student and with several students in group activities.

1. The students work in pairs. Taking turns, one watches to see how the other concentrates to use tension and relaxation to shape his or her body to make the changes described by the teacher. Suggestions for changes include: apple to applesauce; uncooked spaghetti to cooked spaghetti; cube of butter to melted butter; soft snow to snowman; and pair of jeans in washing machine to jeans on the clothesline. Following the activity the students, in pairs, discuss whether they were able to concentrate to make the changes of the imagined objects.

2. The students work in pairs. Taking turns, one watches the other to see if he or she can concentrate to tense and relax muscles at the same time in different body parts to achieve the shape of an imagined object. The participating student concentrates and responds as the teacher names the following objects: bird hopping with broken wing; steel flag pole with flag attached blowing in the wind; and brick fireplace with fire flaming and leaping. Following the activity students discuss whether they were able to trust themselves to concentrate, imagine, and create actions for each object.

3. The students organize into small groups of five and sit in a circular formation on the floor. The students are shown a piece of brightly colored fabric about the size and shape of a small bath towel called "magician's cloth." The teacher demonstrates that its magic comes from the fact that its size and shape may change as it is moved in different ways. The teacher not only turns the cloth into an object such as a tablecloth but he or she creates an action to show that it is an imagined tablecloth. The teacher then gives the "magician's cloth object" to a student who uses it to repeat the exact action of the teacher. The student then manipulates the cloth and concentrates on its changing shapes until it turns into a different object. This student uses the object by creating an appropriate action and then gives the object to another student who receives it by repeating the exact action done with the object. The problem is to concentrate on the moving cloth in order to perceive the shape of an imagined object such as a bowl or bow and arrow, or whatever someone imagines its shape to be.

The "cloth" goes around the circle several times, changing into a different object with each student. If a student cannot get the "cloth" to change, the student passes on the "object" that he or she received. After the second time around the students discuss their responses to their concentration and the "magician's cloth."

4. The students continue the above experience when their concentration skills have been strengthened by using the "invisible magician's cloth" of air. It is more flexible in size, shape, weight, and flow than is the physical fabric.

SUGGESTED ACTIVITIES FOR ADULT STUDENTS

1. With a small group of peers, examine the conceptual design used to structure a child's exploration of concepts in the role of the player. Identify and discuss specific ways in which each concept draws upon a child's resources.
2. Select three games that meet the specific requirements for an activity to assist children to relax, concentrate, and build trust. Prepare guidelines for presenting each of these games to a group of children or adults. Be ready to present them whenever it seems most feasible in an adult or children's group.
3. Refer to the learning experiences in this chapter:
   a. Select three learning experiences that have been designed to involve children in exploring a specific concept: relaxing, trusting, and concentrating. Prepare guidelines and instructional materials if needed. Guide a group of peers to participate actively in each of the experiences. Evaluate their responses and your guidance to determine the effectiveness of each experience for its intended goal.
   b. Design three learning experiences of your own to be used with children for the same purposes as above. If possible try them out with children and evaluate their effectiveness.
   c. With a group of five or six peers explore the learning experience with the "magician's cloth" to see whether the students are able to concentrate and perceive imagined objects as the cloth is moved and manipulated.

6
Exploration of Body Movement in the Role of the Player

Experience is the child of Thought, and
Thought is the child of Action.

BENJAMIN DISRAELI

A child's environment is filled with movement. Things move. People move. Human movement is both functional and expressive. In drama a main concern is with expressive body movement. Children need to learn how to use and control their physical selves to enable them to use body movement expressively to give form to their impulses and imaginings. Children need experience to gain an ever-increasing knowledge of *what* their bodies can do, *where* and *how* their bodies can move in and through space, and *how* their bodies can move in relationship to persons and things. Thus a child needs to gain a conscious awareness of the elements of movement and how they are related. These include: (1) the physical body, (2) effort factors, (3) space and shape factors, and (4) movement relationships.

The purpose of this chapter is to identify concepts in each of these elements and to provide learning experiences designed to guide children to explore each concept. The structural framework presented here is the result of research and exploration with many children over a number of years (Figure 6). The structure is based on a simplification of the comprehensive analysis of movement included in the movement theories of Rudolf Laban.[1]

[1] Rudolf Laban, *The Mastery of Movement*, 2nd ed., rev. by Lisa Ullman (London: MacDonald & Evans, 1960).

Figure 6 Outer Physical Self: Concepts of Body Movement.

· CONSIDERING THE PHYSICAL BODY AS A MEANS OF EXPRESSION

A child who does not know needs to learn that the body can move in different directions—forward, backward, sideward—when traveling through space. The child needs to learn that the feet serve as the moving base for the locomotor movements of walking, running, jumping, hopping, leaping, and combinations thereof. Other body parts may be used to move the body through space, including, for example, hands, knees, and back.

Nonlocomotor movements need to be explored so a child learns that the body can move by remaining in a stationary position while one part of the body serves as a base around which other parts move. With the feet remaining stationary, the body can move in space in a variety of ways. Body parts can move in space alone or in various combinations together in the nonlocomotor movements of bending, stretching, twisting, turning, swinging, shaking, bouncing, pulling, and pushing.

· GOAL AND LEARNING EXPERIENCES FOR LOCOMOTOR AND NONLOCOMOTOR MOVEMENTS, AND DIRECTIONS

· *Goal*

The student is able to move the entire body and body parts in a variety of directions by using locomotor and nonlocomotor movements.

· LEARNING EXPERIENCE PROBLEM

To identify a need to explore and learn movement skills in the processes of drama.

1. The students sit together in a circular formation to discuss the question: Why do you think you need to discover some new ways to move when you already know how to move? The teacher summarizes the responses to point out that whenever they make up plays they need to use movements to tell the story and to show different kinds of meanings and feelings.

· LEARNING EXPERIENCE PROBLEM (LOCOMOTOR MOVEMENTS)

To explore locomotor movement by using the feet to walk in a variety of ways and directions, and as an impetus for imagining characters in action.

1. The students are guided to find personal space by responding to the following directions: "Walk through the open space of the room by walking in a forward direction from where you are now. Each time you hear the drum, walk in a different direction." The students discuss with a partner the different directions in which they moved.

2. Continue the above experience by guiding the students to respond to the following directions: "Walk forward in open space on your tiptoes. Continue to walk on your tiptoes in a different direction each time the drum signals you. Walking on your tiptoes through open space, imagine you are a person or thing different from yourself walking in this way for a particular purpose." The activity is continued by guiding the students to proceed in a similar way by walking on their heels.

3. The students are guided to walk forward in open space with their toes straight ahead, toes turned out, and toes turned in. They are guided to experiment by walking in these ways and in different combinations to imagine they are persons or things different from themselves. The students discuss their imaginings with a partner. Continue by guiding the students to walk on the outside of their feet, inside of their feet, on heels, and on toes. They are then to experiment by walking in different combinations to see if they can imagine they are persons or things different from themselves.

4. The students are guided to move into open space to respond to the following directions: "Imagine you are a clown who walks with shoes that are five times longer and five times wider than your own shoes. Imagine and walk as if you are a clown who walks with shoes that are five times smaller than your own shoes. Find a partner and agree who will be the clown with big shoes and the clown with little shoes. When you are ready, imagine your two clowns walk together in a parade as you move through open space."

· LEARNING EXPERIENCE PROBLEM (LOCOMOTOR MOVEMENTS)

To explore the use and coordination of body parts other than the feet alone for locomotion.

1. The students are guided to organize into two groups by counting off one and two. Ones organize in a straight line side by side at one end of the room, while the twos do the same at the opposite end. The students in each group are guided in turn to follow the teacher's directions: "Travel through space to the other end of the room by using three different ways to travel using your feet or other body parts. Now travel to the opposite end of the room using any body parts to move you except your feet." The students discuss their different ways of moving.

2. Continue the experience with the following directions: "Move to the other end of the room by traveling through space by walking on your hands and knees. Imagine who you might be as you continue to move this way. Travel now to the opposite end of the room by rolling through space. Imagine you are a person or thing traveling in this way for a purpose. Discuss the movement and imaginings with a partner. From a position on the floor, move yourself through space by using only your hands and arms. Imagine who you might be moving in this way. Discuss with a partner."

· LEARNING EXPERIENCE PROBLEM (NONLOCOMOTOR MOVEMENTS)

To explore the nonlocomotor movements of bending body joints and stretching and twisting muscles to move body parts and as an impetus for imagining characters in action.

1. The students are guided to move into open space and respond to the following directions: "Bend fingers, wrists, elbows, shoulders. Bend the waist, shoulders, neck. Standing on one leg, bend the other knee, ankle, toes. Standing on the other leg, repeat the bending movements of knee, ankle, and toes. Begin again by bending fingers and thumbs. Continue to bend them and each time the drum signals you, add another bending movement. See how many body parts you can continue to bend at the same time."

The above experience is continued with the following directions: "Stretch arms outward and forward, then bend arms backward and upward against your chest. Repeat the movements to establish a rhythm. Continue this rhythm and imagine you are a machine or robot doing these movements for a particular purpose. Following the activity, discuss with a partner."

2. Continue with the following directions: "Standing on one leg and keeping your balance, bend the other knee upward, bend ankle upward, then downward, and bend the knee downward so you stand on the floor. Repeat these movements several times. Do the same movements using the other leg. Imagine, now, you are a bird standing at rest on one leg. Standing on both feet, bend your knees forward and downward, then upward to a standing position. Repeat several times without losing balance. Imagine you are a machine or mechanical object doing this continuous movement. Following the activity, discuss with a partner."

3. Guide the students to continue by using bending or twisting movements to say "hello" to an imaginary person, first using one finger, then finger and thumb, hand and arm, head and eyes, foot and leg, and two arms. Have the students use the same body parts and movements to say "yes" and "no."

4. Continue with the following directions: "Standing on two feet and keeping your body balanced, stretch your arms upward; stretch your whole body until you are as tall as is possible for you. Imagine you are the tallest person in the world walking to see what is in the second story windows along an imagined city street. Discuss your stretching and imaginings with a partner. Continue by standing on your feet and, keeping your body balanced, stretch your body as wide as is possible for you. Imagine you are a clown walking to a circus tent for a performance. Discuss your stretching ability with a partner. Continue by standing on your feet with arms stretched upward above your head. Stretch your body forward and downward until your fingers touch the floor. Repeat this movement several times. Imagine you are a person or thing different from yourself. Discuss your imaginings with a partner."

5. Continue: "Make combinations of bends and stretches with different body parts. Change combinations with each drum signal. 'Freeze' into a position when the drum sounds three beats. Hold the position to imagine you are a statue. When the drum beats again imagine the statue comes alive, moving through open space. Discuss this activity with a partner. Continue by lying on your back on the floor. Stretch your arms upward. Imagine you are the movement of waves when the tide comes in and gets stronger before ebb tide sets in. Relax and rest. Imagine now that your arms and legs are the movement of a camp fire starting to burn, then flaming upward, and then slowly dying down. Relax and rest. Turn over on your stomach and do as many bending and stretching movements as possible from this position. Repeat from a sitting position. Repeat from a standing position."

· CONSIDERING EFFORT FACTORS: WEIGHT, TIME, SPACE, FLOW

Whenever a person moves, the body must adjust to the factors of weight, time, space, and flow. These factors are controlled by the purpose of movement. Weight refers to the tension of the body muscles and the degree of strength needed for the movement, which may be heavy, light, or degrees in between. Time refers to the speed of movement, which may be fast, slow, or speeds in between. Space refers to the pathway of movement in space, which may be straight, angular, curved, twisted, or a combination of these. Flow refers to the flow of body action, which may be free and flowing movement or stiff and bound movement.

· GOAL AND LEARNING EXPERIENCES FOR EFFORT FACTORS

· *Goal*

The student is able to control body movement and personal expression by moving in relation to weight, time, space, and flow.

· LEARNING EXPERIENCE PROBLEM (WEIGHT)

To explore the factor of weight with locomotor and nonlocomotor movements using imagery as a stimulus.

1. The teacher says to the entire group of students: "Move into open space by walking with big, heavy steps and pressing your feet downward on the floor. Imagine you are a thirsty giant in the land of giants searching for a stream of cold water. When you find the stream, lower your heavy body so your giant may drink from the stream.

"Move into open space by walking lightly with small steps imagining yourself to be a menehune (elf) in Hawaii. Sneak into a pineapple field to do a good deed by lifting heavy stones to change the course of a stream of water."

2. The students organize into four groups by numbering off. Each group sits in a different corner of the room with each student imagining he or she is a giant. Giants practice for a few minutes to make heavy sounds by moving different body parts. For example, they clap hands together, clap hands on knees, pound fists or heels on the floor. Each group agrees upon a message of no more than four movement sounds to send to the other giants. Other groups catch the message and, in turn, repeat the message exactly as it was sent. Variation is introduced by having giants stand and send messages by using heavy foot and leg movements, and by sending different kinds of sound messages to signal such things as warning or victory.

3. The students sit in circular formation and each selects a brown or green sheet of paper as they are passed. The students are guided to

imagine they are Hawaiian menehunes preparing for a victory celebration by making light rhythmic sounds using the paper. For example, they may use their fingers to tap on the paper or tap the paper lightly on the floor. The students then use their hands to explore ways to make light rhythmic sounds: clapping hands together; clapping hands on knees, face, top of head; and snapping fingers and thumbs together. Menehunes with green paper stand to form a smaller circle inside the larger circle. Menehunes who are seated make a variety of light, rhythmic sounds for the standing menehunes to move to. Moving menehunes step lightly to the sounds as they move through the circular space and use the paper to make light sounds by imagining the paper to be a musical instrument. Each student creates sounds individually with no intention to establish a group rhythm. Similarly, each student inside the circle moves individually in response to the sounds rather than following a group pattern. Variation is introduced by using triangles, bells, or shakers (if available) to make the sounds. Continue with the students alternating roles.

· LEARNING EXPERIENCE PROBLEM (TIME)

To explore the factor of time in relation to rhythm and tempo with locomotor and nonlocomotor movements, using imagery as a stimulus.

1. The students sit in a circular formation. Using a drum, the teacher beats a steady rhythm. The students listen and clap on every beat. The teacher changes the *rate of speed* frequently. Variation is introduced by guiding the students to respond to the beat by tapping feet, snapping fingers, and clapping hands together on knees or on the floor.

2. The students listen to the beat in a musical recording. They clap on every beat as they move through open space individually, each moving and clapping to the beat. Vary by asking the students to use imaginary jump ropes to jump to the beat; bounce imaginary balls to the beat; and by using a different recording at slow speed. The students imagine they are orchestra conductors moving their hands and arms as they conduct an imaginary orchestra. The recording is first played at fast speed, followed by regular speed, and slow speed.

3. The students are guided to say their names simultaneously in their usual speaking voices. As each student, in turn, then says his or her name individually, all students repeat the name and clap the rhythm of the name exactly as it is spoken. Vary by guiding the students to respond to the rhythm of names by moving heads, shoulders, feet, or entire selves as they say each name. Vary further by asking the students to respond to the rhythm of names by moving through space in a way that matches the rhythm of the name they speak. For example, a student may probably run or hop in four short steps to the name *Al-ex-an-der*, and may either walk or jump in two movements to the long beats in the name *Jane Jones*.

4. The students move into open space and organize as partners. In

each pair one student starts a forceful bending, twisting, or turning movement using arms, legs, or the entire body and repeats the movement again and again in fast or slow time. The partner then starts a forceful movement and continues to repeat it, moving near the first student to relate to the other movement in imagining they are a machine working together. When the partners have their rhythms established and their fast or slow movements relating, each student makes a sound to match the force and rhythm of his or her movement. The experience continues by guiding one pair to move slowly through space to relate to the movements of another pair. The four students continue to move and sound as if they are parts of the same machine with some parts moving quickly and others slowly. The problem is to keep the individual rhythmic movements and sounds going in relation to the movements and sounds of the other parts. The audience problem is to see if each part keeps its distinctive movements and sounds and to see which part spontaneously establishes the steady beat.

Vary by having three, and then four pairs combine their movements and sounds into one big machine, and by guiding the students to provide a purpose for their machine. For example, the machine produces power such as steam or a product such as pizza, spikes, popcorn balls, or bikes. Continue by guiding the entire machine to move in slow motion, then in fast motion, and finally back to its original speed.

5. The students imagine they are circus clowns driving little trick cars that have two speeds: fast and slow. Every time a horn honks, the *speed* of the car changes. Clowns start cars in slow speed and drive slowly until they hear a horn and then change to *fast* speed. The experience is varied by guiding the clowns to change directions as well as speed every time they hear a horn. The problem for students is to listen and respond with changes in time and directions. Following the activity students discuss with a partner their responses to the time changes.

· LEARNING EXPERIENCE PROBLEM (SPACE: PATHWAYS)

To explore the factor of pathways in space with locomotor and non-locomotor movements using imagery as a stimulus.

1. The students organize into two groups: players and audience. Players find personal space and respond to the following directions: "Find a straight line on the floor where you are that is six or eight feet in length. At one drum beat, walk in a straight pathway by walking forward on the straight line. Walk backward on the same line and then forward again imagining yourself to be a circus performer walking on a tightrope at the top of a circus tent. The player's problem is to walk by staying on the same straight pathway. The audience problem is to see if the players solve the problem." The players and audience alternate roles after which the group discusses the experience in relation to the imaginings and the straight pathway.

2. The students organize as partners and move into open space. In

turn, each partner responds to the following directions: "Imagine you are the Crooked Man who walked a crooked mile. Using the open space of the room see if you can walk part of a crooked mile by walking in large and small zig-zag, crooked (angular) pathways to cover most of the open space. Your partner watches to see how the problem is solved." Following the activity the partners discuss their responses to the problem.

3. Organization and procedure for this and the two following activities are the same as that used in the previous one. The teacher gives these additional directions: "Imagine you are a little car on a magnetic course in an amusement park." At a signal the car moves in forward-backward-sideward-diagonal directions, but only in *straight* and *angular* pathways. Cars begin in a straight pathway and forward direction. They change pathways and directions every time a horn sounds.

4. "Imagine you are a clown looking for your pet mouse who always runs in *curved* and *twisted* pathways. In the open space, imagine you follow mouse tracks by running in large and small twisted paths until you cover most of the open space to find your imaginary pet at the end of the path."

5. "Imagine you are a champion skater on ice or roller skates. Skate through open space to make: a large circular path; a small circular path; a large and then small figure eight. Skate to write in large letters the first initial of your first name and then the first initial of your last name. Skate in *time* to a musical recording by skating in open space to use different pathways and different combinations of pathways."

· LEARNING EXPERIENCE PROBLEM (FLOW)

To explore the factor of flow with locomotor and nonlocomotor movements using imagery as a stimulus.

1. The students choose partners and move into open space. In turn, each partner responds to the following directions: "Watch the stiff, bound, jerky movements of a toy robot [or mechanical toy] as it moves on the floor. Imagine you are a large robot who has been built to wash imaginary windows whenever an imaginary bucket of sudsy water is placed in one hand and a paper towel in the other. Your problem is to move with bound jerky movements as a mechanical object to do what you are built to do.

"Imagine you are now a person, a window washer who takes pride in washing windows. Your problem is to wash a large imaginary window by using free-flowing movements to demonstrate how to do it for your partner." After the activities the partners discuss the difference in their feelings between the bound and free movements.

2. Organization and procedure are the same as that used in the previous activity. "Imagine you are a mechanical toy bird in a cage. Whenever a key is turned the bird lifts its wings and flaps them up and down twice. Next, the bird turns its head sideward to one side and back again to the other side. Last, the bird bends its head downward to eat a red cherry as

the key clicks off. Your problem is to move with bound, jerky movements as your mechanical bird does each of the actions, in turn.

"Imagine you are now a living bird flying freely in open space until you land on the branch of an imagined cherry tree. You do the same three actions that the mechanical bird did but after eating a cherry you fly freely through open space before coming to a stop."

3. The students organize into two groups: players and audience. The players move into open space and organize in a circular formation. Each player imagines he or she is a string puppet who walks with stiff bound movements. The puppets parade in the circle to the beat of a drum. Suddenly, with the sound of music (recording) the strings no longer hold the puppets and they become persons walking in free-flowing movements as they parade by swinging their arms, moving their heads, and lifting their knees. They parade now through open space moving lightly in different directions and pathways.

Suddenly the music stops. Persons change to string puppets again, walking with bound movements to the beat of the drum. Finally, with a loud drum beat, the strings let each puppet fall into a clump on the floor where each sits with legs outstretched and head and arms bent downward. The players' problem is to follow the directions and move in response to bound and free-flowing movements. The audience's problem is to see how each player solves the problem. The players and audience alternate roles.

· CONSIDERING SPACE AND SHAPE FACTORS

Movement is shaped by *extending* the body or body parts in space in relation to the *size* of a movement, which may range from *small* to *large* or degrees between. The body may *open* by extending body parts outward, sideward, or upward into space, and *close* by bringing them back again near the body.

The body may also move upward and downward in space. It moves in different space levels, including the high level above the shoulders; the low level below the hips; and the middle level, the center of the body between the shoulders and hips. As the body moves in space it can form different shapes depending largely on direction, levels, weight, and extension of body parts. Basic body shapes include an angular or arrow-like shape, a solid wall-like shape, a rounded ball-like shape, and a twisted spiral-like shape.

· GOAL AND LEARNING EXPERIENCES FOR SPACE AND SHAPE FACTORS

· Goal

The student is able to control movement and expression by shaping movement in and through space.

· LEARNING EXPERIENCE PROBLEM (EXTENSION)

To explore extension in a range of body movements in space by changing body size and shape and by using imagery as a stimulus.

1. The students find their own personal space. Each student checks the space by standing in usual way and turning in a complete circle with arms outstretched to see that he or she does not enter the space of another person or thing. They spread legs far apart while keeping balance to imagine they become larger in a solid wall-like shape as they reach their arms upward stretching toward the sun. They return to usual standing positions. Each student folds arms by crossing them lightly upon chest and placing hands on shoulders; kneels downward with both knees to touch floor; bends head downward and imagines he or she becomes small and round by curling up to bring body into smallest possible space. Each unfolds body slowly and returns to usual standing position. Each now thrusts body forward on one leg keeping the other leg firmly on the floor and stretches one arm forward and the other backward to form an arrow-like shape. Each returns to usual position and repeats this action using the other leg. The students repeat the entire experience to imagine they are persons or things different from themselves as they each form different shapes. Students discuss their responses.

2. The students sit in circular formation to look at a deflated balloon, and to watch the balloon change its size and shape as it is blown up and filled with air. The students discuss with a partner the changes the balloon makes in size and shape. Each student then moves into personal space to imagine he or she is a deflated balloon. At a given signal each imagines the balloon fills up with air at the count of ten until the balloon forms a large round shape. At a signal, the students slowly change sizes and shapes at the same count to return to the deflated balloon shape. Discussion then centers on the changing sizes and shapes.

3. Organization and procedure are the same as that in the previous activity. The students watch to see how a fan changes its size and shape as it is unfolded and folded up again. The students imagine they are big fans folded up by beginning from any body position each student chooses. At the sound of five handclaps the students move their body or body parts to cause the imagined fan to unfold into the largest fan possible. The fan folds quickly to the beat of five quick handclaps. The activity is repeated several times with different beats and rates of speed. Activity is varied by: having the fan move backward and forward or sideward in space to fan the air; and having the students imagine they are small fans. Discussion then centers on different ways the problems were solved.

4. The students organize into two groups: players and audience. The players find personal space and listen to the following directions: "Imagine you change from one object to another as if the action is happening slowly in a dream. Imagine you are a large rock that slowly changes into a flying rocket that explodes on target; imagine you are a

large round yo-yo moving upward and downward in space and you slowly change into a flying kite; imagine you are a large castle door opening and closing slowly that changes into a frozen, twisted climbing vine." The players' problem is to change into different sizes and shapes with slow smooth transitions. The audience's problem is to see how the players solve the problem. Players and audience alternate roles, after which a discussion centers on the students' responses to their abilities to make the changing sizes and shapes.

· LEARNING EXPERIENCE PROBLEM (LEVELS)

To identify and explore high, low, and middle levels as directions of the body in space, and to use imagery as a stimulus for imagining characters in action.

1. The students find personal space and respond to the following directions: "Imagine you are elevators in a building that has three shopping levels. The low level is the basement and is near the floor. The middle level is the first floor and on the level where you are now standing. The high level is the second floor and is on a level above your shoulders. At the sound of a bell calling for the elevator on a certain floor show how your elevator moves up and down to the level, and opens and closes its doors each time it stops." The students discuss their abilities to move in different levels.

2. Each student working in personal space is asked to imagine that he or she lifts a heavy suitcase from a low level to a high level by lifting it through three different levels of space to place it on an imaginary shelf. To bring the suitcase down from the shelf to the floor the student is guided to imagine he or she moves the suitcase on four different levels, moving it each time a signal sounds. The students discuss their responses to moving on different levels.

3. Each student working in personal space imagines that he or she is a huge pancake being cooked and flipped over whenever a signal is given for the imagined frying pan to be ·lifted quickly. The students discuss their abilities to move their entire bodies quickly from a low level to a higher level and back again.

· LEARNING EXPERIENCE PROBLEM (SHAPE)

To explore body shape by shaping space through the use of directions, levels, and extension, and by using shape as a stimulus for imagining characters in action.

1. The students organize into two evenly divided groups: A and B. The students in each group sit on the floor with the two groups facing each other with an approximate six feet in between. All are guided to look at different shapes by the way each person's body occupies space. The students in Group A stand up and walk around students in Group B to observe and identify differences in body shapes when viewed

from the front, side, back, and from above. Repeat with Group B. The students discuss their observations from the viewpoint of shape.

Continuing with the above experience, the students in Group A move into personal space, where each student relaxes on the floor. Group A moves in slow motion to continually change individual positions as they remain on the low level of space. Group B walks around the students in Group A to observe changing body shapes. The students in Group B discuss changing shapes with a partner. The groups alternate the activity.

2. The students find personal space and respond to the following directions: "At each beat of the drum bend a different body joint to make a body shape that is angular. 'Freeze' into this position and imagine you are an ugly witch, wizard, or monster. Holding this position, move through space imagining you are searching for food and water. Relax, and discuss the activity with a partner." Discussion centers on whether the students were able to "hold" their angular body shapes and whether their body shapes stimulated their imaginations. This activity is continued to use: curved movements to form a round body shape; twisted movements to form a spiral body shape; and open movements to form a solid wall-like shape.

3. The students find personal space, and are guided to respond to the following directions: "Change from one body shape to another by using slow flowing movements as you hear the names of the following objects: (a) triangle–circle–rectangle–ball; (b) orange–watermelon–grape–banana; (c) car–boat–train–plane; and numbers 1–7–6–0." Students discuss their responses to the changing shapes.

· CONSIDERING MOVEMENT RELATIONSHIPS

Children need to learn to move in relationship to another person or persons. They need to learn to adapt their movements to another person or persons. In moving with a partner, a student may imitate the partner's movement, oppose the movement, or do a movement together with the partner. In a group, students may move by following the movement of a leader, all persons may move together, or all members of the group may move in response to or in opposition to one member of the group.

· GOAL AND LEARNING EXPERIENCES
FOR MOVEMENT RELATIONSHIPS

· Goal

The student is able to move in and through space with or in opposition to another person or persons, and knows how to use relationships as a stimulus for imagining characters in action.

· LEARNING EXPERIENCE PROBLEM (RELATIONSHIP IN PAIRS)

To explore body movement with and in opposition to that of another person and as an impetus for imagining characters in action.

1. In pairs, the students walk *beside* each other to follow each other's movements exactly as they respond to the following directions: "Walk forward, backward, and sideward by staying in step together." The students imagine they are two clowns walking together to marching music as they walk, in turn, in different levels, directions, and with different size steps. Vary by repeating the activity in slow motion and then in fast motion. The students then discuss their abilities to move together.

Continuing in pairs, one student moves *behind* the partner to follow the partner's movement exactly as the partner travels through space by walking, running, jumping, and hopping in forward and sideward directions. When partners are able to move together, they imagine they are clowns doing these movements to music to entertain an imagined audience.

2. Working with a partner, one student imagines he or she is a mirror and the other student a person standing in front of the mirror. The person begins by making slow movements with one hand and arm to see if mirror can follow the movements exactly. When the student, as mirror, follows movements exactly, the person uses the other hand to make movements as well. The partners alternate roles often, and continue by using hand and head movements. When the students can follow each other's movements exactly one follows the other through space by moving in different directions, with different times, pathways, and levels.

3. Working with a partner, each student stands facing his or her partner and they place their hands on each other's shoulders. Each student tries to *push* the other across the room while *opposing* the pushing movement of the other. Vary with each student holding his or her partner's hands while each tries to *pull* the other across the room in a steady even pull without jerking hands or arms. The students discuss their responses to solving the problems.

4. Working with a partner, the first student walks for five steps in any direction. The second student walks exactly as the first student did but in the *opposite* direction. The first student continues to walk for five steps, each time walking differently in relation to a movement factor: direction, weight, level, time, or flow. The second student follows each walk by walking exactly *opposite* the partner.

· LEARNING EXPERIENCE PROBLEM (GROUP RELATIONSHIPS)

To explore the adaptation of movement with and in opposition to several persons, and as an impetus for imagining characters in action.

1. The students organize into groups of four or five. Starting from a standing, sitting, kneeling, or lying position, they work together to form the shape of a big balloon. The students imagine the balloon is filled with helium and floats lightly upward in space moving in large curved paths before it is gradually pulled back again to land lightly on ground. The students discuss their abilities to move together.

2. The students organize into groups of seven. Each group, working independently of the other, forms spontaneously the shape and movement of the following objects:

a. An old car that starts its motor and moves slowly down a street until the motor dies.
b. A huge firecracker that explodes when its fuse is lighted, sending fire and scraps of paper in different directions and on different levels.
c. A water sprinkler that is suddenly turned on and sprinkles water until it is turned off again.

3. Students in a large group of ten or twelve organize into two evenly divided groups: A and B. Group A moves to one end of the room while Group B moves to the opposite with an approximate twelve feet between them. The students' problem is to imagine they are waves at an ocean beach at high tide moving in opposition to each other as the waves run in and out on the beach. The students experiment to solve the problem of moving in opposition to each other. After this problem is solved they improvise the movements and sounds of the waves as they wash on the beach at high and low tide. The students discuss their abilities to move in opposition to each other as a group.

SUGGESTED ACTIVITIES FOR ADULT STUDENTS

1. With a small group of peers, examine the conceptual design for exploration of body movement. Identify and discuss different ways it may assist a teacher who wants to provide movement experiences for children.
2. Select three learning experiences described in this chapter, each to be used to guide children to explore a different movement concept. Prepare guidelines and any instructional materials needed. Share each activity with a group of children or peers. Evaluate the effectiveness of each experience by the response of the students in relation to achievement of the intended goal.
3. Design two learning experiences to be used to guide children to explore each of the following movement concepts:
   a. Locomotor movements of running or jumping;
   b. Nonlocomotor movements of swinging or bouncing;
   c. Effort factors of weight and space;
   d. Effort factors of time and space;
   e. Factors of body shape and size with an extension of body parts;
   f. Movement relationships in a small group.

7
Using the Five Senses in the Role of the Player

History is nothing more than the belief in the senses.

FRIEDRICH NIETZSCHE

Children's modes of sensory perception for the most part are sharp with a freshness that is unique to them. By nature they use their senses when they imagine by making believe that something not real is real. For example, in her make believe play five-year-old Julie sees and smells a cake as she presses sand into a small tin lid. She goes through the physical actions of pretending to bite, taste, and swallow, and in so doing she makes herself and everyone watching believe that the cake she imagines she eats is a real cake. In this experience she uses her senses, her memory, and her expressive abilities to recreate the sensory experience as she perceives it.

In the role of the player the child continually draws upon life experiences. The child needs to form the habit of becoming consciously aware of what he or she *sees, hears, touches, smells,* and *tastes.* The purpose of this chapter is to provide learning experiences to assist the child to learn to use the five senses as tools to create actions that give reality to imagined objects and environments.

· GOAL AND LEARNING EXPERIENCES FOR USING THE FIVE SENSES

· Goal

The student is able to consciously use the senses as tools to give reality through improvised action to imagined objects, environments, and events.

· LEARNING EXPERIENCE PROBLEM (IDENTIFYING THE SENSES AS TOOLS)

To identify the five senses as tools for the player, and to identify a need to collect sensory impressions in one's memory for use in drama.

1. The students sit together in a circular formation. The teacher shows them a nickel and asks the following questions: "How much is this worth? What is the difference between five cents and five senses? How much do you think your five senses are worth to you? What is the difference between a savings bank where you save nickels and dimes and a memory bank where you save memories of things you see, hear, touch, smell, and taste? Why do you think people who do drama and make up plays need to learn to use their senses perhaps even more than most people do? How do you think your senses and memories would help you to create actions to show you are eating an ice cream cone?"

The teacher summarizes the discussion by using responses to point out that food and objects and most things in a play will not be real things. The players use their senses to show actions that cause food and objects to seem real for themselves and others.

2. Continuing with the above experience the teacher suggests: "Let's see how many of your five senses each of you uses to show the action in a short incident in a play called 'A Magic Hood.'[1] Let's imagine you are girls and boys in the village and I am a Candy Vendor who comes to sell candy. When I stand in the village square and call out, 'Candy, candy, sweet drops, sour drops, cherry, lemon, rice,' each of you will hurry to buy a piece of candy. You will buy it, unwrap it, smell it, and eat it."

After the children explore this action the teacher starts a discussion on how the senses are used to show with actions that make-believe candy is real. Following the discussion the children are guided to create the action again to show that they *hear* and *see* the Candy Vendor, *see* the candy and *look* at it as they unwrap it, and *smell* the candy as they *taste* and *eat* it.

3. The students organize as partners and sit beside each other. The partners discuss the following questions: "If you found you could no longer hear, what kinds of sounds do you think you would miss most? What three different ways do your ears help you during the day and during the night? What one pleasant thing have you heard today? Close your eyes to listen to different sounds that are being made in this room right now. Open your eyes and tell the sounds you heard to your partner. Listen again, but this time close your eyes and listen to hear sounds going on outside the room. Open your eyes and discuss the sounds with your partner."

4. "Find a different partner and sit beside each other. Someone is

[1] Masayuki Sano, "A Magic Hood." See Appendix B.

going to make sounds inside the room by doing regular classroom activities. Close your eyes and put your hands lightly over them. Listen to hear what is going on inside the room right now. When you are asked to open your eyes discuss with your partner the sounds you heard and the order in which you heard them." Suggested sounds: person walks to window, opens window, taps on window, rings small hand bell.

5. The teacher continues this activity by inviting the students to take turns in making a series of four sounds that occur in regular classroom activity. After a sound series is completed, the student who made the sounds chooses a volunteer to identify the sounds by repeating the activity. [Examples: (a) open door from hallway, close door, walk to desk, place books on desk; (b) walk to chalkboard, write on board, erase board, drop chalk and eraser.]

6. Working with a different partner, the students listen to a series of four one-minute tapes that have been recorded from happenings in the environment. Following each recording, the partners identify and agree upon the sounds by discussing with each other. The students, in pairs, volunteer to identify the sounds for others by acting out the environmental happening by improvising actions and sounds to match the recorded sounds. Suggestions include: (a) person pushing lawnmower to cut grass, (b) firefighter driving fire engine with siren sounding, (c) birds chirping or seagulls screeching, and (d) kittens meowing. Following the activity the students are asked to volunteer as partners to record one-minute environmental sounds with the tape recorder. Recordings will be used later for a continuation of this activity.

· LEARNING EXPERIENCE PROBLEM (USING THE FIVE SENSES)

To explore the five senses by using them in real experiences and to recreate experiences by improvising actions that give reality to imagined objects.

1. The students find personal space and sit on the floor. Each student is given three peanuts (in the shell) and asked to concentrate to see how each of the five senses are used as he or she cracks and eats the peanuts. Following a discussion students are guided to improvise actions to give reality to imaginary peanuts by using each of the five senses. Vary this experience by using other real foods such as popcorn, carrots, and drinking water in a paper cup.

2. Using a procedure similar to that in the above experience, the students are guided to perceive how they use their senses in daily activities. They are then guided to improvise actions to recreate the sensory experience. Suggested activities include: (a) washing and drying hands, (b) putting on and taking off a sweater or coat, (c) opening a door to listen to a particular sound, and (d) turning on a television to see and hear a favorite program.

3. The students organize as partners and sit beside each other. The

teacher gives the following directions: "Trusting yourself to keep your eyes closed, discuss the answers to these questions with your partner. How many windows are in this room? How many doors? What color is the chalkboard? What color is the floor, the ceiling, the walls? What is the shape of the room, the window, the chairs, the tables? Is there anything in this room that has a circular shape? Is anything in this room shaped like a triangle? What is the shape of the lights? How many are there?" Following their discussion the students are asked to open their eyes to *see* the room again to observe the different shapes, colors, and objects.

4. The students are guided to experience a ten-minute "Sound Walk" outdoors. Although the group walks together, each student walks apart from the others so that he or she may listen, perceive, and collect sounds individually. The students are guided to listen to sounds they make as they walk; to sounds other people make; to sounds made by animals, machines, or from something different in the environment. While walking, the students are guided to find a place to sit where they close their eyes to listen. Whenever a student hears a distinctive sound the student listens to identify characteristics of the sound. When the students return to the room the teacher guides a discussion of "Found Sounds." The students identify by telling or improvising a sound that each found.

5. Variation of the above experience is introduced by experiencing a "Touch Walk." The students are guided to collect, in their memories, textures and temperatures of different objects they touch or of something that touches them (rain, snow, cobwebs). Upon their return to the classroom the students organize in small groups, where each student improvises actions to recreate one of the "touches" he or she found. For example, a student may improvise actions to show the experience of walking barefoot on hot pavement or wet grass, or of touching and smelling a flower.

Ten-minute walks to make careful observations with each of the senses may later be extended to longer walks to different environments. The purpose of the observation may be changed to focus on observing characteristics and actions of human behavior particularly to see body shapes, actions, walks, and mannerisms. Upon their return to the room the students, in small groups, improvise actions to show a particular observation rather than discussing it.

· LEARNING EXPERIENCE PROBLEM (SENSORY RECALL)

To use the senses in recalled experiences by improvising physical actions to give reality to imagined environments, objects, or events.

1. The students organize into groups of five. In each group students recall and agree on a familiar environment where they enjoy working or playing such as a playground, garden, or ski slope. When a place is agreed upon each student decides on an imagined object to work or play

with. The problem for each student is to recall the size, shape, and weight of the object and how it is used in order to improvise actions to give reality to the object. When ready, the students in the small group improvise their actions spontaneously but independently of each other to show the imagined environment and what each does in it.

After a brief discussion of how they solved the problem, the students in each group, in turn, concentrate to again improvise their actions in the imagined environments. The other students who become the audience observe the players' actions to identify the objects and the environment. If the audience is unable to do so, the players tell where the environment is. The players improvise the action again in slow motion with each student concentrating to show more clearly the size, shape, and weight of the object being used.

2. The students organize into groups of six or seven with each group working in a different space of the room. All of the students listen to the same one-minute musical recording to recall an environment associated with the music. For example, a recording of spirited band music may stimulate the children to recall the environment of a rodeo, circus, parade, or a sports event. After listening the students in each group exchange responses and agree upon an environment and a group activity that is happening in the environment. (Activity may be that of the band, of vendors, or of performers.)

Each student decides upon an object to use in the imagined activity. The player's problem is to recall the object's size, shape, and weight and to improvise actions to give reality to the object. While the recording sounds, the students in the small groups improvise actions spontaneously to show where they are and what activity they do. After a brief discussion of how they solved the problem, the students in each group, in turn, concentrate to again improvise their actions in the imagined activity. The other students who become the audience observe the players' actions to identify the activity, the objects, and the environment. Suggestions for recordings include: calliope music, seashore sounds, and Indian or African drumming.

3. The students organize into groups of five or six and sit in a good-sized space in the room. They are guided to recall experiences in which they have worked or played in environments where there were particular substances such as sand, snow, mud, and water. After each group agrees on a particular environment each student decides what he or she will do with or in the imagined substance. When ready, the students in each group, in turn, improvise actions to show where they are and what they do. The players' problem is to improvise actions to give reality to the imagined substance. The audience's problem is to observe the actions to identify the substance, the environment, and the actions.

4. The students organize into groups of five or six and sit together.

The students in each group agree upon a single picnic food such as strawberries or fried chicken. The students discuss the food to recall the size, shape, temperature, weight, smell, and taste. When ready each group, in turn, eats its particular food. The players' problem is to concentrate to improvise actions in relation to its sensory qualities to give reality to the particular food. The audience's problem is to concentrate on the players' actions to identify the kind of picnic food being eaten.

5. The students organize into two groups. Each group, in turn, participates in the role of players and audience. The students as players organize in a large circular formation with an approximate three-foot space between each student. The students, as audience, sit together at one end of the room to watch to see if the players improvise actions to give reality to the imagined environments. The players walk in a clockwise direction in response to the following directions given by the teacher. "Walk as if you are barefoot walking in a dream on sharp pebbles . . . a bowl full of jello . . . a pathway that gives off electric shocks . . . a pool of warm water . . . a mountain of snow . . . a path of sticky honey . . . a carpet of feathers . . . a path lined with tacks . . . the floor of your bedroom." Audience discussion centers on whether the players concentrated to solve the problem.

6. The students organize into pairs. They work together to recall and concentrate to form spontaneously the following shapes after each is described by the teacher: (a) an airplane moving slowly down the runway, taking off for a trial flight, soaring, and landing again; (b) a train engine and passenger car moving on a track that circles a small lake; (c) a rowboat that moves slowly from one side of the river to the other; and (d) a person pouring water from a water pitcher to fill five glasses.

SUGGESTED ACTIVITIES FOR ADULT STUDENTS

1. With a small group of peers discuss the Nietzsche quote at the opening of this chapter. Discuss, also, the sentence that opens this chapter.
2. Observe children in different kinds of activities to find first-hand examples that illustrate children's modes of sensory perception.
3. Refer to the learning experiences in this chapter:
    a. Select four of the learning experiences and use them to guide your peers into using their senses.
    b. Use these same experiences with a group of children.
    c. Design two additional activities for each of the problems identified in this chapter.
4. Arrange for two or three children to accompany you on a sensory "Sound Walk." Use a tape recorder to guide the children to record a series of four sounds in different categories, or from three or four different environments such as the cafeteria, playground, pet shop, and street intersection. Follow-

ing the walk guide the children to use the recordings with their peers to see if they can identify the sounds.

5. Select several objects of different sizes, shapes, and textures. Place each in a paper bag and ask children to identify each object by using the sense of touch.

8
Imagining Basic Circumstances in the Role of the Player

Imagination is more powerful than knowledge.

ALBERT EINSTEIN

Tom, an eight-year-old, playing alone in the living room of his house, stretches out in a large chair, imagining the room to be a spacecraft and himself an astronaut. His improvised actions show, as he pushes upholstery buttons and walks extremely slowly to manipulate two smaller chairs in front of the window, that he pilots the craft and takes pictures while in flight. In his dramatic play this child imagined *where* he is, *who* he is, *what* he is doing, and *why* he does what he does. These are the most basic circumstances—the essential conditions that govern and affect human action in life events and in drama.

In the role of the player, children need to strengthen their skills and abilities to imagine and improvise actions consciously in relation to basic circumstances. This chapter provides learning experiences designed to assist the child to learn how to identify basic circumstances, and to improvise actions to give reality to these circumstances.

Children need many experiences to imagine basic circumstances and to allow these experiences to influence their imagining and improvising of actions. Children's concentration will strengthen if they learn to keep a point of attention on an object or action within an imagined environment. In exploring this element the child must become so familiar with the imagined environment that he or she becomes a part of it. The child needs to begin by imagining and exploring the environment—the place where physical actions occur and which, by its physical nature, conditions the nature of those actions.

· GOAL AND LEARNING EXPERIENCES FOR IMAGINING BASIC CIRCUMSTANCES (WHERE, WHO, WHAT)

· Goal

The student is able to imagine and consciously improvise actions to give reality to the basic circumstances of *where, who,* and *what.*

· LEARNING EXPERIENCE PROBLEM (IDENTIFYING AN ENVIRONMENT)

To identify what is meant by an imagined environment and to give reality to it by improvising actions that show physical objects in it.

1. The students organize into a circular formation and sit on the floor. Discussion is stimulated by the questions: Let's think about this space and place. What makes this particular space and place a classroom? What makes a store a store? How could we change this space into a family living room for a play? If we had only four objects in the living room what objects do you think they should be? Why these objects? Why are the objects different in each room of the house? If someone wanted to enter the living room from outdoors to go through it to another room, what objects would be needed for this action? How might two chairs be arranged to look as if they were a door that could be opened and closed? . . . a table? . . . a television set? . . . a bookcase? . . . a large chair? How might several chairs be arranged to look as if they were a sofa or davenport?

The students are guided to work in small groups to construct the suggested objects. A demonstration may be needed to show how chairs may be arranged in different shape and spatial relationships. They may be placed back to back, side by side, upside down, on different levels, and in small and large spatial arrangements.

2. Continuing with the above experience, twelve students are guided to organize into three groups with four students in each. The other students organize as partners to become the audience. The problem for the group of twelve is to construct one large imagined living room in the open space. They are to use twelve chairs, one for each student. The students are to arrange the chairs to make four objects and two doorways. One group is assigned to arrange the doorways. The other two groups are assigned to each arrange two objects of their choice. The problem for the audience is to observe the construction process and identify the objects.

When the imagined living room is created the participants become the audience and the audience becomes the players. The players work as partners with each pair taking turns. Their problem is to enter the arranged space and to show that the environment is a living room by the way they use the doors and each of the objects. Following the activity the audience discusses these questions: Did the players' actions show what the objects were? Did each partner use each doorway and all four objects? What were the objects? Did each student concentrate to imagine and show that the objects were real?

3. Continuing with the above experience the students discuss the following comments and questions by the teacher: "In a play a living room is just an empty space until the players turn it into a *place of action.* What do people usually *do* in a living room? What do people do in a living room that is different from what they do when they go into the kitchen? Why might people who don't live in the house want to go into someone else's living room?" Discussion is summarized by using responses to point out that in a play it is the players' actions—what they *want* and *do* in a particular place—that make an environment come alive for players and audience.

4. Continuing with the above experience, the students who constructed the living room and objects are guided to organize into pairs to solve a new problem. The other students become the audience. Taking turns, each pair is to enter the living room to show through actions that it is a *place of action.* Each pair imagines and agrees upon what they *want* to do and what they will *do* to get what they want. The problem for each pair is to use the environment and the objects to show what they *do* in the imagined living room. The audience problem is to watch to see if each pair uses the objects to show where they are and what they do. After each pair completes their action, the discussion centers on these questions: Did the players' actions show where they were and what they were doing? Did they concentrate on using each object? The players and audience alternate roles. Suggested actions in a living room include: to find a lost object, to try out new furniture, to set prices on furniture to be sold, and to play checkers or read a book.

5. Continuing with the above experience, the students organize into groups of three. Each group is to use three chairs or three scenic objects to construct an imagined environment. The environments may be suggested by the students. Or the students may choose a slip of paper from a box that names an environment. These include such places as: a tunnel with two openings, a cave with an entrance, a campsite, and a movie theatre. When the environments are constructed each group, in turn, shows its imagined environment. The students enter it, one at a time, to improvise actions (without words) with an object or objects to show *where* they are, and what they *do* in the imagined place of action. The audience watches to identify the environments through the actions of the players.

· LEARNING EXPERIENCE PROBLEM (IMAGINING A PERSON
  OR THING IN ACTION)

To imagine and improvise actions of a person or thing (different from oneself) to show basic circumstances (where, who, and what).

1. The students organize into small groups of three to construct an

imagined environment within an open space in the room by using no more than three concrete objects. Objects include scenic blocks, cardboard cartons, tables, chairs, benches, and small ladders. The students are guided to select the objects in different combinations and to manipulate them by arranging them in different shapes and spatial arrangements to suggest an environment.

The students are then given the following problems: (a) imagine and agree upon who you are as persons or things in this environment and what you do; (b) show through your actions where you are, who you are, and what you do. The audience problem is to watch the actions to identify the basic circumstances. Following the activity the discussion focuses on the questions: Where were they? Who were they? What did they do? Was their concentration on the imagined objects complete?

In this experience the students need to imagine and use *imagined objects* to show the basic circumstances. For example, they may arrange three ladders to construct a rowboat to imagine they are Indians fishing in the imagined water environment. As Indians, the students need to improvise actions to show that they probably use *imagined* objects such as oars, fishing poles, and other objects.

2. Twenty students organize as partners. Each pair numbers off from one to ten. The partners from one to five move to one end of the room to work within the imagined environment of a house. The remaining partners move to the opposite end of the room to work within the imagined environment of the yard outside the house. The partners in the house environment organize the space and agree that each pair will work in a different room: (a) kitchen, (b) dining room, (c) living room, (d) bedroom, and (e) laundry room or basement.

The partners in the yard organize the space and agree that each pair will work in a different area: (a) carport, (b) garden, (c) basketball area, (d) swimming pool, and (e) picnic and fireplace area. The problem for each pair is to imagine who they are and what they do with no more than three *imagined* objects to show their particular environment. The audience's problem is to observe one pair to identify who they are, what their relationship is, and what objects they use in the imagined environment. The discussion centers on these questions: What action and objects did two players cause you to see? Where were they? Who were they?

Variation is introduced by: (a) changing partners after two experiences with the same partner, (b) guiding the students to improvise words as well as actions in an imagined relationship where one person teaches the other to do something, and (c) changing the environment so it becomes a different environment; for example, a circus tent with performers and workers practicing or preparing for circus events.

3. The students organize into groups of four and each group works in a different space in the room. Each group chooses a paper bag with

four similar costume pieces in the bag. For example, these may be work gloves, baseball caps, shirts, aprons, hats, or dental uniforms. As the students put on the costumes they are guided to imagine who they might be different from themselves. When one student is ready he or she moves into open space to improvise the actions of the imagined character doing an activity. The other students join in, one at a time, by imagining themselves to be persons participating in the same activity. As they join the activity, a student must relate his or her actions to the actions of the other player or players. The students do not know in advance what activity the first student will do. The experience is complete after the fourth player has entered the environment and participated in the activity. The experience continues with another player in the same group starting an entirely different activity as an imagined character. Variation is introduced by guiding the students to choose costume pieces from a different paper bag or bags.

4. The experience continues in a similar procedure but the students select a single imagined object to stimulate their imaginations. Rather than using real objects, one student in each group selects the name of an object from a hat. For example, an object-name may be: a basketball, grocery cart, cafeteria tray, or diving board. The student who selects the object-name, such as a basketball, imagines that he or she is a basketball player. The student moves into open space imagining the area to be a basketball court. He or she bounces the imaginary ball and shoots it through an imagined hoop. A student watching enters the environment by relating to the first student and improvising actions to show that he or she uses the imagined object. The other students join the activity, one at a time, by relating to the other players and using the object. The experience is complete after the fourth player enters the environment and uses the object. The audience's problem is to identify the basic circumstances.

· CONSIDERING THE NEED FOR THE PLAYER TO PLAY WITH PURPOSE AND BELIEF

Human action is caused by a desire or purpose. Likewise dramatic action is caused by a desire or purpose. A child needs to learn that the player must have a purpose whenever the player is in a story or play in the place of action. The child needs to know what the purpose is. The purpose comes from what a character in a story or play *wants to do* or *has to do* within the circumstances of the play.

Stanislavski introduced the concept of the "magic if" to help the player turn the character's aim into the player's aim.[1] A child needs to learn

---

[1] Constantin Stanislavski, *An Actor Prepares,* trans. Elizabeth Reynolds Hapgood (New York: Theatre Arts Books, 1948).

to use the *magic if* by forming the habit of self-questioning with the basic questions: What is my purpose? *If* I were this character in these circumstances what would I do to get what I want?

Belief is present in the "dramatic play" of children when they are absorbed in their play. A young child employs belief when the child imagines a doll is a living baby by the way the child treats the doll. The child *acts as if* the doll were a baby. However, as a player and play-maker with peers, the child needs to learn to believe in the reality of the play. The child needs to learn to concentrate to believe and act as if other persons in the play are not themselves but the characters they imagine themselves to be. For example, in playing the story of "Jack and the Beanstalk" the child, imagining himself to be the character of Jack, knows that one of his peers is not really the Giant. But the child needs to concentrate to believe and act as if the other person were the Giant.

· GOAL AND LEARNING EXPERIENCES FOR PLAYING WITH PURPOSE AND BELIEF

· *Goal*

The student is able to identify a player's purpose and to imagine and improvise actions in relation to that purpose. The student does this by treating persons and things in the imagined circumstances with belief *as if* they were real.

· LEARNING EXPERIENCE PROBLEM (PURPOSE)

To identify the need for the player to always have a purpose.

1. The students sit together in a circular formation to discuss these questions: Why did you come to school today? Why did you go to the cafeteria today? In this class, why are you given a problem or told what to do? The discussion is summarized by using the children's responses to point out that action is always caused by a purpose, and the player needs to know the purpose in order to know what to do.

2. The students are guided with the teacher's statement: "This is your purpose. Move into open space to find your own personal space." No further purpose is given. The teacher observes the students for one or two minutes before asking the following questions: "What is the trouble? What are you waiting for? If you're waiting for a purpose each of you give yourself the purpose of relaxing and 'warming up' your body, your senses, and your imagination. Take one minute to do this in your own way." A brief discussion centers on the question: What is the difference in what you do when you have a purpose and when you have no purpose?

3. The students are guided to move into open space. The teacher gives them the problem of seeing if they can organize themselves into three smaller groups in one minute. The next purpose for each group, in turn, is to walk in open space from the time they hear one drum beat until they hear two drum beats signaling them to stop and sit down. The third purpose for each group, in turn, is to walk in open space from where they are to the opposite side of the room. They are to touch the wall to identify its texture and temperature and then return to their places and sit down. A discussion centers on the differences between just walking and walking with a clear purpose, and then on the texture and temperature of the wall's surface.

· LEARNING EXPERIENCE PROBLEM (IDENTIFYING PURPOSE)

To explore a player's purpose by identifying it and improvising action in relation to it by using the magic *if*.

1. The students are given a purpose to be reached in one minute. They are guided to organize into three evenly divided groups and sit at one end of the room. The teacher explains: "First, each is to imagine you are a high school student. You couldn't be a high school student because you are you. See if you can imagine and *act as if* you are a student with a strong feeling of pride for your school baseball team. Next, imagine the environment (open space) is the school grounds leading from the bus to the bleachers. Each group, in turn, will have a different purpose. The first group's purpose is *to cheer* for your team as you go from the bus to the bleachers to watch the game. The second group's purpose, returning to the bus after the game, is *to blame* the umpire for causing your team to lose the game by one point. The third group's purpose, returning to the bus after the game, is *to celebrate* the victory after your school won the game by one point." The problem for the students in each group is to imagine and act *as if* the environment and circumstances are real. The audience's problem is to watch the players' actions to see if they show *where, who, what,* and *why*.

Discussion following each playing centers on the questions: Did the players' actions show *where* they were and *why* they did what they did? How did the different purposes change the actions? The experience continues until each group acts out each purpose. In the second and third playings, the students are encouraged to improvise words with their actions.

2. The students organize into four evenly divided groups. Each group is given a large card that describes a set of circumstances but does not include the purpose for the action. After reading the card the group agrees on the purpose. When ready each group improvises for the others to show the basic circumstances. Cards include the following sets of circumstances:

a. Characters: astronauts; Environment: moon's surface where space-craft has landed; Action: collect samples and take pictures; Purpose: Why?
b. Characters: fishermen and women; Environment: fishing boat on ocean near coastline; Action: use telescopes and cameras to identify "something" on shore; Purpose: Why?
c. Characters: senior citizens; Environment: workroom; Action: arrange bouquets of flowers; Purpose: Why?
d. Characters: men and women; Environment: open space of land; Action: digging, shoveling, clearing brush; Purpose: Why?

3. Continue with the above experience by guiding the students to: (a) improvise actions for each set of circumstances by agreeing on a purpose different from that used by the others; (b) design similar cards to describe sets of circumstances including purposes; and (c) improvise actions for sets of circumstances designed by peers.

· LEARNING EXPERIENCE PROBLEM (BELIEF)

To explore belief in the imagined reality of physical objects and the circumstances of a story or play by improvising actions using the magic *if*.

1. The students organize into groups of four or five. Each group shows that a physical object is a live person or thing by imagining, believing, and acting *as if* the physical object is the real person or thing. Each group works with a single chair, but each group imagines and believes the chair to be a different thing. For example, it may be: (a) a baby bassinet with a three-day-old baby in it, (b) a trained police dog on guard, (c) a bird cage with an angry parrot inside, or (d) a wheelchair holding an injured refugee child who does not speak English.

Each group first agrees upon what the chair will be, and then upon the basic circumstances (*who* they are, in relation to the thing and to each other; *where* they are; *what* they do; *why* they do it). When ready, each group in turn improvises actions to communicate the basic circumstances by imagining and acting *as if* the chair is the real person or thing. Improvisation is complete when the audience agrees upon the chair's imagined identity and the circumstances.

2. Continuing with the above experience the students are guided to plan and improvise basic circumstances by using an object different from a chair to stimulate imaginations and belief. For example, objects may include a length of coiled rope, a small chest with a lock on it, a large hoop, a wrapped package, or objects children bring.

SUGGESTED ACTIVITIES FOR ADULT STUDENTS

1. With a small group of peers, discuss the Einstein quote at the opening of this chapter.
2. Refer to the learning experiences in this chapter:

    a. Select four experiences and prepare guidelines and instructional materials if needed. Arrange to work with a group of children, eight years old or older, in a classroom or recreational program for an hour or for two thirty-minute periods. Use these experiences to guide the children to explore concepts related to the imagining of basic circumstances. Evaluate the children's response in relation to their achievement of the goals.

    b. With a small group of peers originate and design four different learning experiences to be used with children to explore these same concepts. Try out the experiences with your peers before sharing with children. Revise the guidelines if needed.

3. Refer to the learning experience in which the "sets of circumstances" cards are used:

    a. With a small group of peers, discuss and agree on the purpose for each set of circumstances. Improvise actions spontaneously to communicate the purpose in each set of circumstances to other students.

    b. Design similar "sets of circumstances" cards to be used with children at a selected grade level. Correlate the "circumstances" with content in children's literature or to social studies. If possible explore the use of the cards with children.

9
Language, Voice, and Speech in the Role of the Player

Perhaps of all the creations of man language is the most astonishing.

GILES LYTTON STRACHEY

Unique to human beings is the development of language and speech. On the one hand, it is believed that a child's language, including speech, develops naturally. On the other hand, it is believed that this development is extended and refined with opportunities for the child to use language by interacting with the environment. What seems most important in language development is for children to interact with others, particularly with peers and persons in addition to those the child interacts with at home.

Speech and language are fundamental in the art of drama. This chapter provides learning experiences designed to assist the child to use language and speech and to perceive how it may be used to communicate effectively. Four concept areas are explored. These are: (1) listening and discriminating, (2) talking and speaking spontaneously, (3) communicating with meaning, fluency, and projection, and (4) constructing (creating) language and speech with flexibility.

Listening and Discriminating

To listen refers to a child's conscious effort to hear and identify environmental sounds and things to which words refer including the speech and sound of human voices. To discriminate refers to the child's ability to make a distinction of human speech from other sounds, from one vocal sound to another, and to identify these vocal sounds with the things they stand for. To discriminate among sounds includes also the ability to interpret what is heard by identifying meaning through words, tone, and intensity of vocal sound.

· GOAL AND LEARNING EXPERIENCES FOR LISTENING AND DISCRIMINATING

· *Goal*

The student is able to hear, identify, and respond to environmental sounds including speech.

· LEARNING EXPERIENCE PROBLEM (LISTENING)

To explore the ability to listen to hear environmental sounds by identifying sounds that communicate meaning.

1. The students sit together in a circular formation. The teacher moves into the center of the circle to give a friendly greeting with a hand gesture. The teacher then beckons to the students to enter the open space of the circle. It they do not respond to the nonverbal communication the teacher beckons to several children individually. If the students do enter the circle, the teacher communicates with a friendly hand gesture for them to move back to the outer circle. The teacher then speaks to start a discussion with comments and questions similar to the following: Did you get the three messages I communicated to you? What were they? Does anyone else want to communicate a message to us through sign language? Why do you think people invented language? How do people learn to speak? Why do people need to learn *to listen* in order to speak?

2. The students organize as partners and move to a space in the room where they can listen to sound messages communicated by each other without interference from others. The students take turns being the communicator and the receiver. The communicator sends a sound message to the receiver, who listens with eyes closed to receive the message. After perceiving the message the receiver repeats the sound message exactly as it was communicated. Suggested sound messages are: knock twice on the door, pound lightly on the table three times, draw a long line on the chalkboard and erase it, and tiptoe to the door and back again.

3. The students organize and stand in a large circular formation to play the game "Simon Says." The teacher in the center becomes Simon and says, "Simon says, 'Sit down.'" Students follow the command. Simon continues to give verbal commands and the students do whatever action he says. If he omits the words "Simon says" preceding the command, the students *do not follow* the command. Those who do the action join Simon and sit inside the circle to listen and watch the others. Simon mixes commands and actions at a rapid pace so the students must con-

centrate to listen to receive his communication. The student who stays in the outer circle the longest becomes the next Simon. Suggested actions include nonlocomotor movements varied with factors of time, weight, and levels of space. When the students are familiar with the game it may be played in groups of six or seven to increase listening and communicating.

· LEARNING EXPERIENCE PROBLEM (LISTENING AND CONSTRUCTING SOUNDS)

To explore the ability to hear environmental sounds by identifying sounds and creating vocal sounds.

1. The students organize into groups of six and sit on the floor in a circular formation. They all are guided to warm up their voices simultaneously to become instruments in a sound symphony orchestra. Warm-up begins with each student opening his or her mouth to make a big 0, then yawning, taking a deep breath, and exhaling by putting lips together and humming. The students then listen to a one-minute recording to identify sounds they will create. Each group chooses a conductor, and each student chooses the sound or sounds he or she will make and practices them alone. The students next practice with each other to put the sounds together. The conductor works with the students to give signals for the instruments to make the sounds heavy, light, fast, slow, single, in pairs, or together. All groups practice simultaneously.

When the orchestras are ready, each group in turn plays for the others to see if the listeners can identify the "sound symphony" selection. "Sound symphonies" recorded in advance include: (a) kitchen sounds at breakfast, (b) seashore sounds at high tide, (c) city traffic at the morning rush hour, and (d) farm sounds at feeding time.

2. Continuing in the same group, each orchestra composes its own sound symphony selection. The students agree on a title, and construct sounds from memory. The students organize and practice with a different conductor. When ready, each orchestra plays for the others to see if they can identify the symphony selection. Groups may decide on their own title or choose from among the following: (a) Halloween night in a haunted house, (b) zoo at feeding time, and (c) veterinary clinic.

· LEARNING EXPERIENCE PROBLEM (LISTENING AND RESPONDING TO VOICE AND SPEECH)

To explore the ability to listen to the voice and speech of self and others, to respond by following directions and/or improvising sounds and action for imagined characters.

· 1. The students organize into pairs and sit in a circular formation to discuss the following question: When a person speaks do you think the person's voice tells you almost as much as the words? The students listen to a tape recording of "voice inflections" made in advance by the teacher. The recording is in three bands. In each a person says one or two words with four different inflections to communicate four different meanings: happiness, sadness, fear, and anger. The order of the different inflections is changed in each band. The words are: (a) no, (b) come here, and (c) all right. After listening to each band the students discuss and agree between themselves on each meaning. The students are guided to choose a single word such as "hello" and to take turns using their voices to communicate different meanings.

2. The students organize into small groups of six or seven and sit in a circle to see if they can *listen* to send secret messages. The teacher starts a four or five-word message by whispering it in the ear of one of the students. The student receiving it whispers it exactly as it is received to the student on the right. The message continues to go around the circle. The last student whispers the message to the entire group who then carries out the message. If it is incorrect it cannot be carried out. The problem is to listen, receive, and whisper the message correctly. Suggestions for messages include: (a) look out a window now, (b) imagine you eat ice cream, (c) stand, yawn, and stretch, and (d) shout "Hip, hip hooray!"

3. The students organize into pairs and sit on the floor. They listen to the names of different objects called by the teacher. As soon as the students hear the named object, each makes a sound with his or her voice that the object makes and shows in action what the thing is or does. After each list of things has been named the partners share with each other the sound and action of one thing each enjoyed creating. The students then rest for one minute by sitting still with eyes closed to listen to silence and sounds inside and outside the room. The partners identify and discuss the sounds they hear. Suggestions for objects in different categories include: (a) dog, cat, snake, horse, cow; (b) wind, hail, rain, breeze, blizzard; (c) telephone, radiator, electric fan, clock, doorbell; and (d) popcorn, bubble gum, rice krispies, and egg being beaten.

4. The students organize into small groups of four to discuss the following questions: Have you ever wondered how your voice sounds to others? Do you think you speak in a high, low, or medium-pitched voice? The students agree on a short rhyme they know and enjoy saying such as a jumping-rope rhyme, chant, or poem. Each student chooses a line to say alone and practices it. The students then use a tape recorder to record their voices. Next they listen to the recording so each student hears his or her voice and that of others to identify the differences in pitch. They record the rhyme again, this time imagining themselves to be giants speaking in low-pitched voices. After recording, they listen to hear the differences in their low-pitched voices. They record the rhyme again imagining they are elves speaking in high-pitched voices. They listen again to hear their voices. They record the rhyme for the last time with each student using his or her voice with the pitch each prefers. They listen to the recording to discuss the sounds of their voices.

Talking and Speaking Spontaneously

Children develop language and learn to speak by talking and speaking in a variety of different kinds of circumstances, both real and imagined. Children need opportunities to talk to themselves, to a partner, and to persons in a group.

· GOAL AND LEARNING EXPERIENCES FOR TALKING AND SPEAKING SPONTANEOUSLY

· *Goal*

The student is able to make spontaneous verbal responses by commenting and questioning in a variety of real-life and imagined situations with another person and persons.

· LEARNING EXPERIENCE PROBLEM (SPEAKING SPONTANEOUSLY)

To explore abilities to think and speak spontaneously by commenting on personal actions, feelings, and perceptions.

1. The students organize into pairs and sit in a circular formation as the teacher demonstrates how the shape of a newspaper may be changed into an imagined object by moving it in different ways (folding, twisting, opening, crunching). As the teacher changes the newspaper shapes and pretends each to be an object by improvising actions to relate to the object, the students are guided to comment by talking out loud to themselves, the teacher, and their partners.

Each student then works with a newspaper to change its shape and to improvise actions to relate to the objects. The students are guided to talk out loud and comment on the object, to show it to the partner, or to improvise actions and words in relation to the object.

2. The students sit beside a partner. Volunteers read messages by using a microphone or megaphone to make it seem as if the message is being announced from the office. As the students hear each message the partners do and say what they would honestly do and say if the announcements were official. Suggested messages include:

a. There is a power shortage. School is closing now.
b. An envelope with ten dollars was lost on the playground. If you know anything about this, please come to the office.
c. The cafeteria will serve pizza, pop, and peanuts free for everyone today! . . . This is a joke. The cafeteria operates as usual.

3. The students are guided to select a puppet from the puppet box. Each student is to take the puppet to a place in the room where the student can talk to the puppet to get acquainted with its personality to find out its name, how it talks, moves, and if it can sing or do other entertaining.

The students organize as partners to plan a short puppet show just for the partners and puppets to enjoy together. The partners find a place for a puppet stage. Each puppet asks questions to find out about the other puppet, who answers. Puppets may ask their own questions, or choose from the following:

a. Ask a riddle to see if I can answer it in two guesses.
b. Can you teach me how to dance? how to sing a song? how to tell a joke?
c. Have you heard of a puppet who helps you with your problems? There is one. You write, "Dear Petunia" and ask her what to do, and she puts the answer in a puppet newspaper. What problem would you send if you knew where to send it?

Communicating with Meaning, Fluency, and Projection

Children need experience to help them improve incorrect speech habits. They need to gain confidence and enjoyment in expressing orally with an awareness of good speech and voice qualities. Oral communication refers to an ability to extemporize face-to-face conversation by two or more persons in which there is verbal collaboration and an exchange of ideas and meaning.

Fluency refers to an ability to speak smoothly and easily with a flow of language. Individuals have their own individual vocal pace, and each person needs to learn to fit the pace of the voice to the pace of the mind. Fluency appears to be acquired with the development of a child's mental faculties and language. It seems to occur with vocabulary development, skill in word association, and with practice in speaking with another person and persons.

Projection of intensity refers to an individual's ability to speak with feeling and purpose to communicate to another or others without straining the voice. Children need to learn how to project by becoming aware of how to use their natural resonators and vowel sounds. Children need to learn how to avoid putting undue stress on vocal cords.

· GOAL AND LEARNING EXPERIENCES FOR COMMUNICATING WITH MEANING, FLUENCY, AND PROJECTION

· Goal

The student is able to communicate with meaning, fluency, and controlled projection by extemporizing speech in conversation with another person or persons.

· LEARNING EXPERIENCE PROBLEM (COMMUNICATING WITH MEANING)

To explore the ability to communicate to another person or persons by extemporizing speech in a variety of different kinds of speaking experiences.

1. Ten students are guided to organize the space into a supermarket with five shopping areas: (a) meat counter, (b) dairy products, (c) canned and packaged goods, (4) fresh vegetables, and (e) the check-out stand. The students organize into pairs with each pair working in one of the areas, either as a store clerk or a customer. The clerk's purpose is to help the customer with shopping questions and problems. The customer's purpose is to ask about the quality and price of two items before buying. The audience listens to see if the players solve their problems. The discussion centers on whether the players succeed in creating meaningful conversations. The audience and players alternate roles. Similar shopping circumstances may be planned by changing the environment to an ice cream parlor, pizza parlor, or department store. Circumstances may be changed to that of returning an item or complaining about items or service.

2. The students organize into groups of six and choose partners within each group. The partners use toy or imaginary telephones to improvise telephone conversations. The problem for the players is to communicate first in the "wrong way" and next in the "right way." "Wrong way" means that one of the players fails to communicate the message correctly. "Right way" means that both communicate the information correctly. After practicing, the partners share with the group both ways of communicating one conversation. Suggestions for conversations include: (a) child reporting a house fire to the fire department, (b) teenager calling police to report a car accident, (c) magazine editor calling long distance to inform a nine-year-old that a parrot will arrive by plane—a prize for winning a contest.

3. The students organize into groups of three to improvise actions and speech in the given circumstances. They agree upon who each player will be, and arrange the imagined environment. Given circumstances include: (a) Two teenagers and a shopper are in a supermarket where the shopper loses a wallet. The teenagers find the wallet, containing two dollars. One teenager wants to keep the money; the other wants to give it to the store manager. Each talks to convince the other to do what he or she wants. Finally, the worried shopper returns to look for the wallet, and the teenagers return it. (b) In a family living room a child enters and turns on the television to watch a favorite program. The child's older brother or sister enters the room and changes the dial to watch a program for a school assignment. The younger child turns the dial back to get the favorite program. The older child changes the dial. An argument starts in which each tries to convince the other to watch the program each wants to see. A parent hearing the argument enters to find out what causes the trouble, and then settles the argument.

Similar conversations with three persons may be planned in different environments, including a playground, dining room, road, or garage. Circumstances to be developed into arguments that need to be settled by a third person include making decisions concerning: (a) who gets to use the playground equipment, (b) what to get for a parent's birthday, (c) which turn in the road to take to get to desired location, and (d) whether to keep or sell a large box of junk (family heirlooms).

· LEARNING EXPERIENCE PROBLEM (FLUENCY)

To explore the ability to speak with fluency in communicating orally with another person or persons in actual and imagined circumstances.

1. The students are introduced to two puppets: Hans and Gerda. After the puppets leave, the teacher explains that the puppets have come for help because they have trouble speaking to others. When Hans returns the teacher asks him what he would like to do if he were a real person. The teacher talks for Hans by speaking at a fast pace to interrupt the language flow: "If I were a real live . . . uh . . . uh . . . you know . . . person, I . . . uh . . . uh would like . . . you know, you know . . . to whistle." Gerda enters to answer the same question. She speaks at a slow pace: "Well . . . hmmm . . . I never thought of it uh, uh . . . before but uh . . . I think I'd like, uh . . . uh someone to scratch my back."

Hans returns and they listen as the teacher guides the students to discuss and identify the puppets' problems as that of *pace in speaking.* The students organize into pairs to speak to each other at their individual paces to show the puppets how to do it. The students tell each other what they would like to do most of all if they were puppets. Puppets listen to see if each student speaks with an uninterrupted language flow.

2. The students choose a different partner as they continue to show the puppets how to speak at an individual vocal pace. Each student, in turn, speaks for one minute to answer a question. When a bell rings, the other student answers the same question. The problem for each student is to speak at his or her own pace. Each student listens to the flow of speech and counts the number of times the partner stops the language flow. Questions beginning with: "What would you do if . . . ?" include: (a) someone gave you five dollars to spend, (b) you were the classroom teacher for one day, and (c) you could do the craziest thing you can think of.

· LEARNING EXPERIENCE PROBLEM (PROJECTION)

To explore the ability to speak by controlling projection in oral communication.

1. The students organize into pairs. They are guided to put their hands tightly over their ears as they greet each other, and then to repeat the greeting with their hands removed from their ears. They are guided to repeat the same action twice and then to discuss the differences they noticed in their voices each time. The teacher concludes the discussion by explaining that human beings have built-in sound resonators in their

heads that help make voice sounds. The students are guided to hum softly and loudly as they experiment to use their resonators.

2. The students continue in a similar activity by choosing a different partner. The students are guided to put their hands firmly against their throats as they speak to say "hello" three times, softly, loudly and then in a medium voice. They then remove their hands from their throats to discuss with their partner how their fingers felt each time they spoke. The teacher concludes the discussion by explaining that persons have built-in resonators, also, in their throats to help make their voices loud, soft, or medium.

3. The students are guided to stand at one end of the room while the teacher stands at the opposite. They listen to the vowel sounds voiced by the teacher to see if they can hear how the sounds are projected by the voice resonators. They are then guided to *echo each sound* exactly as it is voiced by the teacher. Following this, the students listen and *echo* the words and voice exactly as the teacher speaks a sentence. The sentence is spoken three times: loudly, softly, and then in a normal speaking voice. A discussion centers on learning how to use the resonators to speak in different ways without forcing or rushing the sound. Suggested sentences include: (a) Take the old road; (b) Fight team, fight, fight; and (c) Hurry, I need help.

4. The students, in pairs, imagine and speak as if they are imagined characters. The problem for the students is to project their voices to communicate to each other without forcing or rushing voice sounds. Suggestions for imagined circumstances include: (a) Parent calls from the front door of the house to give a message to a teenager who is in front of the house in a car with the motor running; (b) Patient in the hospital room calls to the nurse for assistance without waking other patients who are in the same room.

Constructing Language and Speech with Flexibility

Children need to learn to adapt to the speech of others with flexibility and confidence. They need opportunities to present ideas, to communicate to others in structured situations, and to interact informally in both real and imagined circumstances.

· GOAL AND LEARNING EXPERIENCES FOR CONSTRUCTING LANGUAGE AND SPEECH WITH FLEXIBILITY

· Goal

The student is able to alter individual speaking patterns by adapting with flexibility to the speech of others and by improvising language and speech to correspond to that of imagined characters.

• LEARNING EXPERIENCE PROBLEM (FLEXIBILITY)

To explore the ability to alter individual speaking patterns by adapting to the speech of others and by improvising speech and language to correspond to that of imagined characters.

1. The students organize as partners and sit in a circular formation. They are guided to think in response to these questions: If you could be *any person* who is now alive or who lived in the past, who would you be? What kinds of questions does an interviewer ask to get factual information from a person? Following the discussion the students agree upon who is to be the imagined person and who is to be the interviewer for a television program. The problem for the student is to imagine and improvise speech and language that corresponds to the character in the imagined circumstance. The problem is completed when the interviewer succeeds in getting three informational facts. Following the activity, the discussion centers on how the students solved the problem.

2. The students are guided to organize into groups of six. The teacher gives the following directions: "Today we are going to learn to be announcers of action events by announcing action as it happens in a baseball game. Everyone who wants to be an announcer will have a turn. One group is to be a baseball team playing against another team of six. The third group of six organizes into partners. Each set of partners forms a sportscaster team to announce the game's action. Other groups of six organize to become spectators to cheer for one of the teams."

The announcers are guided to arrange themselves in three different parts of the room to keep from listening to other announcers. If available, live microphones or megaphones are used to heighten the imagined reality and to assist in projecting voices without straining. The students, designated as teams, arrange a baseball diamond in open space and each team organizes its team positions with six players. The game is played with imaginary ball and bats, and the teacher serves as umpire. The announcers describe the action to communicate it accurately. As the game continues the announcers are guided to imagine they are experienced sportscasters speaking enthusiastically in rhythmic patterns to match the game's action.

Throughout the game and at intermissions the announcers use the microphones to communicate group and individual comments from the spectators. The experience continues until each group has had a turn at being announcers. The teacher may need to demonstrate how an announcer adapts speech and speaking patterns flexibly to the action as it happens. Following the activity, a discussion centers on the students' abilities to improvise language and speech flexibly and spontaneously.

3. The above experience continues with a similar procedure to involve the students in organizing and planning broadcasts of other imagined events. Suggestions include: (a) basketball, soccer, and other competitive

games; (b) Olympic games events of swimming, skating, and skiing; and (c) races including turtle, rabbit, and frog-jumping contests.

SUGGESTED ACTIVITIES FOR ADULT STUDENTS

1. With a small group of peers, discuss the Strachey quote at the opening of this chapter. Discuss, also, the sentence that opens this chapter.
2. To gain insight into language development arrange to observe children of two and three years of age in a nursery school or day care center for approximately one hour. Obtain permission to record the children's conversations and ways of talking. Observe as well the ways in which the children talk, speak, use words, and form sentences. Following your observation and with the recording, aim to identify and analyze factors that appear to contribute to a child's language development, such as listening, imitating, repeating, and forming sentences in response to a sentence formed by another child or adult.
3. Refer to the learning experiences in this chapter designed to involve children to explore the four basic concepts:
   a. Select a learning experience for each concept, and prepare guidelines and instructional materials if needed. Share each experience with a group of peers. Following each experience evaluate the students' responses in relation to the intended goal and to your guidance.
   b. Arrange to use these same experiences with a group of children. Obtain permission to record the experiences. At a later time listen to the recording to evaluate the children's response and your guidance.
   c. Design new learning experiences to be used with children to involve them in exploring each of the four concepts.
4. With another student make the following recordings to be used in these learning experiences: (a) "sound-symphonies," (b) "voice inflections" with words and sentences, and (c) excerpts from sportcasters' broadcasts of different sports events.

10
Building a Character in the Role of a Player

And the little girls, of the age and size that little girls always are, turned their backs on their grownups and played at being mothers, as little girls always play; and poured out little-girl love to wooden dolls in buckskin dress with wooden, staring faces.

EDITH LAMBERT SHARP
Nkwala[1]

Children spontaneously imagine and make believe they are persons and things different from themselves. Sometimes they make believe they are parents, teachers, pets, their heroes—and persons and things they fear, and hate, and yearn to be. When children impersonate others their entire selves become involved in the process. Sometimes children are stimulated to impersonate from strong inner feelings and sometimes children's imaginations are sparked from outer stimuli such as something that they see or touch or a particular sound or sounds they hear.

Although children impersonate spontaneously they need to learn how to consciously originate and build a character by using both their inner and outer selves. This is the purpose of this chapter. It provides learning experiences based on concepts related to building a character from the outside in and from the inside out.

· GOAL AND LEARNING EXPERIENCES
  FOR BUILDING A CHARACTER

· *Goal*

The student is able to originate and form a character and character actions with the entire self by using outer and inner stimuli.

[1] Edith Lambert Sharp, *Nkwala* (Boston: Little, Brown, 1958), p. 90.

· LEARNING EXPERIENCE PROBLEM (OUTSIDE IN)

To explore the ability to originate and form a character by using the physical body and body parts as an impetus for imagining a character in action.

1. The students sit together on the floor in a large circular formation to discuss these questions: When you watch a play or look at a cartoon, how can you tell one character from another? How can you tell whether a character is old or young or good or bad? The teacher summarizes the discussion by using the children's responses to point out that a character in a play, just as a person in life, shows the kind of person he or she is by the way the character looks, moves, talks, and acts. The teacher explains that the students will explore different ways to use their bodies to form images to build a character's physical appearance.

2. The students move into personal space and respond to the following directions: "Squat down near the floor. Notice how your knees are now out of line with the rest of your body. Lift your body upward slowly by straightening your knees and bringing them directly above your feet. Straighten up so your body parts are lined up in a fairly straight vertical line as you stand in your usual way. Now move your neck and head forward out of line with the rest of your body. Holding your neck and head forward in this position, let your head lead you as you walk through the room. Concentrate on imagining you are a person different from yourself who walks this way and talks in the way you imagine this person talks. Greet each person you meet by saying a single word, such as: hello, cinnamon, or vinegar."

The students relax and discuss with a partner the kind of character each imagined he or she was. The students continue to explore the exaggerated extension of body parts to stimulate a character image. The students, in turn, use their stomachs, elbows, and feet and knees thrust outward in different exaggerated lines. The students' problem is to concentrate to hold the body position to allow images and impulses to assist in imagining a character.

3. Continuing with the above experience, the students organize into groups of three. Each student exaggerates a different body part to imagine he or she is a character such as a simpleton or a goon with a single-track mind. The students discuss and agree upon imagined circumstances with an activity requiring the cooperation of all three such as pushing a stalled car, carrying a table from one room to the next, or lifting a heavy sofa into a moving van. As simpletons, failing to plan their efforts, they work in opposition, determined to get the task done. The student's problem is to hold the character's physical position and image while improvising actions and words to get what the character wants in the circumstances. The problem for the audience is to see how each student creates the character's outer appearance. Discussion centers on how students solved the problem.

4. The students organize into groups of five. One student volunteers to be the leader. As in the game of statues the leader, in turn, swings the players in space, and lets them go so each "freezes" into an individual body position. Each player concentrates to imagine a character in action. In slow motion the players "holding" their body positions come alive and move as imagined characters to tell each other who they are. With the help of their leader, the players agree on the basic circumstances (*who* they are in relation to each other, *where* they are, *what* they do, and *why*). As imagined characters, the players improvise actions to act out their purpose. When the characters complete their purpose they return to their statue positions as a part of the action.

The players' problem is to imagine and build characters by using body positions to improvise character actions in the basic circumstances. The audience's problem is to identify the characters by their actions and physical appearance. The discussion that follows centers on these questions: Who were they? Where were they, and what did they do? Did their characters build out of their actions? Did the imagined characters grow naturally out of the statue positions? Was their concentration complete? Examples of characters created by nine-year-olds include: family members cleaning house, deep sea divers taking pictures, baseball players playing a game, and firefighters fighting a forest fire.

· LEARNING EXPERIENCE PROBLEM (OUTSIDE IN, PHYSICAL OBJECT)

To explore the ability to form a character by using a physical object to stimulate the imagining of a character in action.

1. The students organize into groups of five, move into open space, and agree upon a leader. The leader arranges six pieces of fabric of different lengths, widths, textures, and colors on a table. The players each select one fabric and arrange it on themselves in relation to line and shape by putting it on their shoulders, head, or one part of their body (waist, arms, leg, foot). The leader assists when needed. As the students arrange the material they are guided to let the color, shape, or line stimulate their imagining of characters. When ready, the players discuss with each other who they are and agree upon basic circumstances (environment, action, purpose).

The problem for the players is to let their characters build through their action, purpose, and relationships. The problem for the audience is to identify the characters, their relationship, the environment, and action. The discussion centers on these questions: Who were they? Where were they, and what did they do? Did their characters build out of their actions in the environment? Did the characters grow naturally out of the use of the fabrics? Was their concentration complete? The experience is continued with the use of other fabrics. Examples of characters created by ten-year-olds include: (a) doctors and ski patrol leader examine skier's broken arm in ski lodge, (b) rock band musicians prepare for a show, (c) shopkeepers sell beads to customers at street fair, and (d) scientists eat lunch at excavation site.

2. This experience follows the procedure used in the previous experience with the exception that "properties" are used instead of fabrics. Properties include such objects as a telephone, lantern, coffee pot, purse, and jewel chest. The students select three objects to stimulate their imagining of characters, and then agree upon basic circumstances. The experience is continued by using different kinds of properties including objects such as blueprints, computers, stethoscopes, cameras, and objects the children bring. Variation is introduced by having all of the properties be the same object; for example, four artificial roses, canes, or umbrellas.

· LEARNING EXPERIENCE PROBLEM (INSIDE OUT, EMOTION)

To explore the ability to form a character with a strong emotional quality.

1. The students sit together on the floor in a large circular formation to discuss the questions: When you watch a play, how do you know whether a character is happy, sad, afraid, lonely, or mad? What is the difference in the way a person behaves if the person is happy or mad? The teacher summarizes the discussion by using the children's responses to point out that a character in a play, just as a person in life, shows inside feelings on the outside. Sometimes feelings are shown in a person's face, hands, feet, voice, different parts of the body, and in what the person does.

2. The students organize into groups of three. Each group selects an Action-Feeling Card that states an action and an emotion. The players read the card and then agree upon *where* the action takes place and *who* they are in a relationship (family, friends, workers, neighbors). Each group, in turn, improvises the action. The problem for the players is to let their characters develop out of their emotional involvement with the action. The problem for the audience is to identify the characters, the action, and the feeling. The discussion centers on the questions: Where was the action? What was it? Did the characters develop from their feelings with the purpose of the activity? Was their concentration complete? Suggestions for Action-Feeling Cards include: (a) Action: bury a pet; Feeling: sad; (b) Action: read a letter that brings good news; Feeling: happy; (c) Action: enter an empty cabin at night; Feeling: fear; and (d) Action: clean the house or yard; Feeling: mad.

The experience is continued by guiding the students to use the same action cards but to change the feeling for each action. Variation is introduced by guiding children to design Action-Feeling Cards.

· LEARNING EXPERIENCE PROBLEM (INSIDE OUT, PURPOSE)

To explore the forming of a character from within by improvising action in relation to the character's big purpose and related units of action.

1. The students sit in a large circular formation on the floor. The

teacher brings a large apple on a paper plate with a knife and paper towel. The teacher explains that the first big purpose of the class is to eat the apple by sharing it with everyone to get many reactions to the taste of this particular apple. The teacher asks for suggestions as to how to divide the apple. Responding to suggestions the teacher cuts the apple into equal parts and asks a student to pass the plate of apples slices to everyone. The teacher asks the students to discover the taste and texture of the apple as they eat it. The teacher asks for responses to its taste. Following this activity, the teacher asks: What was my big purpose in relation to you and the apple? (To eat the apple to get many taste reactions.) What little actions did we do to reach the big purpose?

The teacher lists student responses on the board by phrasing responses in the *infinitive verb form*. Responses will probably be phrased somewhat similar to the following: (a) to ask for suggestions to divide the apple, (b) to slice the apple, (c) to ask someone to pass the apple slices, (d) to eat the apple slices to explore taste and texture, and (e) to share the taste reactions.

The teacher explains that in a story or play the smaller actions, just listed, are called little units of actions within the big purpose. If a player were to play this "apple scene," the player would need to know the big purpose and the little units. The teacher asks: Why do you think a player in a play needs to know these? The teacher summarizes the response to point out that if a player knows the big purpose and the little units, the player knows *what to do* because *each unit has a purpose* that *fits into the big purpose.*

2. Continuing from the previous discussion, the students organize into three evenly divided groups. Each group agrees on two or three persons in the group to become the audience for the others who become players. The players act out the "apple scene" in relation to the big purpose and the units (listed on board). The players, however, agree on a different environment (where) and character relationships (who). The problem for the players is to let their characters build by improvising actions and words in relation to the big purpose and the little units. The problem for the audience is to see if the players build believable characters. The players are guided to look at the board to read the big purpose and the units before and during the playing if needed. The discussion following the playing focuses on the questions: Who were the characters? Where were they? Did the players let their characters build from the big purpose and the related units?

The experience continues with the audience and players alternating roles. The students build characters from one or more of the following suggested character relationships: (a) apple growers and buyers in conference room, (b) owner and cooks in caramel apple factory, (c) judges at county fair in an exhibit hall, and (d) Johnny Appleseed and a farm family on a roadway.

3. The students sit together near chalkboard. The teacher explains that they are going to improvise action in relation to a purpose and units. They need first to agree on a purpose and *divide* the big purpose into smaller related units. The teacher asks: "What was your big purpose for today when you woke up this morning—your super purpose for today? If it was *to go to school,* because you are here, what other main things did you have to do to reach your super purpose?" The teacher lists the students' responses on the chalkboard, phrasing them in the *infinitive verb form.* They include probably the following or similar units: (a) to wake up and get up, (b) to wash or shower, (c) to dress, (d) to eat breakfast, (e) to walk or ride to school, and (f) to enter the building and go to the room.

The teacher asks the students to look at each of the units to find ways in which they are alike even though each unit is different. The teacher summarizes the responses and points out that each unit is listed as *an action* and each begins with *to,* so a player can think of each unit as *an action with a purpose.* For example: I want *to eat* breakfast so I can *go to school,* or I want *to walk to school* to be there on time. The teacher concludes by explaining that when the students are ready to act out a story or play, they will see how it helps a player to divide the character's action into a super purpose and little units, each with a related purpose.

4. Continuing with the above exploration, the students organize into pairs. Each pair, working with another pair, in turn becomes players and audience. The players act out the super purpose (to go to school) by improvising action in the related purposes in each unit (listed on board). The players first agree on the environment and character relationships. Suggested characters and actions include: (a) mother and child at home get ready for the mother to drive them to school where the mother will serve as a teacher's aide; (b) two teachers, in an apartment, get ready and walk to school, (c). teenager and kindergartner, at home, get ready for teenager to take brother or sister to school on a motor bike.

The discussion following the playing focuses on the questions: Who were the characters? Did the players let their characters build from the super purpose and the related purposes in the units? Did the players' actions show their purposes in each unit?

5. The students listen as the teacher reads or tells the play of the old folk tale, "Henny-Penny."[2] After hearing it the students, with the teacher's help, divide the story into its big purpose and the little related units for the characters of Henny-Penny and Foxy-Woxy. The teacher guides the students to identify Henny-Penny's big purpose as: to go and tell the king of the calamity (sky's a-going to fall). The little units for her character are: (a) to tell everyone she meets of the calamity includ-

[2] See Appendix B.

ing Foxy-Woxy (a dangerous enemy), (b) to listen and follow Foxy-Woxy's plan for a shorter way, and (c) to listen to Cocky-Locky's call and run away to think about the barnyard calamity.

Foxy-Woxy's big purpose is to eat the poultry by outfoxing them. His little units are: (a) to watch as they join in their panic to travel to the king, (b) to suggest the "proper way" to go to the king, (c) to eat all except Henny-Penny, and (d) to scramble after her only to loosen a rock from the cave, which brings calamity upon himself.

The students are guided to organize into two or three groups to build characters by improvising the story action and words. The students create characters by using the big purpose and the related purposes in the little units. After their first attempts the students are guided to discuss and then to play the story again. The students need many experiences to discover how the purpose and related units help them to build believable characters.

The experience continues with the students exploring the physical appearance of each of the characters. They are guided to use their physical selves in relation to the line, shape, and rhythmic movement of each of the characters. Following this activity, the students again improvise the story action and words. The problem for the students is to create believable characters by concentrating on both the inner and outer characteristics of the character.

6. The teacher assists the students in selecting short stories and story-telling poems that are appropriate for beginning experiences in characterization. Criteria for selection are based on the following drama elements: (a) a limited number of clearly defined characters with distinctive physical characteristics and clearly defined purposes, (b) an economy in the number of plot incidents required to tell the story, and (c) a worthy theme with content that appeals to the children and satisfies their developmental needs. Suggested anthologies from which stories may be selected include: *Stories To Dramatize*[3] and *Children's Literature for Dramatization*.[4]

SUGGESTED ACTIVITIES FOR ADULT STUDENTS

1. With a small group of peers, discuss the quote from Edith Lambert Sharp's *Nkwala* at the opening of this chapter. Discuss, also, the paragraph that introduces this chapter.
2. Arrange to attend a theatre production to enjoy the experience. At a later time reflect upon the play and two or three of the characters. Identify and describe specific ways in which each of the characters was developed

---

[3] Winifred Ward, *Stories To Dramatize* (Anchorage, KY: Anchorage Press, 1952).
[4] Geraldine Brain Siks, *Children's Literature for Dramatization* (New York: Harper & Row, 1964).

through physical appearance and inner qualities. Identify and state the super purpose and the related units for each of the characters.

3. Refer to the learning experiences in this chapter designed to involve children in exploring concepts related to building a character from the outside and the inside.

    a. Select a learning experience for each concept and prepare guidelines and instructional materials if needed. Share each experience with a group of peers. Following each, evaluate the students' responses in relation to the intended goal and to your guidance.

    b. Arrange to use these same experiences to guide a group of children to explore these concepts. Obtain permission to record the experience and at a later time, listen to the recording to evaluate the children's responses and your guidance.

    c. Design two learning experiences to be used with children to involve them in exploring each of these concepts.

4. Select a short story for children of a given age level that meets the criteria for beginning experiences in characterization. Identify the required drama elements by listing or stating each of the following: (a) limited number of clearly defined characters, (b) economy of plot incidents, and (c) story theme. Analyze the distinctive physical characteristics and super purpose of each of the characters; list the story units and state the characters' purpose in each; describe briefly the story content; and identify reasons for its probable appeal to children.

11 Playmaking

"First of all, Pop, what is a play?"

"Many things. But what it always is, as well as,
many other things, is people in trouble."

WILLIAM SAROYAN
Papa You're Crazy[1]

For children to progress from the role of player to that of playmaker
they need to perceive how drama elements are used in the playmaking
process. This chapter investigates the structural, conceptual, and learning aspects of playmaking. It first considers an introductory procedure
that differs from that used in the process-concept structure approach.
This procedure, which emphasizes children's reading, is an extremely
simplified form of Reader's Theatre. It has been used to introduce
children to the structure presented here.

Reader's Theatre

To implement the objectives two fifteen-minute periods each week are
designated as Play Time. An hour prior to the scheduled time, the
teacher announces the name of the play and the number of participants
needed. Volunteers are selected, and each receives a copy of the script.
The children sit together, reading the play silently. After the first
reading the teacher asks each child to draw a slip of paper from a hat
for a part—character or director. In the second reading, which is done
orally, each child reads for his or her character. The director reads the

---

[1] William Saroyan, *Papa You're Crazy* (Boston: Little, Brown, 1956), p. 150.

title, cast of characters, setting, and any descriptions of action that are given.

In the third reading the players, with the director's help, get the play "on its feet" by working in a designated area of the room. In most instances this is a corner approximately 9' x 12' which has been sectioned off temporarily from the rest of the room with brightly dyed sheets hung from portable pipes or rods. The director uses objects in the room for scenery if needed. As the players read they imagine their characters' actions and walk through the imagined environment. When a player has problems, the director offers suggestions.

The fourth reading is the Play Time, with the other children in the class becoming the audience. A one-minute musical recording (selected by the teacher) sets the mood of the play. The director opens the curtains, tells the audience the name of the play and cast of characters, and describes the play's setting. The director then turns off the room lights so only the playing area is lighted, and the play begins. After it is over, the players and director sit together to listen to responses and questions from the audience.

After ten or twelve such experiences children generally express desires to make up their own plays. If, however, children seem content just to read, the teacher makes the suggestion. Thus, this procedure serves as a transition from script reading to exploring concepts in the roles of the player and playmaker.

· EXPLORING PLAY STRUCTURE

· Elements of a Play

To involve children in playmaking in the process-concept structure the teacher needs to understand the basic elements of a play, and how they are structured to form a play. Although play structure is relatively flexible, most well-made plays follow traditions established by Aristotle. In his *Poetics* he indicated that drama is comprised of six elements: (1) plot, the dramatic action; (2) characters, the people within the play who enact the dramatic action; (3) thought, the message of the play; (4) language, the words spoken by the characters; (5) melody-sound, the tone and rhythmical quality of the play; and (6) spectacle, the visual image of the play (Figure 7).

The first three elements are internal to the forming of the play, while the last three are external but essential in forming a dramatic production. All six elements are included in the playmaking process with children.

· EXPLORING PLOT CONCEPTS

· Plot Concepts

Plot is defined as the series of incidents through which the characters move and thereby reveal a dramatic story. At the heart of plot in drama

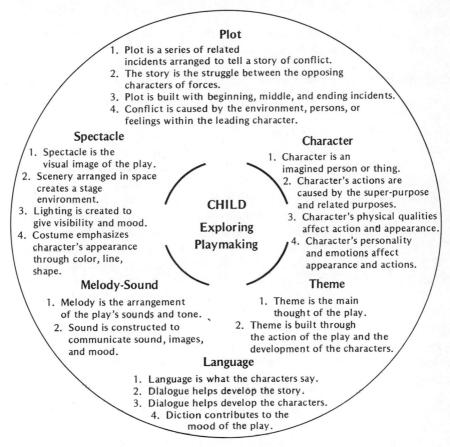

Figure 7 Playmaking Elements and Concepts.

is a character who has a problem and struggles to resolve it. Plot provides the framework for the problem-struggle-resolution sequence. It must be complete in itself, and have a beginning, middle, and end. Exposition incidents show or tell the basic circumstances. The *beginning incident* is the incident that opens the plot to start the conflict. *Middle incidents* are those that show the struggle and move the action to a climax and turning point between the opposing characters. *Ending incidents* are those that bring a resolution to the character's conflict.

To perceive how to form a play children need to explore the most fundamental concepts of plot essential to its construction.

Plot is a series of related incidents arranged to tell a story in which there is conflict.
The story is the struggle between the opposing characters in the conflict.
Plot is built with beginning, middle, and ending incidents in logical sequence.

· *Goal*

The student knows that plot is a series of related incidents arranged to tell a story in which there is conflict.

· LEARNING EXPERIENCE PROBLEM (PLOT)

To identify a need to learn to construct plot as a story with related incidents of action.

1. The students sit in a circular formation. Using a small string puppet and a small bundle of sticks, string, and cloth the teacher asks the following questions: "What is the difference between these two? What needs to be done to put these parts together to make a puppet? Why do the parts have to be put together in a certain way? Now think about making a play. There are three main parts that need to be put together, too—characters, action, and theme. Why do you think these parts have to be put together in a certain way to form a play? How do you think it is done?" The discussion centers on the concept to point out that the *plot is the story* that weaves all the parts (elements) together.

2. Continuing with the experience, the students are guided to listen to the Mother Goose rhyme, "The Queen of Hearts," to discover how characters and action incidents are plotted or put together in a story. In pairs, the students identify the characters and action incidents. The discussion centers on the plot concept as a story of characters in action incidents that are related or tied together.

3. Continuing with the experience, the students are guided to discover how and why the incidents in a story need to be connected or plotted together. Each of the three incidents in the rhyme "Humpty Dumpty" is printed on a large card. Holding the cards up for the students to read, the following questions are asked: In what order do these action incidents need to be placed to tell the story of Humpty Dumpty? Why this order? Can the incidents be arranged in a different order to tell a story that makes sense? The discussion points out that plot is a series of *related incidents* arranged to tell a story that makes sense.

· LEARNING EXPERIENCE PROBLEM (PLOT)

To identify that a dramatic plot is a story with characters who are in a conflict.

1. The students organize into pairs. The teacher explains that it is possible for the incidents in "Humpty Dumpty" and "The Queen of Hearts" to be connected together because of the conflicts in each story. Conflict is explained as an obstacle or problem that a character faces. The students are guided to listen again to "The Queen of Hearts" and identify the conflict. They are to decide first which character faces the obstacle, and next what the obstacle is. The pairs identify these two aspects of the conflict, after which the entire group identifies the character as the queen and the obstacle as the knave.

2. The students, in pairs, are asked to identify whether the following story read by the teacher has a conflict: "Once there was a happy king named Percival who ate onions and sauerkraut every Monday. Quite often the king jumped rope and occasionally he jumped backwards all day. The king was known throughout the kingdom as 'Peculiar King Percy.'" The partners agree that the story has no conflict. In group discussion the students are asked to identify the two basic requirements needed in a story to qualify its plot as dramatic.

3. The students organize into groups of five or six. Each group reads the same short story silently or aloud. The students then examine the plot to identify: (a) the characters in the conflict, (b) the obstacle that causes the conflict, and (c) the series of incidents that tell the story. When the groups finish, two groups join together to exchange their findings. Stories for younger children include folk tales such as "Teeny Tiny"[2] and "Three Billy Goats Gruff."[3] Stories for older children include Aesop's fables, "The Shepherd Boy and the Wolf"[4] and "The Wind and the Sun."[5]

· *Goal*

The student knows that plot shows the struggle between the opposing characters in conflict.

· LEARNING EXPERIENCE PROBLEM (PLOT)

To explore the ability to form a plot by identifying and showing the struggle between the opposing characters in a conflict.

1. The students organize as partners. All pairs play Squat Tag at the same time within designated areas. The partners agree upon who is to be It and who is to be Free. Free's problem is to stay free; It's problem is to become free by tagging Free. Free may, when absolutely necessary, assume a squatting position and be safe. After two minutes, the partners exchange positions. Subsequent discussion focuses on the questions: Did the game bring about a rather evenly matched struggle between partners, or was it too one-sided? When you were It what did you want most of all?

Using the children's responses, the teacher points out that in a good tag game, just as in a good dramatic plot for a play, there should always be a fairly even fight. The characters must really struggle for what they want because the enjoyment of the play lies partly in its struggle.

2. The students sit in a circle and organize as partners. The teacher

---

[2] In Geraldine Brain Siks, *Children's Literature for Dramatization* (New York: Harper & Row, 1964), pp. 107–109.

[3] In Winifred Ward, *Stories To Dramatize* (Anchorage, KY: Anchorage Press, 1967).

[4] In Ward, op. cit.

[5] See Appendix B, Plays for Use in Playmaking With Children.

reads or tells a story and asks the students to identify plot incidents that cause the struggle. Beatrix Potter's "The Tale of Peter Rabbit"[6] is good for younger children; the play form of "The Wind and the Sun"[7] is good for older children. After the partners discuss the incidents, the group identifies those that cause the struggle.

3. Continuing with the experience the partners move into a space in the room where they work without interference from others. Players agree upon who will be each of the opposing characters in the story they have just discussed. The players act out the struggle incidents by improvising action and words that make their characters work to get what they want in the conflict relationship. After the first trials the students discuss these questions: Did each player work to get what his or her character wanted in the struggle? Did a struggle happen, or did the players give in too soon? The students try again with the same incidents.

· *Goal*

The student knows that a plot is built with beginning, middle, and ending incidents in a logical sequence.

· LEARNING EXPERIENCE PROBLEM (PLOT)

To explore the ability to build a plot with beginning, middle, and ending incidents.

1. The students sit in a semicircle. The teacher draws a large equilateral triangle on the board and asks the students to imagine what it might have to do with playmaking. The teacher explains that the triangle is a line drawing that shows how the plot of a play is built (Figure 8). The teacher briefly describes the process.

2. Continuing with the experience, the students organize into small groups of six or seven to read a short story and then to identify the beginning, middle, and ending plot incidents. Suggested for younger children are "The Three Billy Goats Gruff"[8] and for older children "The Conjure Wives."[9]

3. Continuing this experience with "The Three Billy Goats Gruff," younger children organize themselves into three groups of four. The first group is called "the beginning," the second "the middle," and the third "the ending." The first group identifies, imagines, and improvises actions to show *only* the beginning plot incident. The second group shows *only* the middle plot incidents, and the third group shows *only* the ending incident or incidents. The audience's problem is to watch as each group improvises and identify whether the players solve the

[6] In Ward, op. cit.
[7] See Appendix B, op. cit.
[8] In Ward, op. cit.
[9] Ibid.

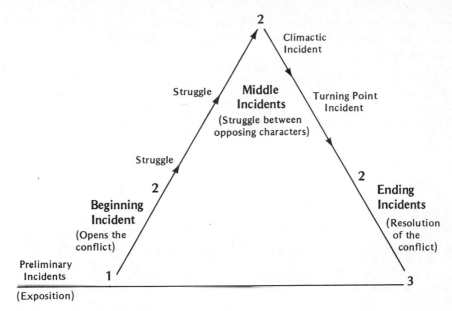

Figure 8 Structuring the Plot.

problem. The groups organize the physical space of the room so they act out the plot in a logical physical sequence as well. While one group improvises, the other groups remain silent and still as characters in a picture book. A similar procedure is followed with older children, who use the story of "The Conjure Wives."

4. The students organize into groups of five and listen to the same music (two minutes or less).[10] They are to imagine that the music is a soundtrack for a short play in which the conflict is caused by a person or environmental factor. After listening the students exchange ideas and agree on a plot with beginning, middle, and ending incidents that show a character's conflict-struggle-resolution. The students organize the space for their play, decide who the characters will be, and improvise actions (without words) to match the music. The students continue with each group, in turn, communicating its plot to the others. The audience aims to identify the plot and the characters.

· EXPLORING CHARACTER CONCEPTS

· *Character Concepts*

The child has learned from the role of the player that a character in a play is an imagined person or thing with human characteristics. The character who moves the story forward by struggling to resolve the conflict is called the leading character. The character who opposes the

[10] See Appendix C, Audiovisual and Instructional Materials.

leading character is referred to as the opposing character. The child needs to explore and apply the following fundamental concepts required to build a character.

A character is created through the action of the play.

A character's actions are caused by the character's big purpose and related purposes in the play and units of the play.

Physical and personality qualities affect the character's appearance and actions.

· Goal

The student knows that a character is created through the character's actions in the incidents of the play.

· LEARNING EXPERIENCE PROBLEM (CHARACTER)

To identify and create a character by improvising his or her actions in the story of the play.

1. The students organize in a circle to discuss the questions: What is meant by the statement: *a play is a story shown through the actions of the characters?* What is a character? What causes a character's actions in a play? The teacher summarizes the discussion to clarify the goal.

2. The students continue with the above experience. The teacher reads a short story or play in which a leading character is created through the actions of the story. The students identify and describe the leading character's actions in each of the action incidents. Suggested stories or plays include: "Jumping Beans"[11] and "The Tree Angel"[12] for younger children and *Fortunately*[13] for older ones.

3. The students organize into players and audience. The players move apart from each other so that there is no interaction. The teacher reads *Fortunately*.[14] Each player must listen, imagine, and improvise actions for the character of Ned as the story is being read. The audience must ascertain whether the characters are believable. The players and audience then alternate roles. Discussion focuses on the believability of the kinds of characters created through the actions.

· Goal

The student knows that the character's actions are caused by the character's big purpose and the related units in the incidents of the play.

[11] Judith Martin and Remy Charlip, *Jumping Beans* (New York: Scholastic Book Services, 1969).

[12] Judith Martin and Remy Charlip, *The Tree Angel* (New York: Scholastic Book Services, 1968).

[13] Remy Charlip, *Fortunately* (New York: Scholastic Book Services, 1966).

[14] Ibid.

• LEARNING EXPERIENCE PROBLEM (CHARACTER)

To identify the character's big purpose and the related units in the incidents of the play, and to improvise character actions to achieve the character's purpose.

1. The students organize into pairs and sit in a circle. The teacher explains: "In a play the action is planned to show a particular kind of character. I will read a story in which the leading character does many different things, all of which are to show the character's big purpose. As you hear the story, ask yourself what that purpose is."

Suggested for younger children are "Raggylug"[15] and for older children "The Wise Ones."[16] There is discussion between partners and then within the group. Student responses are used to guide the students toward the big purpose of the character.

2. Continuing with the experience, the students listen to the same story again. This time students identify the beginning, middle, and ending incidents, and the leading character's purposes in each incident. The partners discuss. In the group discussion that follows, the teacher lists the related incidents and the character's purpose in each on the chalkboard. The students then identify the big purpose and related units of the *opposing* character.

3. Continuing with the same experience the students organize into groups of five to improvise character actions as they act out the story. Each group, working in a good-sized space, arranges that space for the environment of the play. The students cast the characters. Each player imagines and improvises actions in relation to the big purpose and related units.

· *Goal*

The student knows that the character's physical appearance and personality qualities affect the character's actions.

• LEARNING EXPERIENCE PROBLEM (CHARACTER)

To explore the ability to spontaneously select and use a character's distinctive physical and personality characteristics in the creation of a character's actions.

1. The teacher explains that the students are going to experiment with a form of Story Theatre to see if they can create characters on the spur of the moment. Each player is to spontaneously create a character's actions as a story is told. There are three basic rules:

(1) *The rule of the theatre.* The students are simultaneously players, playmakers, and audience in the play. The players aim to communicate

---

[15] In Siks, op. cit.
[16] See Appendix B, op. cit.

a character to the audience entirely through action. Everyone sits in a large semicircle on the floor facing the playing area except the storyteller, who sits on a stool slightly to the left of the audience.

(2) *The rule of instant action.* As soon as the storyteller says the name of a character a player moves instantly into the playing area and improvises the character's actions as the story is told. As soon as that character is no longer in that part of the story, the player returns at once to the audience.

(3) *The rule of instant cooperation.* When the storyteller names a character several players may jump up; the players need to cooperate instantly, giving way to one player so the action can continue uninterrupted. If, however, the character can be formed effectively by more than one player, the students create the character together; for example, the tree in *The Giving Tree*[17] or the mountain in the play *The Tale of Oniroku.*[18] The players must cooperate in giving everyone a chance to participate.

The teacher suggests they use the very short story of "Humpty Dumpty" to explore this form. With the space arranged and students seated the teacher-storyteller begins the rhyme: "Humpty Dumpty . . ." Instantly a player jumps up and moves into the playing area. The storyteller continues: "Humpty Dumpty sat on a wall." As the player shows Humpty Dumpty walking to sit on an imaginary wall, several students in the audience might impulsively move to the playing area to form the Wall. All of the students in the audience might join in. This is permissible and, in fact, encouraged *if* players cooperate instantly and concentrate on creating a believable imaginary wall. Without pause the storyteller continues: "Humpty Dumpty had a great fall." When Humpty falls, the wall, no longer needed, returns at once to the audience. After the player has improvised Humpty Dumpty's actions, the storyteller goes on, "All the King's horses and all the King's men."

Any number of players may immediately become the king's horses and men. While these characters try to help Humpty, the storyteller, following the players' actions, says, "Couldn't put Humpty together again." Instantly these players return to the audience while the player improvises actions to show what Humpty does to end the story and return to the audience.

The teacher then leads a discussion to solve problems or answer questions the students may have. In a second trial of the same story the emphasis is placed more clearly on the character's physical appearance and personality.

2. The students continue to explore the character concepts by using

[17] Shel Silverstein, *The Giving Tree* (New York: Harper & Row, 1964).
[18] Joanna Halpert Kraus, *Seven Sound and Motion Stories and The Tale of Oniroku* (New York: New Plays for Children, 1971).

Story Theatre form with the folk tale of "Henny-Penny,"[19] Charlip's *Fortunately*,[20] and Sendak's *Where the Wild Things Are*.[21]

· EXPLORING THEME CONCEPTS

· *Theme Concepts*

The theme is the core of the play. Developed through the dramatic action of the play, it is revealed through the plot and the interaction of the characters. "What is the play about?" is a key question used to probe the elements to discover the theme.

The most basic concepts of theme in the process of playmaking with children are the following:

The theme is the main thought of the play.
The theme is built through the plot and the development of the characters.

· *Goal*

The student knows that theme is the main thought of the play and is built through the plot and characters.

· LEARNING EXPERIENCE PROBLEM (THEME)

To explore theme to understand what theme is and to identify a play's theme.

1. The students organize as partners and sit together in a circle. The teacher asks for volunteers to tell a favorite joke to see if the others are able to get the point of it. The teacher has two or three ready should the children not be able to think of jokes on the spur of the moment. After each joke is told the partners discuss the point of the joke. The teacher then leads a group discussion stimulated by the questions: Why do you enjoy a joke when you understand the point of it? Why do you think people make up jokes about human beings? Why do you think playmakers create a play around a main thought about human beings? Discussion emphasizes the theme concept.

2. The students listen to a story told by the teacher. In pairs, they identify the theme and share their ideas with the group. A story for young children is *The Little Engine That Could*[22] and for older children "The Musicians of Bremen."[23]

---

[19] See Appendix B, op. cit.
[20] Charlip, op. cit.
[21] Maurice Sendak, *Where the Wild Things Are* (New York: Harper & Row, 1963).
[22] Watty Piper, *The Little Engine That Could* (New York: Platt & Munk, 1961).
[23] In Ward, op. cit.

· LEARNING EXPERIENCE PROBLEM (THEME)

To explore theme by examining how it is built through a play's action and characters.

1. The students sit in a circle, organize as partners, and listen to the folk tale of "Teeny-Tiny."[24] They identify the theme by discussing these questions posed by the teacher: What did Teeny-Tiny do in the opening incident that started her conflict? What did she do in the middle incidents that caused her to struggle? Why did she put her head out of the covers and tell the Voice to TAKE IT? What is all of the action in the story about? After partner and group discussions the following theme is arrived at: A guilty person is haunted by his or her conscience.

2. The students continue with the experience by organizing into small groups of four each composed of two sets of partners. Next each group plans how to act out the story of "Teeny-Tiny," and decides who each of the players in turn will be. The students then improvise character actions and dialogue to build the theme. After each group has had a first trial, one group joins another, each acting out the story for the other. The players aim to show the theme through the actions of the characters. Discussion focuses on how the players solved the problem and whether knowing the theme helps the players to act out the story.

· EXPLORING LANGUAGE AND DIALOGUE CONCEPTS

· *Concepts of Language and Dialogue*

The verbal expression of a play is language, which consists of the words spoken by the characters as they talk in dialogue and in other kinds of speaking relationships. Diction is concerned primarily with the way the players speak for the characters, and it contributes to the tone, clarity of speech, texture, and mood of the play.

The most basic concepts of language in the process of playmaking with children are the following:

Language is the words spoken by the characters of the play.
Dialogue helps to develop the plot, characters, and mood.

· *Goal*

The student knows that language is the words spoken by the characters in the play, and it helps develop the plot, characters, and mood.

· LEARNING EXPERIENCE PROBLEM (LANGUAGE)

To explore the ability to create language and dialogue for a character that help tell the story and develop the character.

[24] In Siks, op. cit.

1. The students organize into a semicircle for Story Theatre. The teacher uses the story, "The Peddler and the Monkeys."[25] The rules of this form are reviewed. The students' problem is to create words as well as actions that develop the characters and tell the story.

The storyteller *phrases* the story to stimulate the characters to speak. For example, the storyteller may say, "When the Peddler decided to go to the village he told his plans to his wife but she tried hard to get him to change his mind." If the players do not speak, the storyteller *assists* by providing a different suggestion: "The wife reminded the Peddler of his daydreaming habit." If the players still do not speak, the storyteller *adapts* to the players, for example, "On this particular day the Peddler went on his way for his wife did not feel like talking." When the players create dialogue freely the storyteller allows them to continue unless they digress from the plot, in which case the storyteller *adapts* to their dialogue and interrupts to continue to tell the story.

Concluding discussion focuses on the questions: Did the players solve their problems? Was the characters' language appropriate? Did it help to tell the story? The students play the story again with different players.

2. Continue this procedure with several experiences. Use stories in which dialogue is essential to the plot development.

· LEARNING EXPERIENCE PROBLEM (LANGUAGE)

To explore the ability to create language and dialogue for a character that help tell the story and develop the mood.

1. The students sit in a circle to explore the use of their voices to create the mood for a play. Given the problem to create an eerie, fearful mood they speak simultaneously (but not in unison) the opening line of "The Conjure Wives"[26]: "Once upon a time when Halloween came in the dark of the moon." They repeat the line several times to create different moods, happy and sad as well as lonely. The next problem is to use their voices to create a lonely mood by saying, "Let me in, do-o-o! I'se cold thro-o-o-o an' thro-o-o-o, An' I'se hungry, too-o-o!"

2. Continuing this experience with "The Conjure Wives" in Story Theatre form the students improvise dialogue and actions to create the mood and tell the story. The storyteller and players aim to communicate the strange, eerie mood of the play through voice and dialogue. The audience determines how they succeed. The problem is explored a second time with a student as storyteller and with different players. "Teen-Tiny" is good for younger children and both younger and older children enjoy the challenge of creating a "panicky rumor" mood for "Henny-Penny."

25 Ibid.
26 In Ward, op. cit.

· EXPLORING MELODY-SOUND CONCEPTS

· *Melody-Sound Concepts*

This element comprises the total sound or musical quality of the play's dialogue and the music or rhythms used as a soundtrack or background. Sounds are created to cause the players and audience to imagine they hear whatever sound is necessary in the action of the play. Sounds heighten the mood and serve to strengthen the emotional impact of the dramatic action. The child explores the most fundamental concept:

Melody-sound is the arrangement of the play's sounds and tones to communicate images and mood in the action of the play.

· *Goal*

The student knows that melody-sound is the tone quality of the play and that it is used to communicate images and mood.

· LEARNING EXPERIENCE PROBLEM (MELODY-SOUND)

To explore the ability to identify the sound images in a play and to construct sound to communicate an image and mood.

1. The students are guided to listen to a recording of an improvisation of "Teeny-Tiny" to identify the sounds and images. For example, the sound of Teeny-Tiny's footsteps, the opening and closing of the teeny-tiny door and gate, and later the Voice. Discussion centers on the sounds the students hear, and on the particular sounds used to convey actions, characters, and mood.

2. The students organize into groups of three, each of which receives copies of the play "Henny-Penny."[27] They read the play to identify the sound images in the script, and then select objects from the sound box or from the room to construct the two sounds. Each group, in turn, creates the sound images while others listen with their eyes closed. The students discuss and agree upon the sounds that communicate the sound images most clearly. The group who created these sounds becomes the sound crew for the Story Theatre experience with this story.

The sound crew sits with the storyteller (no scripts used) and improvises the required sounds and sounds to match the characters' walks and actions. The storyteller tells the story by adapting to the actions and the sounds. The players improvise actions in relation to the storyteller and the sounds. Discussion centers on the ability of the sound crew to match the sound with the actions to create images and mood.

---

[27] See Appendix B, op. cit.

· EXPLORING CONCEPTS OF SPECTACLE

· *Concepts of Spectacle*

Spectacle is the element concerned with the visual image of the play. Viewed as the process of bringing the story alive visually, emphasizing its dramatic action, spectacle is formed primarily through scenery, light, and costumes.

The fundamental principles of design used to form a visual image—line, shape, color, and size—are applied in each of the related aspects of spectacle. The most basic concepts of spectacle in playmaking with children are the following:

Spectacle is the visual image of the play communicated through scenery, light, and costume.

The line, shape, color, size, and spatial arrangement of scenic objects create an environment for the play's action.

Lighting gives visibility to the environment and strengthens dramatic action through the use of intensity, color, and distribution.

Costume pieces emphasize a character's appearance through the use of line, color, and shape.

· *Goal*

The student knows that spectacle is the visual image used to strengthen the dramatic action through scenery, light, and costume.

· LEARNING EXPERIENCE PROBLEM (SPECTACLE)

To identify spectacle as the visual image that strengthens the dramatic action through scenery, light, and costume.

1. The students sit together in a circle and discuss the questions: When you go to a play what do you go to *see*? Why do you think scenery has been used in plays for hundreds of years? What else is used in plays to help the audience see and believe in the make-believe of the play? How do costumes and light help? Discussion is summarized to reenforce the concept.

2. Continuing the experience, the students organize into pairs and listen to the teacher read the first four short incidents of "A Magic Hood."[28] The students identify four ways in which spectacle can be used to strengthen the visual image of the play. In discussion the four ways are identified as: (a) lighting to open the play, (b) scenery to communicate the Japanese village square, (c) character action to communi-

---

[28] Masayuki Sano, "A Magic Hood." See Appendix B.

cate the conflict, and (d) costumes to emphasize the characters and to show they are in Japan.

· LEARNING EXPERIENCE PROBLEM (SCENERY)

To identify the scenic requirements for the environment of a play and to arrange objects of proper size, shape, and color to create the environment.

1. The students organize into three groups, and each works in a different part of the room. Each student receives a copy of "A Magic Hood,"[29] and students in each group read the first four incidents aloud. Each group is given a problem: (a) identify the environment; (b) identify the scenic object(s) needed in the action; (c) select appropriate scenic object(s); and (d) arrange the object(s) in the given space to create the play's environment. The groups view each others' stage environments. Discussion focuses on the questions: What is this play's environment? What is the only scenic object needed? Why is it needed?

2. The students consider the *shape* of scenic objects. In "A Magic Hood" the essential scenic object is "a cherry tree in full bloom." Three different tree shapes approximately four feet in diameter are used. The first is a large flat circular shape, the second flat and triangular, and the third, a realistic tree shape. The students discuss the shapes from the viewpoint of design and the environment of the play.

3. The students consider *size* in relation to scenic objects. Three similar but smaller (one foot) objects are compared in size with the other shapes on stage. The students discuss relative sizes, shapes, and projection.

4. The students consider the use of *color*. The reverse side of the circular part of the larger tree shape is shown to be a soft pink, and the reverse side of the triangular part reveals a deep purple-pink. The teacher asks one of the groups to help design cherry blossoms for the realistic tree shape by twisting three-inch strips of brightly colored deep-pink crepe paper to each branch. During this process the other students discuss and consider the color of each scenic object from the viewpoint of the play's requirements.

· LEARNING EXPERIENCE PROBLEM (LIGHTING)

To identify the purpose of lighting and to explore the use of lighting equipment to give visibility and mood to the play's environment.

1. The students sit in the playing area. The teacher refers to the lighting equipment and explains that lighting in a play is used for visibility and mood. Lighting for visibility allows the audience to see the play's action and objects that need to be seen. Lighting for mood strengthens the dramatic action.

[29] Sano, op. cit.

2. Continuing with the experience the students organize into groups of four or five. Using the available equipment the teacher demonstrates the concept of lighting to one group while the others observe. The students in that group demonstrate to students in the other groups. The teacher observes to clarify any points of discussion that arise.

3. The students organize into two groups: A and B. Each group sits in a circle at opposite ends of the room. Each student receives a script of "A Magic Hood."[30] Group A is asked to read the opening incident of the play, which takes place between the characters of the Stage Manager and the Lighting Man. Group B is asked to read the closing incident beginning with the speech of the Candy Vendor, who shouts, "Very well, Master. Ring the fire bells!" and ending with the Stage Manager's speech that begins with "They did a fine deed."

When finished, the students in Group A organize into smaller groups of four while the students in Group B organize into two evenly divided groups. All groups identify the kind of lighting needed in the incidents and then, in turn, construct the required lighting. Finally, the players are selected to improvise action while each light crew, in turn, creates the required lighting for the incidents. Discussion centers on how the players solved the problem in relation to the concept and the available lighting equipment.

· LEARNING EXPERIENCE PROBLEM (COSTUME)

To explore the use of costume pieces in terms of shape, line, and color to strengthen a character's appearance and personality.

1. The students organize and sit in a circle. Using a piece of golden colored satin or some similar material approximately two yards long and a yard wide, the teacher arranges the material in different shapes and lines. The students are guided to spontaneously identify the character images created by the material. The teacher begins by placing the material around his or her neck and shoulders and arranging it to fall in vertical lines, first down the front of the body and then down the back. The material is then arranged in horizontal lines as sashes around the waist. A diagonal line is created by arranging the material over the right shoulder and tying it loosely on the left at the waist. The two ends of the material are then folded together so that it may be arranged over both shoulders as a shawl, over one shoulder as a draped garment, or across the front of the body as an apron or draped panel. The teacher then winds the material around the head as a turban and ties the ends so that they fall vertically over the shoulders. The teacher emphasizes that the material has been selected so that its color and texture correspond to the character's role. Considerations are the character's position in the story relationship and the character's personality.

[30] Ibid.

2. Continuing this experience, the students work in pairs within the circle. Each student selects a single piece of material from a costume box of materials. The problem is to create a variety of costume pieces for imagined characters by arranging the material in different lines and shapes on different parts of the body. The partners discuss the different arrangements each creates.

3. Prior to this experience the students have read or listened to a reading or recording of the entire play, "A Magic Hood."[31] The students organize into groups of four. Each group is given a copy of the director's notes describing the costuming of the characters of the Candy Vendor and the Village Master. The problem is to use a single piece of textured material to create a costume for each of these two characters that emphasizes their opposing character relationship.

The teacher points out that complementary colors on the opposite ends of the color spectrum are often used in costume pieces for opposing characters. The students work as a group to discuss and select appropriate materials according to color and texture. Two students arrange the materials as costume pieces while the other two students become the two characters.

Each group, in turn, shows the other groups the costume pieces they have created. The audience's problem is to determine whether each group solved the costume problem.

SUGGESTED ACTIVITIES FOR ADULT STUDENTS

1. With a small group of peers, discuss the Saroyan quote that opens this chapter. Discuss, also, advantages and disadvantages of using with children the introductory procedure of Reader's Theatre described at the opening of this chapter.
2. Refer to Figure 7, the conceptual design of playmaking elements and concepts. Examine each concept as it is stated by analyzing the statement in relation to its intent to clarify the meaning of each element for the teacher. Suggest any changes, additions, or deletions that you believe need to be made in the concept statements.
3. Refer to the learning experiences in this chapter:
   a. Select six experiences, each designed to involve children in exploring a different concept in each of the playmaking elements. Prepare guidelines and any instructional materials needed. Share each activity with a group of children or peers. Evaluate the effectiveness of each experience by the response of the students in relation to their achievement of the intended goal.
   b. Design six learning experiences to be used with children to guide them to explore six different concepts, one in each of the playmaking elements. Explore the effectiveness of the experiences by using each with a small

[31] Ibid.

group of peers. Evaluate their response in relation to the intended goal and revise the guidelines if needed.

4. Select two short stories, contemporary and traditional, for younger children and two for older children.
   a. Select each on the basis of probable appeal to the children and from the viewpoint of dramatic action.
   b. Analyze each of the dramatic elements in each story to see if they meet the criteria of a limited number of characters and plot incidents, and a worthy theme.
   c. Prepare two of the stories so you may tell them with enjoyment and flexibility.
   d. Use these two stories in Story Theatre experiences to guide your peers to explore a specific concept in the elements of plot, character, or dialogue. Revise guidance if needed and then use each story to explore specific concepts with children.

5. Design six playmaking activities for a Reading Learning Center for children of a given age or grade level.
   a. Specify whether the activities are for one, two, or more players.
   b. Develop the activities to involve children in an exploration of a concept in each of the playmaking elements.
   c. Employ the principles of novelty, manipulation of concrete materials, and interaction with peers.

◆ 12
Audience

There was a child went forth every day;
And the first object he looked upon and received with
*   wonder, pity, love, or dread, that object he became.*
And that object became part of him for the day,
*   or a certain part of the day,*
Or for many years or stretching cycles of years.

WALT WHITMAN
There Was a Child Went Forth[1]

To look upon, receive with feeling, and become. With beautiful simplicity
the poet describes the way children perceive and learn. In their daily
living children listen, see, and respond to a myriad of stimuli and happenings in the environment. They imagine, and they become.

Learning in the role of the audience is natural to children. Drama
being created—coming alive to be communicated to others—is a communal art unique to human beings. The word "Audience" stems from the
Latin verb *audio* meaning "to hear, to listen" and "theatre" stems from a
Greek word meaning "to see, to view." In the art of drama an audience
is a group of persons gathered in a designated place or space to experience a drama. Children who sit together on the floor or in the
theatre to watch a drama coming alive are not unlike human beings
who sat together upon the ground or hillside, in daylight or firelight
thousands of years ago to be entertained by others. There may be
twenty or thirty or fifty or more individuals involved in a theatre experience, if one counts all who create and receive the drama. Yet when

[1] Walt Whitman, *There Was a Child Went Forth* (New York: Harper & Row,
1943), p. iii.

the drama comes alive, the experience unifies all the participants basically into one. The unity and universality that existed in the primitive theatre is an essential aspect of the nature of theatre.

To progress in their abilities to originate and form drama children need to learn the role of the audience. If they are to experience the aesthetic power of drama and learn to appreciate its rich heritage, children need to experience the audience role from several perspectives. The dual purpose of this chapter is to consider the component of audience from the child's role in experiencing it and the teacher's role in guiding the process. First it examines briefly the child as the audience who receives and responds to the created drama forms, and then the child as the creator who communicates drama to an audience.

EXPERIENCING THE AUDIENCE ROLE

Identifying Processes, Concepts, and Goals

The basic elements of the component of the audience are interrelated with the processes of: (1) perception, (2) response, and (3) evaluation. To guide children to achieve specific learning outcomes, the content of the processes and elements of audience has been organized into key concepts. Goals have been formulated from these concepts (Figure 9). These are stated as follows:

1. The student knows that the purpose of the audience is to listen, view, enjoy, and perceive the drama experience.
2. The student knows that an audience responds to drama and theatre experiences spontaneously with applause and other nonverbal means and with evaluative comments following the activity.
3. The student knows that his or her response aims to assess a player's solution of the dramatic problem by evaluating the player's concentration, imagination, and effort; and by giving suggestions to assist the participant's improvement.
4. The student is able to evaluate a theatre experience by giving a personal response, and by making comments based on his or her understanding of the concepts of playing and playmaking.

Learning the role of the audience carries with it a dual responsibility for each individual. First is self-responsibility. As a learner, the child views and listens to peers using skills and employing specific concepts that the child too is in the process of learning. The child needs to learn to concentrate to: observe others; determine whether and how the goals of the player are reached; and recognize that in the creative process there are many alternative and imaginative ways to reach a given goal or solve a problem.

Second is the child's responsibility to peers. Did I reach the goal or solve the problem? How may I improve what I set out to do? These are

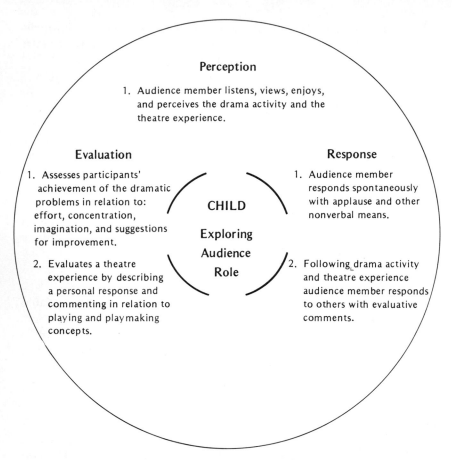

Figure 9 Audience Role: Processes, Concepts, Goals.

unvoiced questions of most conscientious children involved in learning. Children want and expect to learn from their peers. Placing the emphasis on the objective to be reached is essential in this learning process. An objective evaluation, rather than subjective approval or disapproval, is imperative from the viewpoint of interrelated learning roles. In the role of audience the child learns the responsibility of both receiving and responding to peers with honest "feedback" about an activity. In this interactive process, which is extremely affective in nature, the child gains respect and value for the efforts, imagination, and integrity of peers.

Implementing the Goals

The teacher is responsible for interrelating the child's learning experiences in the role of the audience with activities in playing and playmaking. It is through a continual interchange of these roles that the child learns and develops. To implement the audience goals, the teacher follows the same guidance strategies and procedures used for playing and playmaking. However, the teacher specifically emphasizes audience goals in two areas of the teaching-learning process. These are in planning the audience learning experiences and in guiding students following their observation of the participants.

PLANNING EXPERIENCES FOR THE AUDIENCE ROLE

Variety and flexibility should be considered in planning how to organize students for different experiences of the audience role. The size of an audience is determined by the nature of the learning experience. Variety is used in organization to allow students to interact in small groups, large groups, and in pairs. The membership of the audience group should change frequently. Students need to interact with many individuals rather than being allowed to continually interact with one or two friends. Techniques used to organize audience groups include: (a) grouping by ability, (b) division by sexes or sizes, (c) grouping by numbering off, and (d) grouping by inviting children to organize themselves into a specified number of equally divided groups.

Each learning experience for the audience needs to be stated clearly. Even though the problem for the audience is related directly to the problem of the participants, the audience members need to know the specific goal or problem on which to focus their attention. A teacher should frequently ask a child in the audience group to paraphrase the problem or problems they are to solve.

GUIDING THE AUDIENCE TO EVALUATE

The teacher uses procedures that are intended to provide the students with guidelines that will eventually enable them to guide evaluative discussions on their own. First, the teacher guides the students to sit in an arrangement that allows for maximum verbal interaction. A circular arrangement provides for both interaction and eye contact among students. The size of the circle depends on the number of persons involved in the discussion. The place for discussion should vary. Sometimes the participants move into a space to join the audience. Sometimes it is the other way around. The topic of discussion focuses directly on the goals the audience and participants will set out to achieve.

Second, the teacher describes four responsibilities of the audience as they participate in an evaluative group discussion. Each participant is required to: (1) respond, (2) avoid interrupting another speaker, (3) keep on the subject of discussion, and (4) summarize mentally or verbally, reaching conclusions based on the discussion.

Third, the teacher describes the four points of assessment that audience members use to evaluate student participation. These include: (1) whether participants solved the problem, (2) individual imaginative efforts, (3) concentration, and (4) suggestions to assist participants. To employ these the teacher uses two kinds of questioning techniques. The first is direct questioning, in which the teacher asks a question that calls for a yes or no response. For example: "Did the players solve the problem?" This question requires an answer that converges the students' thinking to the question asked.

The other is an open-ended questioning technique that encourages divergent thinking and allows a child to elaborate or clarify a response. For example, "What action did you see that caused you to believe the stage environment was a forest?" A teacher uses judgment in guiding audience members to evaluate student participation. In introductory stages the teacher does not use all four of the points of assessment. Rather the evaluation is focused directly on determining whether the participants reached the goal and on suggestions to assist them in achieving the goal. The teacher concludes and summarizes the main points and aims to keep the discussion brief and purposeful.

Experiencing Theatre

Concurrent with the learning experiences in playing and playmaking, children need to experience the role of audience in theatre productions of excellence. Outstanding theatre experiences serve as models for the child's learning in each of the interrelated roles. For the child to be moved by the aesthetic power of a theatre performance is an integral part of the process-concept structural approach to drama.

Children must have opportunities to discover for themselves how drama communicates to them through theatre productions that represent theatre at its best. This means a theatre production that is created with its own distinctive charm and, to paraphrase James Barrie, has its own "sort of bloom."

Children need quality theatre experiences at periodic intervals during the school year. It is the teacher's challenge and responsibility to arrange for the finest productions available. On the one hand, if there are professional theatres in the vicinity they may be interested in producing for child audiences. On the other hand, if they are not available, other sources should be considered. For example, students in drama and theatre classes in the middle school and junior high school may respond to opportunities to produce two or three different kinds of theatre productions each year for children in the kindergarten and primary school. High school or college students may also be invited to produce a program of theatre for children in the elementary school.

COMMUNICATING TO THE THEATRE AUDIENCE

A strong and immediate outcome of a satisfying theatre experience is the desire of children to create theatre. Children who have experienced the forming of plays through learning experiences in the elements of playmaking will want to create theatre to communicate to audiences other than themselves. In the process-concept structural approach children are encouraged to do so. Children need to experience theatre by taking it in and by giving it out—assimilating and accommodating their perceptions and feelings.

Children's productions need not and should not be elaborate. A five- or ten-minute production offers a satisfying experience for beginners in this step-in-progress learning of drama. Children who create and construct the playmaking elements for short plays such as "Henny-Penny," "The Wind and the Sun," and "Jumping Beans," enjoy the challenging experience of synthesizing the elements and communicating the play to an audience of children in a different grade in the school.

A class of third graders created three different versions of the play "Henny-Penny" and shared it with several different audiences of kindergarten, first-, and second-grade children. One group created the play as a puppet show. Another created it as a traditional play and made costume pieces from newspapers. The most distinctive features of the animal characters were emphasized by a newspaper nose for Foxy-Woxy, newspaper feet for Ducky-Daddles, and a newspaper comb on top of his head for Cocky-Locky. The third group created a Story Theatre production of the play.

What happens to the child player or playmaker when in the process of communicating a play to an invited audience the audience responds? Perhaps the audience laughs, claps, shouts, or responds nonverbally with sighs or sudden starts. Children who have gained security in the skills of concentration, imagination, and adaptation should be ready for the challenge and enjoyment of a live audience responding naturally and honestly. The important consideration is *what* happens to the group of serious collaborators who are committed to the responsibility of forming the dramatic production. What happens when there is a response to a character's imaginative actions? Or a response to lighting, or sound, or arrangement of scenery or costumes? What happens to the playmakers when the play is over? The applause and comments are "music to their ears." Hughes Mearns was perceptive. In *Creative Power* he supports this kind of experiencing: "Just to be—really *be*—another person in an undistinguished play is to make one immeasurably free forever."[2]

Consider this. A child who participates actively in baseball or one of the team sports will as an adult seek similar experiences, most often as a spectator observing others involved in that same sport. Does the same hold true for dynamic, aesthetic theatre experience? Will a child who participates in satisfying drama and playmaking activities seek similar activities as an adult? Will a citizenry who seeks aesthetic ex-

[2] Hughes Mearns, *Creative Power*, 2nd rev. ed. (New York: Dover, 1958), p. 96.

periences in their lives be different from a citizenry to which aesthetic values are of little if any concern? Whitman, the poet, perceived that "To have great poets, there must be great audiences too."

SUGGESTED ACTIVITIES FOR ADULT STUDENTS

1. With a small group of peers, discuss the Whitman quotes that open and close this chapter. Discuss, also, each of the following by identifying reasons to defend or attack each statement:
   a. Learning the role of the audience is natural to children.
   b. To progress in their abilities to originate and form drama as players and playmakers children need to learn the role of the audience.
   c. In the process-concept structure approach the child's learning the role of the audience pervades his or her learning the roles of player and playmaker.
2. Select four learning experiences designed for the role of the player or playmaker in which there has been no stated goal or learning experience for the role of the audience:
   a. Design an audience learning experience for each.
   b. Arrange to share the learning experiences you design (in combination with the learning experiences in the role of player or playmaker) with a group of children or peers.
   c. Apply guidance procedures suggested for the teacher to apply when guiding an audience of children to evaluate.
3. Suppose a group of children plan to attend a children's theatre production. You have been asked to design a procedure with learning activities to prepare the children to receive, respond, and evaluate their experience.
   a. Outline the procedure you will follow to reach this objective.
   b. Specify the processes, concepts, and goals you aim for the children to experience through the theatre production.
   c. Design six learning activities for the children to be used prior to or after the experience.
   d. Employ the principles of novelty and interaction in the activities and your procedure.
4. Design six audience learning activities for children of a given age level to be used in a Reading Learning Center.
   a. Specify whether the activities are to be experienced by two or more students.
   b. Develop the activities to involve students in the role of the audience in each of the processes of perceiving, responding, and evaluating. (The concepts may or may not be directly related to drama elements.)
   c. Employ the principles of novelty and interaction.

Part 3

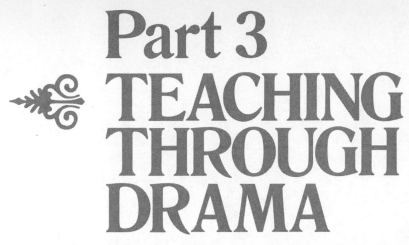

TEACHING THROUGH DRAMA

Children Learn Through Drama When Guided to Explore Content and Concepts of Subject Areas Through Drama Processes and Elements

It is startling to hear noise in an elementary school hallway, but it is even more startling to hear the sound of hoofbeats in an elementary school hallway. What was more startling was to see cardboard horses being ridden by a group of live pilgrims heading for Canterbury. And what was most startling was that these pilgrims were nine-year-olds in the fourth grade.

ALBERT CULLUM
Push Back the Desks[1]

[1] Albert Cullum, *Push Back the Desks* (New York: Citation Press, 1967), p. 189.

❧ 13

Integration of Abilities and Learning Through Drama

This above all: to thine own self be true,
And it must follow, as the night the day,
Thou canst not then be false to any man.

WILLIAM SHAKESPEARE
Hamlet

Drama can serve as an integrative force in children's learning if the teacher knows how to use it effectively as a teaching method. Integration, in a dictionary sense, is a process of bringing together (parts) into a whole. From the perspective of the developing child, integration implies the involvement of the whole person, the individual interacting *in toto*. *Interaction* implies that the individual responds and behaves because of the unifying effects of internal and external forces.

An individual's internal forces lie within the integrity of his or her personality—the distinctively human qualities of each individual. Drama then becomes the external force used by the teacher to provide conditions that will interact optimally with children's internal forces. In the act of creating drama, as in all arts, it is the integrity of each individual that brings significance to the individual, to the group, and to the drama formed. Integration of learning needs always to respect the integrity and uniqueness of each individual's abilities—imagination, feelings, perceptions.

The purpose of this chapter is twofold. First, it is to show the use of drama as an integrative force in the child's processes of learning and developing. Second, it is to demonstrate how the teacher provides integrated learning experiences through drama. To accomplish these purposes six artist teachers present selected experiences in brief essays. Each is a practitioner in the field who works with both children and adults. In an individual writing style each uses personal experience to show how drama has been used to stimulate, involve, and presumably integrate the abilities and learning of children. The theme that unifies the essays is the conviction by each teacher of the effectiveness of the art of drama to promote individualized learning within the scope of the total experience. An implied theme in the essays is the view that drama needs to be included as a central art in the language arts or arts curriculum of the elementary schools in our country, and in teacher education.

Each writer speaks from her own area of experience. Hazel Dunnington focuses on the use of drama as a catalyst to facilitate the development of a child's language and reading skills. Sue Lerner extends this focus. She explains how filmmaking and drama experience serve to improve reading comprehension and language communication skills. Dorothy Prince describes how drama heightened children's involvement in writing poetry and interpreting it. Barbara Salisbury presents an approach to aesthetic education and shows how drama is used as the matrix to stimulate and synthesize children's experiences in the related arts. Wendy Perks reviews the procedures she used in a comprehensive experimental in-service drama program for teachers to discover how the elementary school curriculum could be integrated through drama. Aurora Valentinetti, an artist puppeteer with many years experience in performing and teaching, defends puppetry as a theatre art and offers guidelines for its use as an art in education.

TEACHING LANGUAGE CONCEPTS AND READING SKILLS THROUGH DRAMA

Hazel Brain Dunnington[1]

Each year more classroom teachers in the elementary school are using improvisational drama to teach basic language and reading skills. These teachers are enthusiastic about the use of drama as a strong, natural motivator for involving children in an experiential approach to reading and to exploring related language concepts.

From the children's point of view this approach consists of: (1) experiencing, and observing the recording of their experience in "print" (on the chalkboard in story form); (2) acting out their experiences as set down "in print"; (3) reading their own language in unison from "print"; (4) making line drawings of the story action; (5) rereading the story, this time focusing attention on words as symbols of meaning;

[1] Hazel B. Dunnington, Associate Professor of Drama and Communications, Central Washington State College, Ellensburg, WA, coeditor with author of *Children's Theatre and Creative Dramatics* (Seattle: University of Washington Press, 1961).

(6) experiencing concepts such as sequencing, comparing, and contrasting from a "doing through drama" base; and (7) individuals reading their story again and again from an individual copy "printed" by the teacher for the child to read, to keep, and to cherish.

Questions posed most frequently by curious classroom teachers regarding this approach are: How is drama effective as a facilitator in languaging and reading procedures? How does the teacher proceed? What are the pitfalls? These questions will be considered briefly, first by examining the underlying rationale of the approach, second by identifying fundamental instructional procedures, third by describing two different classroom experiences with children, and finally by looking at possible pitfalls.

Rationale

The approach is based on the following assumptions:

1. Perceiving an environment involves all faculties and, especially, the senses; concrete impressions provide the stimuli for children's expressions, which when written "in print" generate favorable attention.

2. Using the children's "printed" story as a basis for improvised action reenforces and extends personal meaning; thus, children view words as symbols for their own experience.

3. Group reading of internalized action from the teacher's "print" of the children's talk elicits positive response and adds meaning to the reading experience.

4. Making line drawings of the action heightens the children's valuing of reading and reenforces imaging and meaning.

5. Reading the story from his or her own ditto copy facilitates the child's understanding of words as symbols representing meaning and actions.

6. The child benefits (a) by using language that stimulates dramatic action and (b) by dramatizing action that stimulates language.

7. Improvising concepts and acting out story sequences reenforces meaning, as in comparing and contrasting actions in relation to weight (heavy/light), space (up/down), and time (fast/slow); and in grasping the meaning of sequence.

Instructional Procedures

Essentially a teacher's role is one of (a) being alert to children's strong, spirited interaction and talk and (b) seizing upon their personal expressions. Sequentially, the teacher proceeds as follows:

AFFORDS STIMULATING EXPERIENCE

The teacher provides children with first-hand experience (as on a field trip), or with imagined experience (through such stimuli as films, sound recordings, etc.) and seizes upon aspects commanding the children's attention.

STIMULATES CHILDREN'S TALK ABOUT THEIR EXPERIENCE

For instance, on a nature walk children are guided to look for "moving things" and encouraged to talk about them. Upon returning to the classroom children are guided to again talk about things they saw and how they moved.

PRINTS CHILDREN'S LANGUAGE ON CHALKBOARD OR CHART

If the children are beginning readers, the teacher "prints" the most simple of their language structures. For example, in "we saw" stories the teacher selects such children's verbalizations as "worms squirm" or "leaves fall." With more experienced groups the teacher "prints" language structures reflecting the children's capabilities.

FOCUSES CHILDREN'S ATTENTION ON "PRINT"

The teacher shows children that through "printing," experience is recorded, set down, and "kept" for sharing with others and enjoying at a later time.

GUIDES CHILDREN TO IMAGINE AND IMPROVISE ACTIONS

Children are guided (a) to concentrated imagining of the thing or person's environment and its way of "moving" in its environment, and (b) to improvising the action (and sounds or words when these are natural to the experience).

GUIDES CHILDREN TO READ IN UNISON

The teacher guides the group to read the "printed" story together. In the beginning the story may be one brief sentence or even just two words. The teacher may give particular attention to words as name and action symbols.

MAKES DITTO COPIES OF THE STORY

During children's free play or recess the teacher makes a ditto copy of the story for each child.

GUIDES CHILDREN TO READ THE STORY AGAIN

Each child is encouraged to reread the story from his or her own copy in unison, and possibly some singly and some in groups, depending on individual capabilities.

GUIDES CHILDREN TO MAKE LINE DRAWINGS OF THE STORY

In drawing, children recall the actual experience and the improvised experience. They may want to act out the actions again. This kind of experiencing tends to internalize and integrate the child's learning.

GUIDES CHILDREN TO READ FOR SELF AND OTHERS

Children are encouraged to reread the story for their own satisfaction and to take their story home where each child may read it to family members or friends.

REPEATS THE PROCESS

Children enjoy "creating" a book of their own stories, acting them out, and reading them (in small groups, or individually).

ENCOURAGES IMPROVISATION AND DRAMATIZATION

Through improvisation and dramatization the child's understanding of a variety of concepts is strengthened and his or her sight and speaking vocabularies are increased.

A First-Grade Experience

Guided to look for "moving things" on a nature walk, first-grade children became fascinated with the sight of ants building a "hill." As the children watched, one child said, "They're marching." Back in the room, "Ants march" became their first story. For weeks, according to the teacher, the children imagined and improvised actions of marching ants building a "hill," and every child enjoyed reading the two words and learned them. Their next story was "Cars zoom!" and the third one, "Children run. Birds fly."

A Third-Grade Experience[2]

On the first day of school in a third-grade classroom the teacher, Mr. Wilson, genially asked, "What shall we do now, read a story or write one?" Probably partly to test Mr. Wilson's sense of humor a child replied, "Let's write a story—about Mr. Wilson." Objectively, but with a twinkling eye, Mr. Wilson approved, challenging the children. The group was guided to create a story with a problem, and the teacher recorded the following on the chalkboard.

Once upon a time Mr. Wilson went out in the rain.
He slipped and fell into a mud puddle.
A lady saw him.
He was wet and ugh, ugh, muddy.
The lady decided to put Mr. Wilson into the washer.
When the dryer started, Mr. Wilson spun around and around.
The lady took Mr. Wilson out of the dryer, and was she surprised?
Mr. Wilson was now only six inches tall!

[2] By permission of Roy R. Wilson, formerly classroom teacher, Hebeler Elementary School, Ellensburg, WA; currently completing Ph.D. in children's literature, Ohio State University, Columbus, Ohio.

Enthusiasm was high the next day, and the group was guided to improvise action when the teacher suggested, "Maybe we could do a play about our story." The children concurred, and delighted in imagining and solving the drama problem of Mr. Wilson's shrinking from his towering six feet to a mere six inches. Each day, that first week, this group wrote and dramatized a new chapter of *Mr. Wilson's Great Adventure*. Chapter titles were "Mr. Wilson's Problem," "Down the Drain," "Swallowed by the Great Fish," "Saved by the Fisherman," and "Restored to Normal Size."

In the last chapter, Mr. Wilson's big sneeze "inside the fish inside the freezer" pops him out onto the floor. The lady again puts Mr. Wilson into the dryer. This time he is "fluffed up" to normal size again. The final line of the children's story was, "And were the children glad! The teacher the children had while Mr. Wilson was away was very mean. The end."

Every child in the class eagerly volunteered to read a chapter and to act out a part of the improvisation as the group went from room to room in their school and to other third grades in other schools to share *Mr. Wilson's Great Adventure*. This group created other stories and acted them out, including in October *The Spooky Adventure* and in November *Finding Friends*, and so on throughout most of the year.

Pitfalls

To cope with possible pitfalls, the teacher should avoid monotony in prolonging discussion. Keep each experience spirited by involving children in improvisation and dramatic problem solving.[3] Sieze upon children's experiences and responses; utilize *their language*. Avoid belaboring the process. Give the experience the needed dramatic structure according to the children's capabilities. Enjoy the children and the experience.

INTEGRATING LEARNING THROUGH FILMMAKING AND DRAMA

Sue Lerner[4]

As an elementary teacher, I have tried to find learning projects that combine the use of many skills with content from social studies, science, literature, music and/or art. Many projects were rejected because of their impracticality for the classroom, or because they were not sufficiently

---

[3] Mr. Wilson's strong belief and experience in drama result in much dramatizing being done in his classrooms. This may be a factor in children's ready acceptance of his suggestion to act out their story.

[4] Sue Lerner, classroom teacher and reading specialist, Fairwood Elementary School, Kent (Washington) Public Schools, author of "Animate Your Curriculum: A Handbook."

motivating for the children, or too much work for the teacher. However, I discovered a project which solved these difficulties—filmmaking. Without much movie camera experience, I was able to help children produce animated films. Since my first experience six years ago, filmmaking has continued to be a successful classroom project with children from second through sixth grade, and in elective classes in junior and senior high school.

Filmmaking—Valuable Classroom Project

Having made both live-action and animated films with children, I have strong evidence to support its use, first as an effective way to teach basic reading, language, and mathematics skills; and second as a self-motivating classroom activity. To further validate my evidence I surveyed available experimental research on the use of activities similar to film-making to teach or improve reading comprehension. Research leads to the conclusion that filmmaking does, indeed, improve reading comprehension skills. Following is a summary of the synthesis of my findings.

Reading Comprehension Skill	Filmmaking Task	Experimental Teaching Method
Finding main idea	Making storyboard	Self-discovering
Showing sequence	Making storyboard	Visualizing
Interpreting	Writing dialogue	Forming generalizations
Locating descriptions	Making cut-outs	Visualizing
Interpreting author's intent, mood, tone	Cut-outs, dialogue	Visualizing
Inferring pace of story	Making timing sheets	Audio-visual shifting
Construing meaning	Shooting film Following directions	Audio-visual integrating

It appears that similar conclusions may be drawn regarding the value of filmmaking to improve language (communication) skills. Children work diligently toward their end product—a film—while they willingly learn all the skills necessary to making a film. An outstanding value lies in the fact that the necessary skills are just those that the curriculum dictates; and, according to the abilities and ages of the children, many skills may be learned to a much higher level of accomplishment than normally possible because of the high motivation, attitude, and involvement in learning. Students ask often for advice on punctuation and sentence structure because they need the information for their scripts. How often do most students *ask* to be taught these skills?

Two related values, unique to this project, are its provision for continued practice and its high degree of success, no matter what the age of the filmmaker. When children make a film, they willingly write and rewrite, rehearse and rehearse their scenes with and for each other. This procedure requires some teacher time, but the children become quite discerning in their evaluative criticisms of each other, once the teacher has helped them set some basic standards by which to judge. Experience has proved that the less the teacher becomes involved after introducing the project, the more imaginative the children's films become.

Scope of Filmmaking Project

Most teachers are concerned about the amount of classroom time and effort required in filmmaking. Perhaps the best way to consider this is to, first, explain the procedural steps, and second, to offer specific instructions for each step. Time spent on each is related to the needs of the students and the teacher's desires or expectations for the children in a first film-making experience. The project is extremely flexible in this respect. With experience and a minimal amount of help from the teacher, most children will produce more intricate and polished films with each new attempt. Often the teacher needs to encourage simplicity in the making of first films.

STEP I

Prefilmmaking activities are divided into three types: (1) observing and categorizing the elements of shape, color, and texture in a single picture or event (seen or read about); (2) observing, evaluating, selecting, and relating elements in an event or picture to each other; (3) observing, selecting, relating, and organizing single elements which have been combined into a story or event. These three types of activities sharpen sensory perception and improve communication skills.

STEP II

Constructing short, live-action sequences based on content from social studies, science, literature, music, and/or art. This activity prepares children for later work with the camera.

STEP III

Acting out sequences, video taping, or filming sequences. Children work in pairs or small groups to prepare sequences which successfully communicate the intended message. This activity helps the children produce smooth, polished, and well-constructed communications by affording practice of previously learned skills. This step may be the end product, or the learning process may be continued by animating the sequences prepared during live-action rehearsals.[5]

[5] For information on animation handbook, see Appendix C.

Instructional Guidelines for Filmmaking

STEP I. PREFILMMAKING ACTIVITIES (USING HAND PRINTED JOB CARDS ON 4″ X 6″ INDEX CARDS)

A. OBSERVING ELEMENTS IN A PICTURE OR EVENT

A choice of these activities should be given to students:

1. Find a curvy, bumpy object. Shine a flashlight on it. Move the light around. How do the shadows change?

2. Use your own still camera to tell a message to your friends. If you're an expert photographer, try different lighting effects or use an unusual subject.

3. Choose appropriate music to go with a picture, or choose an appropriate picture to go with some music.

4. Look through a glass brick or a glass of water. How is the image distorted? Why is it hard to read through water?

5. How many things can you find of the same color, shape, pattern, or texture?

6. Draw a tree at 9 a.m., noon, and again at 3 p.m. Note the position and angle of the tree's shadow. See if your friend can find the tree you used or tell at what time your pictures were drawn.

7. See if you can make up some double descriptions such as these: flat, crispy = a potato chip, or a fall leaf; camper = a vehicle, or a person camping out.

8. Find something you think is unusual. Why is it unusual? (Is it out of place, odd-looking, unexpected?)

9. How many ways can you describe an object or animal (bug-eyed beetle, grumbly gorilla)?

10. Describe a picture by the way it might taste, smell, or sound.

B. RELATING ELEMENTS IN PICTURES OR EVENTS

A choice of these activities should be given to students:

1. Find two pictures of the same subject matter. Are they alike in mood, texture, lighting, tone?

2. Read or tell a story to a friend. Don't let your friend see the pictures in the book. Let your friend find or draw pictures to illustrate the story. How are your friend's pictures different or similar to those in the book?

3. Decide on a theme (games, weather, best friends, etc.). Collect pictures about the theme. Mount the picture in a collage and let your friends guess your theme.

4. Choose a set of pictures. How are they alike (subject matter, colors, moods)?

5. Put several pictures into story order so they make sense to you. Tell the story to a friend.

6. Illustrate a theme with your own photographs.

7. Using a favorite story character make up a story that places him or her in a new time and situation. (How would Winne-the-Pooh behave in a city today?) Act out the story with no more than four classmates.

8. Use pictures in a collage to let people know how you feel about something (pollution, children's rights, working mothers, worldwide food situation, etc.).

9. First group: tape a conversation. Second group: listen to the tape; transcribe the dialogue. Third group: read and act out the action and dialogue. Listen to the tape again. How has the original conversation been changed? Was the meaning altered or lost? Why?

10. Tape record two people in conversation. Listen to the rhythm of their talk. Is it even or uneven? Loud or soft? Happy, anxious, somber, melancholy?

STEP II. PREPARING A SEQUENCE TO FILM

A. CHOOSING A TOPIC ON WHICH TO BASE A SEQUENCE

1. The most important requirement for the topic is that it be visualizable. Children have chosen topics from social studies (such as, hunting for meat and preparing it to eat in Colonial America), science (such as, how a lever or pulley works), literature (such as, a wordless picture book or an action sequence from a longer story, for example Raold Dahl's *Charlie and the Chocolate Factory*), and original stories.

2. If filmmaking is intended to be used as a motivational tool small groups of children may prepare different sequences based on a central topic. Once each sequence is prepared, the children arrange the sequences in a logical order so they will be ready to be filmed on the same roll of film. In one class the children made a film in social studies based on life in Colonial America. Small groups worked on different aspects of Colonial life such as food, clothing, entertainment, and so on. These sequences were put together on one film, and thus the children shared what they had learned with each other.

B. PLANNING THE SEQUENCE TO BE FILMED

1. Children should first sketch, on separate pieces of paper, the events they will show in their sequence. If sketching is difficult, a short written summary of each event may be substituted.

2. Each sketch, or written summary, is mounted on a board, wall, bulletin board, or some surface where they are all visible at one time. This is called a storyboard.

3. Children find planning easier if they act out their sequences. All during the planning stage the children should be encouraged to improvise for each other, in order to check how accurately the desired message of the sequence is being communicated. Teachers may wish to conduct several miniworkshops in drama to help children experience

basic drama processes and gain basic drama skills in movement, speaking, and in improvising actions. During the planning of the Colonial America film, the children improvised the shooting of a bear. One child played the bear, and the filmmakers noted how the bear should fall and lie after being shot. The children found it helpful to study the bodily structure of the bear and other animals in order to find out how they move so players could improve their improvised actions. The children also found that asking others to identify what is being acted out as they prepare helps the players to know whether they are communicating the intended message. If a message fails to communicate, players explore and experiment with improvisations of actions to improve their communication.

4. Filmmaking techniques and principles and practices used in the visual arts contribute to the success of a film. Children benefit from learning about color, tone, mood, shading, and placement of objects against a background. If the teacher is not equipped to teach these basic practices, willing helpers may be recruited among parents and high school teachers. Several children in each class are usually camera buffs and some have had some art experience in forming compositions that involve sensory qualities and aesthetic visual perception.

5. Music is another subject area that contributes to filmmaking and needs to be planned, for an appropriate soundtrack adds mood and a professional quality to a film. Through filmmaking children may learn about the elements that give a musical piece its mood and tone. Again, teaching specialists and parents may serve as resource teachers.

STEP III. FILMING SEQUENCES OR VIDEO TAPING

A. FILMING REQUIRES SPECIFIC EQUIPMENT

1. A video tape machine or a "super 8" movie camera, film, movie lights, a tripod, and projector are needed to make a film. Most school districts own such equipment, and many families own movie cameras. Film and processing average about four dollars for fifty feet, which results in a three-minute-and-twenty-second film. Usually children wish to pay for their own film and processing, and then keep the film at the end of the school year.[6]

B. DEMONSTRATING HOW TO FILM A SEQUENCE

1. The teacher calls the class together to watch a demonstration of the filming process. When a group is ready to film a sequence the entire class is asked to observe as the teacher shows this group of children how to set up and operate the camera. If the teacher is inexperienced, he or she is advised to follow the instructions in the handbook that accompanies

[6] A Title III Minigrant was used to purchase film and filmmaking equipment in 1974. Information on minigrants is available through the Federal Projects Office of local school districts.

the camera. Mount the camera on a tripod; focus; check to see if there
is sufficient light; and begin to film.

2. Children in the first group become the film teachers for the following groups. Working in this way provides excellent learning experience
for all of the children, and it frees the teacher to go back to the regular
classroom responsibilities.

Classroom Management During Filmmaking Project

This project has been successful in traditional and open-concept settings;
it has also been flexible enough for either tightly or loosely structured
classrooms. To introduce the project I involve the whole class in a
discussion of filmmaking. Children are then asked to work in pairs to
choose a job card describing a prefilmmaking activity. After one or two
hours (not necessarily consecutive) the class meets together to share
what partners have done. Alternating work and sharing periods, the
prefilmmaking activities should take from five to eight hours of class time.
If this appears to be too large a time block, recall how many language and
reading skills the children are experiencing. This project replaces many
regular class lessons in those skills—it does not have to be additional
lessons.

Preparation of the sequences (selecting a topic, plotting it out, doing
the art work, and collecting the needed props) is best begun by small
groups working with the teacher. Reading groups provide a ready
organizational plan. Begin with one group. Get them started while the
other children do their regular reading lessons; then work with the next
group of children. Replace regular reading group work with planning
the sequences, script-writing lessons, and art lessons. Replace regular
seatwork with work in pairs or groups of three to work on the sequences.
(Three children on one sequence is convenient if the teacher is con-
sidering animation later, because three jobs are necessary—animator,
photographer, and director.) It should take the children about an hour
of planning and three to five hours of active preparation to prepare a
sequence. Once all groups have met with the teacher to plan, suspend
group meetings; the teacher is then free to circulate and help as needed
while the children work on their own.

When the first group is ready to act out their sequences, call the class
together to set standards with which to evaluate. Now is the time to focus
on drama processes, concepts, and skills. Emphasize techniques of oral
and visual communication for which you feel your children are ready.
Then let the children go ahead and rehearse their sequences.

When the first group has planned their sequence, they are ready to
make their storyboard. Call the class together again, this time to watch
as the first group acts out a scene and sketches it onto a card. After all
scenes are sketched, cards are made for the title, the credits (names of

the children who worked on the film), and "the end." All cards are mounted in sequential order on the storyboard. From this, the timing sheets are made. Timing sheets are used to record what is happening in the sequence second-by-second. They are necessary for animation but not for live-action filmmaking. Children are generally ready to make their own storyboards once they have seen other children do one or two.

When a group is ready to film, the entire class is called together to observe the process. The procedure follows as previously described. Animation may take place in a corner of the classroom without disturbing the children who are not filming. Live-action filming requires more space, but provides some of the most exciting learning experiences I have witnessed.

TEACHING CHILDREN TO WRITE POETRY AND INTERPRET IT THROUGH DRAMA

Dorothy Prince[7]

I like poetry. I relish it in a way not unlike the way I do a superb gourmet dinner for it seems to me that poetry, like a good meal, is created by persons who respect the combining of particular elements into distinctive forms that evoke aesthetic feelings.

Early in the beginning of each school year (for the last fifteen years), whenever the time seems just right, I share a delicious poem with my children. It isn't always the same one, for it has to be right for the particular children, for me, and for that particular moment. It is always an unexpected occasion, something like a hot buttered biscuit less than thirty seconds out of the oven. As is true with anything that is satisfying to the sensibility, the children ask for more.

My collection of poetry begins with poems about the fall of the year and follows the seasons through to summer. We learn many poems together by choral reading and then, it just happens, children begin to memorize poems on their own. Each morning a few students volunteer to recite their favorite ones. By the end of the year some of the children know as many as fifteen poems from memory. Poems the children particularly enjoy are dittoed near the top of a sheet of paper, leaving a large space below for individuals to draw their responses to a poem— maybe an image they see in the poem or a feeling about it. Some of the poems I share are: "September," by Edwina Fallis, "Billy Goats Chew," by Richard W. Emery, "The Little Elfman," by John Kendrick Bangs, "Who Has Seen the Wind?" by Christina Rossetti, "The Purple Cow," by Gelett Burgess, Walter De la Mare's "Some One," Mary F. Butts' "Water Jewels," "A Valentine," by Eleanor Hammond, "Snow," by

[7] Dorothy Prince, classroom teacher, Greenwood Elementary School, Seattle Public Schools. This essay is recounted in collaboration with the author.

Dorothy Aldis, "Kite Days," by Mark Sawyer, Robert Frost's "The Pasture," and "Catkin" and "I'm Glad," by unknown authors.

Procedures for Involving Children in Writing

There always comes a moment when something seasonal happens that says, "Look, I'm a metaphor." Then I know it's time to beckon the children to the window, where we all look out and I say something, such as, "Some trees are packing up their clothes for winter. Do you see them packing?" And while we continue to look out the window, I say, "Of course trees don't pack up their clothes but it seems to me as if they do." So the children are invited to look out the window or around the room with each trying to find something outside or inside that doesn't really happen, but just seems like it does.

IDENTIFYING METAPHORS

Children enjoy the new word: met-a-phor. They respond to an opportunity to repeat it several times and to a challenge to search for metaphors in their literary readers, in the room, on the way to and from school, at home, in the early evening, or at night. We begin to collect metaphors by writing them out and putting them in a big yellow basket. I invite everyone to sit down on an orange pillow by the basket to relish a few metaphors when they have a few free moments.

SEEING, FEELING, AND WRITING SIMILES

Almost as unexpectedly, similes always show up in our classroom. A day arrives that "is as bright as a flower with dew on it." Or, one of the children—"Brooke is as quiet as a hot October day." The children respond to the new word sim-i-le. We begin looking for and writing similes that heighten the effect of imagery by showing resemblances through the use of the word *as* (as slow as, as beautiful as, as bright as). This theme is enlarged on whenever there is a change in the weather. For example, "Today, the rain falls like . . ." "What?" I ask. The responses come: "Like marbles," calls Floyd. "Like a broken drinking glass," says Gene. "Like specks of silver!" Phyllis offers. We look for persons or things in action and then try to imagine resemblances, such as, "The wind blows like . . . The squirrel darts up the tree like . . . The boys roll and tumble like . . ." The children begin to write similes in single-sentence form and these, too, find their way into the yellow basket.

LIVENING UP SENTENCES

On the chalkboard, I write: "He went down the street." The children are asked to close their eyes to get images or pictures in their minds in response to the following questions: "Was this an old man, a young man, or a boy? Did he shuffle, trot, walk briskly, rush, dash, plod, or trudge? Was there anything special about the way he was dressed? Was there a purpose or feeling that came through in the way he moved?" The children are asked to liven up the sentence, with each one using their images as they write the sentence. Some of the responses are: "The teenager dashed as fast as a ten speed." "The poor man paced back and forth as hungry as a cat." "The worried young man raced down the street as fast as a fire engine."

For the next two weeks the children get plenty of practice in imagining as they work with a new sentence each day. They use metaphors and similes to liven up a simple sentence after they have taken time to imagine the circumstances. Some of the simple sentences are: The wind blew. She fell down. He shouted. A flame shot up. The ground was wet. The fire burned.

STIMULATING WORD AWARENESS

To foster children's awareness of the power of words to express different kinds of feelings and thoughts, I introduce them to nouns, verbs, adjectives, and adverbs. We begin by looking for words that tell the names of persons, places, and things—things that we can see, hear, touch, taste, and smell. We call these "picture words." The children make individual lists of picture words that each discovers. Each child classifies his or her words in personal categories resulting in such classifications as these: "Things I See," "Things I Hear," "Things I Like and Things I Hate," "My Twenty Favorite Things," "Things I'm Afraid Of," "Things That Make Me Shiver," and "Things I Collect Including Meals."

When an awareness of words has been stimulated we discuss how feelings always seem to go with "things." I suggest, for example, "How do you feel when you look at your report card for the first time?" "How do you feel when I tell you that Kurt has the chicken pox?" "How do you feel when you make 'something' and it turns out better than you expected?" "How do you feel when you sing 'The Candy Man'?" Children are guided to individually select a single word and write a feeling sentence about it.

A similar procedure is used for verbs as "action words," adjectives as words that "paint the picture," and adverbs as words that "paint the action" by telling how an action is done.

STIMULATING AWARENESS OF SENTENCE STRUCTURE

To introduce children to the use of words to structure a sentence, I use a novel approach. I gather the children together in a rather secretive, curious mood and explain that they are invited to go quietly into the coatroom to see if they can find something that enjoys them in a very special way. Of course, the children are puzzled. They see nothing unusual in the coatroom. They can't imagine what is there that enjoys them—no animal, no person. I tell them this 'thing' is not alive, but that it delights in all the attention it gets, and it has written a story for them which I have put on the front blackboard under the big map. They hurry back to their seats. Then I pull up the map. Together we read the story aloud to see if any of them guessed right: Your Shiny Fountain!

1. I am your shiny fountain waiting patiently for you happy, thirsty children.
2. I stand by the sink in a corner of the coatroom.
3. You line up in front of me quickly and quietly soon after the bell calls you inside.
4. You wait anxiously for a cool drink from me before class starts.
5. Your leader carefully turns my shiny handle.
6. The water eagerly jumps into your open mouths.
7. I think you like me since you come back often.

REARRANGING WORDS

Children often have trouble reading sentences that begin with adverbs, or with "-ing" words called participles. So learning to write sentences that begin with words other than the simple subject is a big help in getting them over this trouble spot. I suggest, "Can we change the words around in the first sentence, so they are in different order, and still have the sentence make sense?" Soon we get a good sentence, which I write on the board: *Waiting patiently for you happy, thirsty children, I am your shiny fountain.* Then someone notices that you could write the same sentence starting with the word *Patiently.* We are careful not to change the words, just to rearrange them. After doing this with all of the sentences, working together orally, the children are then ready to construct interesting sentences of their own, beginning with such words as these: when, while, as, quietly, soon, after that, at three o'clock, suddenly, just then, and silently.

To involve children in understanding the use of adverbs and phrases in writing sentences, I write out several eight- or nine-word sentences that contain short phrases and adverbs. I put each word of the sentence on a tagboard card, and give the cards to eight or nine children. Children in the group come to the front of the room to arrange themselves so their words form a sentence. Once the sentence is formed, the children are asked to explore different ways to rearrange the words to change the wording of the sentence.

Introducing Children to Haiku

As the children progress a time comes when everyone seems in the right mood to discover what has been described to me as an ancient Japanese custom. It is exchanging thoughts and feelings on certain days of the year. It begins with a person writing a thought or feeling on a narrow strip of rice paper. The person then places the paper on a twig or thin branch of a designated tree by twisting the paper so it will not fall or

be blown away by the wind. Each person who places a message on the
tree may then take a message from the tree. To prepare for this ceremony
I bring a bare tree branch or dried tumbleweed bush to the room, and
place it in a container so it is stable. I explain the custom to the children,
provide them with pastel-colored strips of writing paper, and we proceed
to write and decorate the tree so it "blooms with thoughts and feelings."

After this experience I introduce haiku, a form of Japanese poetry.
I read several short haiku and explain that each tiny verse conveys its
thought and feeling in only three lines. Together, we discover that a
haiku almost always reveals the poet's feeling or awareness of nature
through a picture in action. We discover, too, that the entire poem is
formed with only seventeen syllables, with the first and third lines containing five syllables, and the second line seven. We begin by writing
several haiku together about something we've seen that particular day
or something we feel strongly about. The children's haiku are written
on the board so they can see the haiku form. After a few first trials we
attempt to put a metaphor or simile in each verse.

The children then begin to write their own haiku. They are encouraged
to look for something particular that interests each child in the real
world or in pictures they find in books or in magazines such as *Ideals*.
Here is a beginning attempt written by a boy who saw "something" on
his way to school and hurried in to write it:

Through a bush I watched
a little grey bird resting,
Chirping news to me.[8]

From a list of words I had written on the board, the word *courage*
caught the attention and sparked the imagination of a nine-year-old boy
struggling to establish this very quality within himself. This is his haiku:

Who has courage to climb?
The sun and the moon do;
they do, every day.[9]

Interpreting Haiku Through Drama

For many years I have guided nine-year-olds to write haiku but I had
not realized the powerful and natural motivation that drama offers to
children both in writing and in interpreting poetry until last year. In a
school assembly, drama students from the University of Washington
presented a haiku mime workshop for children from kindergarten through
the sixth grade. The program was presented by four mimes and two
narrators all wearing grey head scarves and brightly colored Japanese

[8] By permission of Geoffrey Wall.
[9] By permission of Billy Studerus.

kabuki aprons over dark sweaters and jeans. Simple Japanese instruments were used by the narrators, who sat downstage near the audience. The instruments included a gong, chop sticks, a wood block, tea cup, chimes, silk fans, and paper. These were used to accompany or introduce a haiku which was recited either by the narrators or the mimes. The program was introduced with one of the narrators speaking and the other creating sound images in relation to the mimed action:

Haiku is an idea (mime . . . sound)
Haiku is a movement (mime . . . sound)
Haiku is a feeling (mime . . . sound)
Haiku is a sound (mime . . . sound)
Haiku puts an idea, a movement, a feeling, a sound together . . .
to make a living picture. Imagine. A rainbow. (mime . . . sound)[10]

Selected haiku were presented that told a story, painted a picture, communicated a feeling, and spoke with shadows. All of the children were impressed by the beauty and humor of the aesthetic experience. My fourth-grade children, who had been writing haiku, asked if the university students might visit our classroom to hear some of the haiku the children had written. The students, inspired by the children's verse, began to work out improvisations from the children's haiku. In a short time the students succeeded in involving all of the children in improvising actions for their own haiku.

The total experience stimulated the children to write new haiku, and to interpret each one through improvised action and sound. The children's writing improved, for their motivation was high, and they became more aware of images as characters in action. Through this experience I perceived that the characters and action of drama are the "picture" and "action" words of poetry, and that each art, seeking to give order and form to feelings, enhances the other. In the process it is really each child and the teacher who, relishing the experience, are enhanced.

AN APPROACH TO AESTHETIC EDUCATION

Barbara T. Salisbury[11]

How many hundreds of sunsets have we seen, but the memory of that *one* is so strong as to cause all our senses to vibrate in recollection?

How many hundreds of meals have we eaten, but we remember *one* in every detail, from the food, to the setting, to the conversation?

---

[10] Designed and developed by Sheri Liberman, Spring 1974; part of work toward master's degree from University of Washington, School of Drama.

[11] Barbara T. Salisbury, Director of Aesthetics, Seattle University and Matteo Ricci College of Seattle University, Seattle, WA; bachelor's and master's degree from University of Washington, School of Drama.

How many children have we seen at play, but watching *one* made the years tumble away and said "All Children"?

What is it that seems to change the ordinary into an Event, an aesthetic experience? Why do we seem to value these experiences so highly? Why don't we have more of them? Must we leave to chance the occurrence of experiences that can enrich our lives just as meaningfully as understanding algebraic equations?

Philosophy and Objectives

Aesthetic education is a process of training imaginative perception— the well from which creativity springs. Imaginative perception transforms the ordinary into an aesthetic experience. All the senses are alive and responding, the mind's eye is viewing, recalling, projecting, connecting. Often the experience is left just as it is, a memory imprinted and re- membered with joy. Sometimes the experience becomes the impetus for a painting, a dance, a poem, or a telephone call to someone from long ago, or a meeting with colleagues to plan something new.

So many things are happening at once in an aesthetic experience that it may be helpful to delineate the process briefly. First, the senses are apprehending. They are aware of the sensory properties of the object or event—properties such as color, light, space, time, motion, sound. Second, the mind is apprehending. It perceives the formal properties— composition, unity, theme, balance, dramatic structure. Third, the imagination is apprehending. It is receiving and responding to the expressiveness, the feeling content, of the object or event. Past experiences and hoped-for experience cause the imagination to focus on and see meaning in the form.[12]

The overall goal of aesthetic education is to help students increase their capacities to experience and make decisions about aesthetic qualities in all aspects of human life. There seems to be a particular atti- tude present in certain people who have aesthetic experiences more often than other people. One could call this an aesthetic attitude except that, curiously enough, the same attitude has presided over many of the great scientific discoveries of humankind. The components of this attitude include time, curiosity, and whimsy. Time—to see, to open the senses (those windows of the human body), to savor the moment. Curiosity—to play with the wonders of nature, to ask. Whimsy—to delight in leaps of thought, and in trying out odd connections. Such an attitude makes aesthetic education a facilitator for discovery.

The arts and the environment provide tools to help sharpen both

---

[12] For expanded discourse on the dimension of the aesthetic experience, see Harry S. Broudy, *Enlightened Cherishing: An Essay on Aesthetic Education* (Urbana: University of Illinois Press, 1972).

children's perceptions and their understanding of form and expressive content. In many ways the visual arts are the easiest to work with because they seem more objective and impersonal. When working with movement and drama, however, one is forced to become involved and to internalize, which can lead to personal insight regarding the aesthetic qualities dealt with. Although the aesthetic qualities are numerous, they include such things as the nature of basic phenomena: time, space, motion, color, light, sound; they include principles of form and structure; and they include understanding of and feeling for direct and indirect expression.

Exploring Aesthetic Qualities Through the Arts

Following are examples of how one aesthetic concept may be taught through an integration of learning experiences in the visual arts, drama, and music. A number of activities are suggested from which teachers may select their own combinations and add their own innovations.

CONCEPT

Space can be manipulated to express strong feelings by the use of "open" and "closed" forms.

OBJECTIVES

(1) To become aware of the sensory properties and expressive potential of manipulating open and closed forms in several arts; (2) to create characters and objects that embody closed characteristics and open characteristics; and, (3) to identify and describe those characteristics as they appear in several of the arts.

TEACHING PROCEDURES

MOVEMENT WARM-UP   Lead the children in opening and closing their hands rhythmically. Ask what other part of their arms they can open and close. Guide them to do this kind of movement with as many parts of the body as possible. Work up to the point where the whole body is closed, including the face, and then work in reverse until the whole body is open. Inhale when open, exhale when closed. End with the entire body closed and, while they are in that position, proceed to the next activity.

DRAMA ACTIVITIES   While they are in the closed position, suggest that they think of what kind of person or thing might be closed like that and why. What might the character be doing? After a few ideas have been given, guide the players to move around as their closed character, trying to get the rhythm of the character's walk. Other questions or suggestions to offer while the players are walking: What kind of mood is the person in? Why? Say "Hello" to other people as you think this person would. Do one thing your character wants to do right now.

After acting, help the players evaluate: When you were all closed up, how did you feel toward other people and the world? At what times do people tend to feel closed and withdrawn?

Guide the players to get in a closed position again, then open their bodies way up as they fill their lungs with air. Repeat several times, ending with the open position, remembering that the face is open, too. Guide the players through the same process they experienced in the closed position. Follow with a discussion about times when people feel open.

Optional activity for those who have had some experience in improvisation: Examine how the open person and the closed person might react to the same situation. For example, they are both in a jumbo jet waiting to take off. First, they decide where they are going and why. Then they start a conversation with each other. Their speech and the way they sit and move will reveal the personality and feelings of each character.

ART ACTIVITIES   Sometimes people are closed when they feel sad. Ask the children to use their hands to express sadness. Ask them to fold a piece of paper so that it expresses sadness. The purpose of using the hand and then the paper is to help them abstract the idea of sadness into a shape. The shape is not intended to represent a real image but rather a feeling.

Encourage the children to work with clay or some other moldable substance. Ask them to think of a time when they have felt sad and then to express the feeling in clay. When they are finished, have them put the objects aside and repeat the exercise, but with a happy, open feeling. When both are completed, discuss the difference between the shapes of the sad pieces and the happy pieces. In general, the open, happy pieces are likely to reach upward in vertical or diagonal lines, whereas the closed or sad pieces may be low, more horizontal and earthbound.

Which colors seem closed? Which seem open? Usually a combination of line and color express the feeling. The children may experiment with various colors and shapes on paper to express open or closed.

The children may examine pictures or photographs in magazines and books to find examples of open and closed shapes and feelings.

MUSIC ACTIVITIES   Guide the children to select a piece of music that would be an appropriate accompaniment to their art pieces. Or they could use "found-sounds"—sounds made by themselves with anything available and suitable, from vocal sounds to chalk screeches. Discuss the music or sounds. Are they slow or fast, erratic or rhythmic? Do they cover a wide tonal range, or do they seem to stay within a certain narrow spectrum of tones? Are they minor chords or major chords? Are they loud or soft?

When the children have combined the sound and object, what story do they seem to tell? Children who are watching may share their story impressions as well.

By exploring and developing the facets of a single aesthetic concept, children learn to expand their perceptions and increase their understanding. With many such experiences, children should be able not only to appreciate the real value in aesthetic qualities but also to make decisions about them.

INTEGRATING THE ELEMENTARY SCHOOL CURRICULUM THROUGH DRAMA

Wendy Perks[13]

Classroom teachers in the elementary school, where I am a drama teacher and coordinator, requested an in-service course in drama to be conducted during an entire school year. These teachers, aware of children's enthusiasm for drama classes, wanted to use drama in their classrooms as a means to involve children in learning through drama.

The in-service program was organized on the following premise: drama in the elementary school can become both a catalyst for curriculum integration, and a teaching methodology that provides the teacher with a means to encourage children's deeper involvement in learning. The premise focused on two objectives: first, to determine whether through in-service experience classroom teachers could gain significant insight into the philosophy and fundamentals of the art of drama, and second, to determine whether their in-service experience would enable them to use drama as an integrative force in the established elementary school curriculum.

What were the outcomes? With the limitations necessitated here, the question will be considered first by briefly viewing the nature of the in-service program, then by examining the instructional procedures used in one learning unit, and finally by drawing some conclusions.

Teacher Preparation

The in-service program was organized to include the following varied experiences:

Active participation in weekly drama workshops conducted by drama
    coordinator to explore drama processes and concepts;
Investigation of underlying philosophy through selected reading of

[13] Wendy Perks, Drama Coordinator, Keith Country Day School, Rockford, IL; master's degree from University of Washington, School of Drama.

college textbooks and evaluation of instructional materials planned
for use with children;

Observation of children exploring drama processes and concepts under
the guidance of drama coordinator;

Designing drama activities to correlate with subject areas and to explore
their use with children in the classroom;

Regular seminars with drama coordinator to discuss procedures and
problems;

Individual planning conferences with drama coordinator.

As the program developed the teachers began to comprehend the
philosophy of drama as an art through active participation and involvement in the drama processes. These processes imply problem solving.
A problem is discovered and must be worked through by "playing with"
various solutions. The solution takes form. It is communicated to others
and is evaluated by all those involved in the process.

It was comparatively easy for most of the teachers to design activities,
largely because the teachers had already participated in drama explorations. With their experience, teachers could perceive ways to design
activities to relate to children's needs and capabilities and to the
subject matter of the established curriculum.

Integrated Learning Unit in Sixth Grade

Through cooperative efforts the classroom teachers and I developed a
flexible yet structured approach to integrating drama with the basic
curriculum at every grade level. The approach consisted of the development and implementation of drama-oriented learning units. To illustrate
this approach, a learning unit developed by Dan Kocher, a sixth-grade
teacher, is described here in outline form.[14] Through cooperative efforts
Mr. Kocher and I planned a unit entitled *Man—The Question-Maker*.
The unit, which expanded into a four-month time period, used drama
as the integrative force to combine social studies, science, and language
arts. The academic areas of art, mathematics, and music were also
integrated into the unit at various times during the semester.

Man—The Question-Maker began in the drama classroom with the
drama coordinator working with the sixth-grade students. The classroom
teacher observed the drama coordinator's teaching procedures and the
student responses (Figure 10). As the unit grew the teachers and coordinator teamed their teaching efforts, working with the students in the
drama classroom. After the sixth week, the classroom teacher, familiar
with drama processes, returned to his classroom and continued to develop the learning unit with the students. Class time for the unit varied

[14] By permission of Dan Kocher, Keith County Day School, Rockford, IL.

Figure 10 (Left) Imagining Character Stimulated by Costume Piece. (Right) Improvising Dialogue (Photographs courtesy Andy French, Rockford, IL).

from forty-five minutes to an hour and a half according to the student involvement.

OVERALL UNIT GOAL

To develop the students' abilities to ask precise, open-ended questions, and to then search for ways to begin to answer those questions.

CURRICULUM CONTENT

SCIENCE   Atoms, Molecules, Radiation, Conduction, Aristotilean Concepts of the Universe, Galilean Concepts of the Universe

SOCIAL STUDIES   Greeks, Renaissance

LANGUAGE ARTS   Thinking, Talking, Listening, Speaking, Communicating, Reading, Writing

OTHER   Art, Math, Music (not planned on regular basis)

Outline of Drama Classes and Instructional Procedures

CLASS ONE ACTIVITIES

Movement, Sense Awareness

FOCUS   Wondering "Why"

MOTIVATION   An Old Wooden Bowl

BASIC ACTION

1. Based on sensory observation, each child shares "why" questions about an old bowl, for example, Why is the bowl so many colors? Why does the bowl have so much empty space? Why does the bowl have a jagged line in the middle?

   2. All students act out, in pantomime, one action that shows how the bowl might have become marred.

TO THINK ABOUT FOR NEXT MEETING   Students are asked to come with twenty-five "why" questions that they feel have no answers.

CLASS TWO ACTIVITIES

Sense Awareness, Pantomime

FOCUS   The Greeks told myths and created gods to explain "why" the world they lived in was the way it was.

MOTIVATION   Question: If the bowl were changed into a Grecian urn what would it look like? How might it be used? (Picture or real Grecian urn is examined.)

BASIC ACTION

1. Establish through pantomime the details of the environment in ancient Greece.

   2. Establish through pantomime the kinds of commoners in Greece who used the imagined urns.

   3. Establish through pantomime what kinds of things in nature that affected their lives.

TO THINK ABOUT FOR NEXT MEETING   What questions might the Greek farmers have asked that they would need to create myths or gods to answer?

CLASS THREE ACTIVITIES

Improvisation, Characterization

FOCUS   To experience how a myth might have been created to answer a scientific "why" question in Greece.

MOTIVATION   A collection of sea shells, driftwood, stones.

BASIC ACTION

1. Through discussion followed by pantomime students recreate the environments of a Greek seashore and hillside.

   2. The drama teacher role plays Democritus (Greek philosopher who first defined and described the atom and molecule); the students role

play Democritus' disciples and interact with him by improvising action and words.

3. The classroom teacher and students discuss informally the modern definitions of atoms and molecules and their functions in relationship to each other.

4. Using rhythm and movement the students imagine and become atoms of oxygen and hydrogen to form a water molecule machine. The students explore bonding and positive and negative charges in this manner.

CLASS FOUR ACTIVITIES

Characterization, Improvisation, Sense Awareness

FOCUS   The risk involved in trying to find answers to "why" questions.

MOTIVATION   Discussion: What people do you know personally and historically who have been punished for asking "why"?

BASIC ACTION

1. Classroom teacher role plays Aristotle as he tells about his belief in the four elements: earth, air, fire, water. He asks the students, who role play philosopher-kings, to try to prove he is wrong by searching the room to find something that is not composed of those elements.

2. The drama teacher tells the story of Prometheus, a Greek myth in which Prometheus is punished for asking Zeus why man could not have fire.

3. Students improvise dramatic incidents from the Prometheus myth, including the creation of Pandora, who brings hope to man.

CLASS FIVE ACTIVITIES

Characterization, Emotional Awareness

FOCUS   How feeling motivates humans to search for answers to "why" questions.

MOTIVATION   Pictures from *The Family of Man*[15] Students are asked to identify the one emotion each sees in the person or persons shown in selected photographs.

BASIC ACTION

1. Students are involved in movement and pantomime activities aimed at stimulating a deeper awareness of how emotions affect physical actions.

2. The drama teacher tells the story of Theseus, the great Athenian hero who succeeded in killing the Minotaur, a powerful monster, half

---

[15] *The Family of Man,* created and compiled by Edward Steichen for the Museum of Modern Art (New York: Maco Magazine Corp., 1955).

bull, half human, who devoured maidens and youths. This is another opportunity for the students to understand through a myth the human nature to question.

3. The students organize the story into scenes to create a play.

CLASSES SIX THROUGH TEN

Activities aim to involve the students in exploring each of the playmaking elements as they work for in-depth characterization, for spontaneous dialogue, to reveal a theme, and on aspects of spectacle and sound. The goal for the students is to form their own play from the Theseus story.

Continued Semester Activities

A partial list of the students' activities throughout the rest of the semester reflects the depth of student involvement. It shows too the classroom teacher's ability to encourage the learning unit to unfold through several student-initiated projects. The classroom teacher's list reads as follows:

1. In their social studies textbook the students read the chapter describing the Middle Ages to better understand why the Renaissance was a rebirth of many Greek concepts and thoughts.
2. Some students created an imaginary debate between Aristotle and Galileo. Other students role played the parts of scientists, jury, and judge, and attempted to decide which man held the most acceptable theory regarding the universe.
3. Through pantomime the students formed tableaus of Renaissance and Medieval paintings. The students were able to recapture the essential innovations in Renaissance art through body positions, facial expressions, and manipulation of the light in the room.
4. Oral reading time at the end of the day focused on the Greek myths, and always involved spontaneous dramatization of incidents.
5. In small groups the students improvised, wrote, rehearsed, and presented their own plays based upon dramatic incidents in the life of Leonardo Da Vinci.
6. The students planned their own ideal community by using Renaissance ideals as a stimulus.
7. The students started a new list of twenty questions all beginning with "why".

Conclusions: Why Drama?

Man—The Question-Maker was structured to meet the needs of a particular group of participants—sixth-grade students, their teacher, and the drama coordinator. Through mutual planning the learning unit stimulated a high degree of student involvement. This was evident in interaction experiences that involved problem solving, decision making, seeking new knowledge, questioning, willingness to try, attempting new ways to express and form thoughts and feelings into action, and requesting feedback and evaluation from peers.

LEARNING UNITS IN OTHER GRADES

Through mutual planning between the drama coordinator and classroom teachers in each of the first six grades, other successful learning units were implemented. Each was drama-oriented and provided a new way for children to perceive the world. Titles of the other units included: "Eggs"—grade one, "Maps"—grade two, "Ecology"—grade three, "The Explorers"—grade four, and "Sound"—grade five.

CLASSROOM TEACHER RESPONSES

Released from more traditional teaching methods and segmented curriculum areas, teachers responded differently. From the start they were enthusiastic, although several questioned their abilities to become involved in drama processes and techniques. At the conclusion all were impressed by the students' involvement and by their own involvement. Teachers agreed that an essential aspect of the experience was the continuing in-service drama program.

As a culmination of the year's endeavor, the classroom teachers began to search for curriculum materials to further assist in the processes of integrating learning through drama. In-service programs have continued. A leading resource is INTERACTION: *A Student-Centered Language Arts and Reading Program*, which employs drama as a common force for an interchange among students, materials, and methods.[16] Our search continues for even more effective ways to use drama as a catalyst for curriculum integration. Our continuing aim is to assist each child in building "knowledge structures," and to become a more thoughtful, feeling, careful questioner and problem solver.

DISCOVERING THE WORLD OF PUPPETS

Aurora Valentinetti[17]

What is a Puppet?

This question was put to a group of first graders and, in the simple straightforward answers that tumbled out, they showed their grasp of the essence of the puppet. "A puppet is fun" . . . "A puppet is something you move" . . . "A puppet is something you make talk" . . . "A puppet is your

[16] James Moffett, senior ed., INTERACTION: *A Student-Centered Language Arts and Reading Program* (Boston: Houghton Mifflin Co., 1973).

[17] Aurora Valentinetti, Associate Professor of Drama, University of Washington, Founder-Director-Producer of the Valentinetti Puppeteers.

friend." What a nice thing a puppet is—fun and a friend! This same
question put to second graders brought forth more sophisticated answers,
which included the classification of puppets, the materials used in making
them, and even some historical facts. But they too defined the puppet
in terms of human response. The children had discovered the secret of
the puppet's success—its universal appeal. A puppet, in its own gentle
way, commands your attention and demands some kind of response.
Few can resist its bidding.

An Ancient Theatre Art Form Revisited

It comes as a surprise to many that the puppet theatre has its own ancient
history, dating well before Christian times. Even more surprising is the
fact that the miniature wooden thespians sometimes predate the human
actor. The road they have traveled through the centuries has been more
rough than smooth, but they have endured and there is no question that
they will continue to do so.

In the past decade there has been a great resurgence of interest in
this art form and a rediscovery of the puppet's dual role of entertainer and
educator. To assess the power of these little performers you need only
watch a group of children responding to puppets' antics. And children do
respond, even to a bad puppet show, because whether young or old, we
all have a need for fantasy. The theatre has always provided an avenue
of escape from the harsh reality of life and, to serve this purpose, the
puppet has no equal. Stripped of the restrictions of the human form,
these creatures know no boundaries in the flight of fancy.

A Child's Heritage

The seeds of imagination must be sown very early in life, and they must
be carefully nurtured if they are to blossom into a profusion that will
last a lifetime. Drama, music, art, dance, the spoken word, the written
word, all these expressions of humans' creative minds should be a part
of every child's inheritance. His or her first glimpse of this inheritance
might well be through the medium of the puppet theatre. The small
scale suits a child well, for it enables a child to explore and experience
the various arts on an intimate basis. A well-planned puppetry project,
by its very nature, can serve as an introduction to all the arts, not as
separate entities, but as an integrated whole.

Integrity in the Art

While teachers, like children with new toys, delight in rediscovering the
puppet's role, puppeteers despair. Why? Because all too often the well-
meaning but ill-prepared teacher gives scarcely a nod in the direction of

either *art* or *theatre*. To ignore these factors is to deny the true spirit of the puppet.

Let us return to the original question: "What is a puppet?" A puppet can be any inanimate object that is given "life" through movement, through sound, or both. It can be as abstract as light played against a screen, or as concrete as a detailed reproduction of the human figure. But a puppet is nothing until it is given an opportunity to make a statement, no matter how simple a statement. A puppet must be given a reason for being, and this can only happen when it is born out of drama.

Many projects initiated in the classroom are less than successful because they are never really brought to a satisfactory close. They stop with the making of the puppet. This is like signing a death warrant for a child before it is born. It denies the puppet the right to "life" and the child the right to a rich and rewarding experience. You can understand the implications of denying a child, but do you smile at the thought of denying a puppet? If so, still another dimension of the definition is needed. A puppet is an extension of a human being who seeks another way to communicate. Puppet and child are one and the same. Serve one well and you serve both.

The Teaching Tool

The puppeteer would be the last to refute the effectiveness of the puppet as a teaching tool, but puppeteers have cause for concern as they see quality give way to quantity. They cannot rejoice when they hear the cry, "Come one, come all, to puppetry, the new pink, candy-coated pill guaranteed to cure all ills!" Through bitter experience the puppeteer knows there is no such guarantee. Like any other tool, this one is only as effective as the person who wields it.

No layman in his or her right mind would walk into a laboratory and begin to mix chemicals at random. The results might well be disastrous. Yet how often we see this happen in the arts. Experimenting, trying, accepting, rejecting are as much the prerogative of the artist as the scientist. The puppeteer asks only that those wishing to experiment with this art emulate the scientist. Gather together a fundamental body of information before beginning. In this way you can avoid "lab" disasters— immediate ones from the standpoint of the classroom, and long-range ones from the standpoint of puppetry as a theatre art form in the future.

The Task Begins

You cannot teach what you do not know, and you will not know until you have a reasonable overview of the entire field of puppetry. Begin by reading. There are a number of well-written and illustrated books which will prove of great value to you, not the "how-to-do" books, but those that will provide background.[18] A sense of history will bring a better understanding of the role of the puppet, and seeing what is possible will lay a springboard for your own imagination.

Only the teacher can determine what will be the most practical approach to puppets for a particular group of children. We are dealing with so many variables that no pat rules can be laid down. The great value of puppetry as a teaching tool is its versatility. There are four major puppet classifications—hand, rod, shadow, string (marionette) (Figure 11). Each type of puppet has its own advantages and disadvantages. Study the possibilities which seem most practical for your needs. For instance, small uncoordinated hands cannot manipulate a hand puppet in the traditional three-finger method (Figure 11). Very few youngsters can handle a marionette successfully unless it is limited to the simple two-string balloon or spool puppet. This classification is best left to the professional. There is no better way to discover what will work best than by doing. Before presenting a project you must go through the entire process of construction not once but several times. Only in this way can you test your own skills and the level at which you can present the project. Rest assured that, once you begin, the learning process will be reciprocal; the children themselves will have much to contribute.

Introducing Puppets to Children

Put a puppet in front of a child, and the child will instinctively pick it up to make it move or say something. The child knows a puppet is a performer, and, as such, the puppet should be introduced. If possible, launch your project by having the children see a "live" puppet show. Since shows of quality are none too numerous or available you may have to turn to film or television. Perform for them yourself with the simple puppets you have made. Introduce the idea of creating some puppets and presenting a show for some other class or outside group. From that point on enthusiasm alone will almost carry the project to completion. But be forewarned; it is just such unbridled enthusiasm that has spelled disaster for so many projects. It will be your responsibility to "rein in" and give direction.

Before actually beginning to construct puppets, the children should be given the opportunity to explore the field as you did. Share with them the books, the photographs, and give them, too, a sense of history. Next let them use the various types of puppets, which can be those you have made, those that the children may have of their own, or some of the less expensive commercial ones. Let them improvise little playlets and let them discover just what each kind of puppet can do. Again, only you

[18] See Appendix A.

Figure 11 Four Kinds of Puppets (Courtesy Deborah L. Hammond, Seattle, WA).

can decide in which direction you wish to go. Decide and then gently guide.

The First Project

Having been given some background, the children are now ready to begin. The first project, at whatever grade level you are working, should be a simple one that can be completed and given "life" within an hour.

Instant success with a feeling of accomplishment is desirable, particularly at the primary level. At this point the quality of craftsmanship is far less important than the completion of the project. With proper guidance the quality of each successive project will improve.

Paper plate, paper bag, and balloon puppets are good beginning projects. They represent three basic types and they require essentially the same materials for completion. These materials include: construction paper, crayons, felt markers, white glue, paste, rubber cement, and miscellaneous trimming materials. The paper plate works best as a *rod puppet* with a tongue depressor, fastened with masking tape, for a control. Any flat stick or heavy hardboard may be substituted. The paper bag is best utilized as a *hand puppet,* with the folded flap making the movable jaw. The balloon puppet lends itself well to a simple (but sometimes short-lived) two-string *marionette.* Features and appendages are secured with rubber cement. The puppet is strung with black carpet thread and suspended from a stick or heavy piece of cardboard.

The paper plate and paper bag puppets of the "Three Pigs and the Wolf" illustrate how simple these puppets can be (Figure 12). If you study the drawings you will see that the basic design of the pig is made up of circles, parts of circles, and triangles—a good example of how you can teach several arts at one time through this single medium. Preschoolers can make these puppets without too much trouble if they are shown samples and then given an assortment of precut shapes to put together as they choose. Whether you make one or all three of these puppets is for you to determine, keeping in mind that it is folly to try all three at the same time.

The Debut

In this initial performance each child is a "star" eagerly displaying his or her creation. With the younger ones you must be close at hand to give support if it is needed. With the older ones you sometimes need to be at hand to keep things from getting out of hand! Whether the performance is a simple "show and tell," the recitation of a rhyme, or the singing of a little song, encourage a "theatre" atmosphere. Expect the children to give their attention to the performer and to show their appreciation with applause. As youngsters are exposed to more advanced and complicated theatre forms, their own enrichment and satisfaction will be in direct proportion to their ability to listen and absorb. Training in concentration cannot begin too soon.

Following the individual performances, you may want to organize children into small groups of three to six and let them improvise short scenes. Let them talk about stories they would like to do next. During this period you will be able to single out the leaders and the followers, and you can make your preliminary plan for expanding that unit of work or moving on to the next level.

Figure 12 "Three Pigs and the Wolf" (Courtesy Deborah L. Hammond, Seattle, WA).

Choosing a Play

When ready to move to the next level, the preparation and presentation of a play, your greatest challenge will be to keep things simple. There is a logical progression that will help in this respect; going from nursery

rhymes to fairy and folk tales, to legends and myths, to contemporary
stories and, finally, to an original script. Introduce and follow through
with this plan of action and you will give the children direction and
lighten the burden of your own task. Working with existing stories provides the foundation of plot and character upon which the play can be
built. Learning the basic principles through the familiar will make the
transition to original material easier.

Among the many advantages of the puppet show is the limitation of its
size. Only so many little bodies can be accommodated in one stage, which
can be anything from a packing crate to a blanket in a doorway. This
happily eliminates the classical "villagers and townspeople" of children's
theatre. No child wants to be an "extra"; each wants to feel that his or
her involvement is really important. And so it should be. To provide
each child with this opportunity, you must do not one but several plays.
Through observation and discussion of a number of plays, the learning
experience will be enhanced.

At first let imagination run wild, let the children stretch as far as
possible, even to the absurd. Later, the ideas can be simplified and
refined. Prepare a scenario for each story and let the dialogue develop
as it will. A written script is not necessary, but you will need to set some
limitations or each play will turn into an epic!

Choosing the Players

The play and players cannot really be separated, for one depends on
the other. Some puppets lend themselves better to one kind of drama; the
hand puppet, for instance, is the clown of the puppet family, while
the rod puppet is more dignified. Choose the type of puppet that serves
the action of the play best. With older children you might want to try the
same story with different types of puppets. It will illustrate vividly
the unique properties of each type and stimulate creative solutions to
the problems to be solved in the telling of the story.

The Original Script

Once the children have learned the principles of creating a play by
adapting stories, they can create their own plays. Those given for pure
entertainment will often be a faintly disguised retelling of a classic or
something they have seen on television. Now is the time to move to the
area of social studies, applying what has been learned and finding new
problems to solve. Since the company of actors has already been created,
you will probably not need too many additional puppets. A change of
wig, a different costume and your villain becomes a hero, your princess
the girl next door. You will find the puppets and children eager and
ready. All they need is a signal that says, "Go!"

The Challenge

Have you been overwhelmed with ideas? Have you wavered between
interest and discouragement—between the desire to try and the decision
to let it lie? Good. You should be fully aware of the responsibility of the
task before you undertake it. This bare touching on a few points is only
an indication of the greater task of doing. Interest and enthusiasm are
not enough; certain skills are required. If you do not have all the
requisites (and few have), that alone should not deter you. What you
lack can be provided by others. A puppetry project *does* serve as an
introduction to all the arts, and if you feel insecure in an area do not be
shy about calling on your colleagues. They may need to call on you at
some other time.

　　You as the teacher cannot do it alone, anymore than the child can.
Where will you go for your resources? To the library and to your some-
time-critic, the professional puppeteer. Accept criticism gracefully and
then, like the puppet, demand attention. The professional-in-name-only
may demur for fear of exposing his or her own inadequacies, but the true
artists *will* respond. They see the wisdom of sharing their art and the
possibility of inspiring at least one person to carry on this art after they
are gone.

　　There is one other resource, the most important of all, and that is *you*.
In the final analysis *you* are really the only one who can feed the fire
of imagination after it has been lit. *You* are the only one who can hone
your skills after they have been demonstrated. *You* are the only one who
will be in direct contact with those with whom you wish to share your
knowledge. If your desire is strong enough, you will find the time and
the way. A puppet is indeed *Master Teacher*, so powerful that we sometimes forget that without a "back-up man" it is only an empty sack—a
little bundle of sticks. It is nothing. Someone must provide the breath of
life, and that someone is *you*. Accept the challenge.

SUGGESTED ACTIVITIES FOR ADULT STUDENTS

1. With a small group of peers, discuss each of the following to arrive at a
   conclusion to be exchanged in a larger group discussion:
   a. Drama can serve as an integrative force in children's learning if the
      teacher knows how to use it effectively as a teaching method.
   b. In the act of creating drama it is the integrity of each individual that
      brings significance to the individual, to the group, and to the drama
      formed.
   c. Drama becomes the external force used by the teacher to provide
      conditions that will interact optimally with children's internal forces.
2. Read Hazel Dunnington's essay. Identify specific language concepts and
   reading skills she cites as a rationale for the inclusion of drama with children
   in language arts. Read again the descriptions of children's drama workshops

in Chapters 1 to 4 to identify additional language concepts and reading skills children experience through drama.

3. Read Sue Lerner's essay to identify reading skills that she cites as being those children use in experiences in filmmaking and drama. Identify the chief reasons for the justification of the children's time spent on drama-filmmaking projects.

4. Read Dorothy Prince's essay to identify specific ways in which drama can be used to stimulate children to read, write, and interpret poetry.

5. Read Barbara Salisbury's essay. With a friend develop a rationale to be used at a parent-teacher-student meeting to explain aesthetic education and to justify its inclusion in children's basic education.

6. Read Wendy Perks' essay. Identify several essential ways in which her approach and procedures differ from traditional procedures used to integrate children's learning in the elementary school curriculum.

7. Read Aurora Valentinetti's essay. Identify several basic reasons to justify her conviction about puppetry in education: "Like any other tool, this one is only as effective as the person who wields it."

⚜ 14
Drama with All Children

Though few children are geniuses, all children, I early discovered,
possess gifts which may become later their special distinction.

HUGHES MEARNS
Creative Power[1]

There are millions of children in the world and one of them is Tom, a
lively five-year-old who is commonly referred to as a *typical* child. Joe
is a happy seven-year-old who is considered physically *atypical* because
he is blind and his sister Ginger, an active nine-year-old, is considered
gifted. David, who is ten, is mentally retarded yet David and Joe and
Ginger and Tom all enjoy imagining and pretending in their own
particular ways.

Because almost all children play at make believe and want to interact,
communicate, and relate to other children drama has been included in
many children's programs outside of the elementary school environment.
These include programs in park, recreation, and community centers; art
museums; libraries; language-learning centers; summer camps; Camp
Fire Girls and Girl and Boy Scout programs; and in nursery and pre-
schools. Drama programs have been incorporated into the curriculums of
Sunday schools and religious education. Drama has been used in different
kinds of therapy programs with children.

Chief requirements for adults who want to involve children in drama
experiences are that the adults understand the developmental needs of
the children and of individuals within the group, and that they under-

[1] Hughes Mearns, *Creative Power: The Education of Youth in the Creative Arts*
2nd rev. ed. (New York: Dover, 1958), p. 267.

stand drama as an art. Sue Jennings provides a handbook, *Remedial Drama,* for teachers, social workers, occupational therapists, nurses, and psychologists who seek new ways to incorporate drama activities into their work with children.[2] Jennings clarifies the primary aim: "In preventive and therapeutic work we are largely concerned with improving communication and, in so doing, with assisting individuals and groups to build relationships."[3] Jennings stresses the need to put emphasis on drama rather than on problems, and to create secure boundaries for fragmented groups and individuals.

Emily Gillies in *Creative Dramatics for All Children* emphasizes the splendid learning opportunities that creative drama brought to the special children with whom she worked.[4] Aiming for the creativity and personal wholeness of each child, she describes her experiences with emotionally disturbed and brain-injured children, and with children for whom English was a second language.

To indicate the broad range of possibilities for the involvement of all children in drama, brief essays by four artist-teachers are presented here. Each author, in a personal writing style, conveys a philosophy and teaching procedures based on his or her experience and convictions. The first two essays reflect the extensive scope of drama in programs with children. Sarahjane Hidell describes how she involves very young children in learning through drama. Sister Peggy O'Connell, who for more than a decade has explored the use of drama in the teaching of religion, delineates some of her discoveries. The last two essays consider drama in relation to atypical development. Jeff Brewster relates some of his experiences in using drama with physically limited children. Taras B. Denis, writing from a vast realm of first-hand experience, makes a plea for the inclusion of drama as an art in the education of the deaf child. A unifying theme in the essays is the importance of teacher education in drama as it relates to child development, special education, and aesthetic education.

DRAMA WITH FOUR- AND FIVE-YEAR-OLDS

Sarahjane Hidell[5]

People continually ask why I teach drama to four- and five-year-old children. The implication, of course, is that little children are too young to really learn from drama experiences. This is not true. Research has

[2] Sue Jennings, *Remedial Drama: A Handbook for Teachers and Therapists* (New York: Theatre Arts Books, 1974).

[3] Ibid., p. 2.

[4] Emily Gillies, *Creative Dramatics for All Children* (Washington, DC: Association for Childhood Education International, 1973).

[5] Sarahjane Hidell, Drama Teaching Specialist in community programs and parochial schools in the Seattle area; graduate of University of Washington, School of Drama.

documented the fact that a person's basic character and personality are well established by the age of six years. After that point in time, although obvious growth changes occur, the rate of growth begins to subside and does not continue with the rapidity that characterizes the first five years of life. These are, in fact, the most formative years of personality development. It is rewarding for me as a teacher to witness the joy of the children as they step into the world of creative make-believe, and at the same time to witness them gaining an increased awareness of their own reality.

My purpose here is to offer my rationale and objectives for teaching drama to young children, identify some basic teaching procedures, and describe a beginning drama class with four- and five-year-olds.

Rationale and Objectives

Teaching drama to young children, before it can be safely and properly done, requires a fair balance of theoretical and practical knowledge. It is definitely not a process of "I teach, you learn." The drama teacher needs always to concentrate on guiding in relation to each child's individual personality, interests, needs, and qualities of character.

My overall goal is to help establish each child as a positive growing person, aware and confident of his or her creative abilities and aware of the environment. This, of course, places serious responsibility as well as demands on the teacher.

To prepare for teaching drama to young children, some areas that should be researched, studied, and explored with practical experience are: child development, psychology, sensory perception, expressive body movement and dance, dramatic imagination, mime, acting, improvisation, puppetry, role playing, and dramatic play analysis.

It is important to realize that when a child is involved in the creative process the child expresses inner, secretive aspects of his or her total self. Therefore, the teacher must remain sensitive to the individual child within the scope of the demands the creative drama experience makes upon the child. One technique for maintaining this sensitivity to each player is to adopt the player's perspective. This is achieved by exploring each learning experience and dramatic event along with the players. In this way the teacher experiences first-hand some of the nervousness, hesitation, frustration, and difficulty, as well as the sense of accomplishment, and enjoyment, of each player involved.

Teaching Procedures

My classes are limited to sixteen students who meet one hour each week for a ten-week session. Classes meet in a public library activity room, which provides easy access to appropriate children's literature. In the five years I have taught young children most of the students have signed up for additional classes, with the result that the majority of beginning students remain in the same class over an eight-month period.

ORGANIZING THE DRAMA ACTIVITIES

With a beginning group the class period is generally organized into four distinct learning areas in which the children experience activities centering in: (1) orientation, (2) movement exploration, (3) pantomime, and (4) improvisation. By the sixth or seventh hour most children have gained enough security and drama skills to enable them to enjoy improvising action and words from dramatic incidents in stories they have selected from library books. Or they enjoy imagining and improvising action for new endings to well-known folk tales.

The organizational pattern of activities shifts as the students progress in their abilities. By the tenth or twelfth hour, activities are generally organized to include an approximate ten minutes for combined orientation and movement exploration, fifteen minutes for improvisation, and thirty minutes for story dramatization.

ORIENTATION

Each introductory class begins with ten or fifteen minutes of orientation activity to establish a joyful atmosphere where everyone feels free and safe to listen and to talk about what each individual wants to tell the others. It provides a time to give recognition to individuals and to reaffirm the self-worth of students on a one-to-one basis. The students and I sit in a large circle on the floor. This arrangement tends to make the group more cohesive by making the teacher less imposing and allowing for interaction with persons on either side and opposite. Orientation time allows a free interchange of conversation; children are given opportunities to share feelings, experiences, simply tell about something new, or, if the child so desires, to remain quiet and listen. The circle provides an effective arrangement for learning people's names and identifying names with faces. We play one of several name games at each meeting so everyone becomes better acquainted. Students are made to feel responsible for each player having a place in the circle at all times. This is achieved by positively recognizing a student who notices that another student, for whatever reason, does not have a place in the circle. In classes subsequent to the first orientation, contributions of personal artwork are encouraged, which give the individual a further opportunity for recognition.

MOVEMENT EXPLORATION

Following verbal interaction, students need to explore rhythm and body movement. For control during this activity I have found that the hand clap (one clap means to freeze the motion, two claps means to sit down) is acceptable and effective. Movement exploration is planned to alternate between vigorous and quiet activities.

PANTOMIME

In beginning classes four- and five-year-olds are more comfortable in expressing themselves through action rather than dialogue. On a social level, group pantomime promotes teamwork, and with it a broader awareness of others, which is essential to the development of a less egotistic behavior than is characteristic of these ages.

IMPROVISATION

Improvisation should be approached from a problem-solving perspective. Opportunities to be physically active while solving problems are especially important for this age group, where physical activity is the norm. Players are guided to explore fundamental concepts of improvisation including: imagining basic circumstances (who, what, where), believing in make-believe, and acting "as if." Exploration of these concepts lends itself readily to the use of concrete materials as sensory stimuli. This enables the players to perceive concepts through the manipulation of physical objects, which is a primary requisite for learning at this patricular age level. Active involvement with concrete materials also fosters the development of drama skills needed for believable story dramatization. Improvisation offers the child a relatively unstructured approach to solving dramatic problems. Dialogue and action are open to the player, and there is no definite right or wrong interpretation.

STORY DRAMATIZATION

Eventually, children ask to "act out stories." We begin by dramatizing beginning, middle, and ending incidents of dramatic stories, or a "dramatic incident" the children select. Story dramatization offers the comfortable structure for action and dialogue that some students require. A more sure sense of accomplishment and a feeling of relative security within the dramatic experience is thus available to the student who particularly needs this security, order, and organization.

Example of a Beginning Drama Class

Following is a simplified breakdown of a typical drama class for a beginning group of four- and five-year-olds.

I. ORIENTATION (10 MINUTES)

II. MOVEMENT EXPLORATION (10 MINUTES)

The focus is on identifying body parts and on limb consciousness. Let the players become aware of their bodies and the interrelatedness of their limbs. Have them "shake out" each part of their body, beginning with the toes and working to the head. Ask them to lie quietly on the floor and in a quiet voice ask them to: "Send a thought-glow to each part of your body as you think about one hand and one arm, the other hand and the other arm . . . one foot and that whole leg . . . the other foot and that whole leg." To show how the body can be relaxed or tensed, guide the students to walk around the room first as wooden soldiers, and then as limp Raggedy Ann dolls. "Try now to be a human puppet shaking one hand, shaking the other, walking slowly on one leg and then the other, and then sitting down as a puppet would."

III. IMPROVISATION AND PANTOMIME (30 MINUTES)

Players are divided into groups of four. Each group is given a particular environment/situation, for example, a day at the beach, landing on the moon, going to an amusement park, or taking part in a rodeo. Each player is given a piece of fabric (cloth material) and asked to make it into "something" other than what it is, and to do something with the object that will help the audience know *who* and *where* the characters are, and *what* they are *doing* (Figure 13).

While players decide what to do within their groups, I visit each group and conduct a "group-think" (Figure 13). Because players of this age solve problems best on an individual basis, each person generally chooses to do something different. In the "group-think" I encourage each player's ideas (appropriate to the assigned environment/situation), and ask for examples of activities they might do. It has been my experience that the majority of these examples have been student-oriented with little help from myself. Some of these, for example, include: (a) at the beach—put on a swim suit, swim, splash, blow up an inner tube, lie in the sun, and find a picnic spot; (b) moon flight—dress in a space suit, walk on the moon, collect samples, and take pictures; (c) amusement park—ride the merry-go-round, eat hot dogs, drink soda pop, eat pink cotton candy, and walk through the mirrors; (d) rodeo—ride a bucking horse, do fancy roping, do steer wrestling, and be a cowboy clown.

When everyone in each group is ready, one group improvises while the other three become the audience (Figure 13).

IV. EVALUATION (REMAINING MINUTES)

Seated again in a large circle, a verbal interchange of responses is encouraged. I comment on the imaginative and positive activities that I observed, and encourage players to relate what they enjoyed most about the experience.

DRAMA IN RELIGIOUS EDUCATION

Sister Peggy O'Connell[6]

Religious educators and liturgists are again turning to drama, as did the churches in medieval times, realizing that here is a medium for teaching

[6] Sister Peggy O'Connell, Creative Drama Specialist for College of Saint Catherine, University of Minnesota, and Archdiocese of Saint Paul; master's degree from University of Hawaii, College of Education.

Figure 13 (Top) Imagining Characters in Action. (Middle) "Group-Think" Conference. (Bottom) Being an Audience (Photographs courtesy David M. Butler, Department of Fine Arts, Seattle University, Seattle, WA).

with vast potential for the fostering of spiritual understanding and attitudes. Since the beginning of humankind people have expressed their relationship to God through rituals of movement, dance, and drama. For several years my colleagues and I have explored the use of improvisational drama with children, youth, and adults in the teaching of religion and in liturgical celebrations. Our goal in education has always been to educate the whole person. We believe that drama helps this goal to be realized. Teachers and principals in our schools are enthusiastic about the inclusion of drama as part of the total education of each person: we see drama as body response and communication of the mind and the spirit reaching out to others.

My purpose here is first to clarify the assumptions on which our teaching of drama is based. Second, it is to describe representative practices intended to aid teachers in using drama to teach religion.

Assumptions for Using Drama in Religion

Three assumptions govern our teaching (which is continually in an exploratory stage):

1. Human beings use their powers of mind and body to recreate and celebrate their sharing in God's creation. Whether the human being wants to tell the good news of God's love for all people, or wishes to praise, thank, or worship Him as Lord and Giver of life, the human being is impelled to respond with his or her whole person, the body directed by mind and spirit in individual creative expression.

2. Persons being taught experience their giftedness and express it with their whole body-soul-selves in a variety of drama forms including movement, speech, acting, characterization, and playmaking.

3. The implanting of values and attitudes must be achieved through direct experience. Moralizing is useless. Drama affords direct experience corresponding to life experience.

Drama Practices in Religious Education

DRAMA MATERIALS IN TEACHING RELIGION

In drama workshops with children and teachers I begin most often with the *content* that lies within the individual. This is done by involving participants in individual expression through action and whole body movement. Often, I give scarves and streamers to players to encourage them to explore and express individual images related to a particular theme such as creation, thanksgiving, or praise. Movement exploration naturally leads individuals to express attitudes by forming statues, first individually and then in groups. In the latter, participants may form and hold a statue to convey an attitude such as forgiveness, mercy, or joy.

Then, I may challenge them to slowly change the statue (at the count of three or four) to convey a different attitude; if the statue is open, I may ask them to close it; if it is on a high level, to bring it to a low level, each time making a smooth transition that results in a different attitude. From movement, I proceed to exploration of character images, again using a variety of religious themes. I encourage participants of all ages *to say what you want to say with your whole body*. Initial experiences in movement are generally put together in prayer services.

MOVEMENT EXPLORATION IN TEACHING RELIGION

To illustrate how individual expression through movement may be related to religious themes several activities that have appealed strongly to both children and adult teachers are described below.

CREATION THEME   Players are asked to form a large circle with each person facing outward. Each player is asked to think of a movement to do with hands and arms that expresses *something in creation* for which the person is grateful. Players continue to repeat the movement until each is comfortable with it. Players then move to find a partner. Without talking, partners, in turn, share their movements with each other. After a few times of sharing individual movements, players alternate and each does the partner's movement. Each player then moves to a new partner to share the original movement. This procedure continues until all players have interacted with each other.

A variation on this theme has been done by beginning with a large circle with all persons facing the center. One person in the circle starts a hand and arm movement to express *something in creation*. All players in the circle mirror this player's movement. Following several repetitions the person who started the movement yields movement leadership to the person on the right, and that person makes a movement which everyone follows. This person then hands movement leadership to the person on his or her right, and the experience continues around the circle. If someone in the circle cannot think of a movement this person hands the movement he or she received on to the next person. For further variation this experience may be done in small group circles, or participants may be asked to use their entire bodies to express a creation idea. An experienced group may continue the creation theme by creating movement to the lines from the first chapter of "Genesis" or to James Weldon Johnson's "The Creation." In doing either of the latter, children who enjoy speaking are encouraged to work out verse choirs in small groups to accompany the movement.

EXPLORING ATTITUDES   Ask participants to divide themselves into small groups of four or five persons. Each group is asked to work out a group movement either in the form of a living statue or a moving picture to express praise, petition, thanksgiving, sorrow, or other attitudes that the children suggest. Groups may create movements for all attitudes, or for just one. When groups are ready, they may combine their group movements into a prayer service for the entire group. The teacher or one of the players may spontaneously create a prayer to combine the attitudes into a unified whole.

EXPLORING FEELINGS   Working individually at the outset, and later in small groups, children are guided to use their entire bodies to express basic emotions such as anger, fear, and joy. Activity may be stimulated by a story or an incident related by the teacher or a child. For example: "Show how the Good Samaritan felt by what he did when he came upon the wounded man on the road; show how the people felt by what they did when the lepers came near; show the fear of the apostles in the boat by what they did when the storm raged." Explore single incidents, strong in emotional content, that are within the children's realm of feelings.

IMAGINING CHARACTER AND IMPROVISING ACTIONS

Whenever children *identify* with persons or things, children readily improvise action and words (or sounds) for the imagined character.

GROWTH THEME   For Lent, spring, or the theme of individual growth, children are guided to discuss the meaning, struggle, and purpose of birth and growth. The children's ideas are encouraged. They include most often the images of a seed bursting and struggling to grow into a tree, plant, or flower; an egg cracking and hatching into a bird, chicken, duckling, or gosling; and a caterpillar growing and changing into a butterfly. In turn, each image is explored and the children improvise actions for the imagined characters. When needed, the teacher may guide the experience with comments to deepen feelings and to establish sequence. With more experienced groups, a musical background may be used. Silence is often preferable with each person experiencing the meaning of birth, struggle, and growth in an individual, meaningful, way.

PRAYER SERVICES   Older children find particular enjoyment in imagining characters and improvising action for "The Lord's Prayer." After discussing the meaning of prayer and this particular prayer, the class is organized into small groups or partners depending upon the number of persons. Each is given a single line or lines of the prayer and asked to work out movement appropriate for their particular lines. When groups are ready, the prayer is put together with each group improvising its movement while the prayer is recited. Following the initial playing, each group teaches its movement to the others so the entire group may do all the movements as the prayer is spoken the second time. Variations on the prayer theme may be used by selecting other prayers including the twenty-third, one-hundreth, and one-hundred-and-fiftieth Psalms, and the Beatitudes.

A prayer service may be used as a way to draw together a unit of study. For example, a group of younger children culminated a study of God's gifts with a dramatic prayer service. The children were guided to identify the different things in the world around them that God gives to make people happy or to provide for the wants of people and other living things. The children were asked, first, to choose the one thing that each would like to be, and, next, they were asked to plan and organize the space for "God's world" with each gift in its place. For instance, children who decided to be mountains, trees, and a lake needed to decide where each should be in the spatial relationship. When each player was in the place that seemed appropriate to the imagined environment, the teacher explained that she was going to create a prayer of thanksgiving to God from the gifts they had selected. When the players heard their gifts spoken in the prayer they were to move to give thanks to God. The teacher paused after each image to allow sufficient time for players to express individually. "Morning" from Grieg's *Peer Gynt Suite* provided an appropriate background mood. Following is the prayer created spontaneously from the children's realization of God's gifts:

Thank you for your world, O God. We are happy living in it.
You made the grass to grow on the hillsides.
You made the trees to give us fruit and to give us shade.
You made rain to help things grow and the sun to warm us and give light.
You made rocks and mountains and hills and gave homes and hiding places
*   for animals and little wild creatures.*
We thank you, O God. You are good.
You put stars in the sky and moving clouds and a lighted moon.
You made winds blow and the waters move.
You made birds that sing and bugs that creep.
You made minnows and whales—butterflies and lions.
We thank you, O God. You are good.
We, your creations, thank you, O God.
It is good to live upon your beautiful earth.

PLAYING AND PLAYMAKING IN RELIGIOUS EDUCATION

The procedure and materials a teacher uses are governed always by the needs and progress of the particular group of children and of individuals within the group. Stories selected from the New Testament may be used to introduce a theme, provide character images, and offer conflict situations for acting and interacting. Stories are used for dramatization only when the players have gained skills in concentration, body control, belief, and adaptability.

New Testament stories should be selected to show the warm, human qualities of Jesus, qualities that children can identify with. If children are to be taught that the life of Jesus is the most creative and stimulating life ever lived, then it must be made real, meaningful, and natural to them. If the life of Jesus is presented as being characterized by super-natural actions, if Jesus is so elevated that he appears not to be a real person at all, then His teachings will have little influence on the modern child. My guidance to teachers is to find the *universal qualities* in the person of Jesus, and help children to discover similar qualities in their lives and the lives of people they know. Stories for dramatization should be used in which the meaning is direct as well as symbolic. The stories of Jesus and the blind man and the Good Samaritan have resulted in effective experiences for children from the viewpoints of both meaning and dramatic form.

Many Old Testament stories offer excellent material for dramatic action and stimulation of imaginations. However, it is essential to select stories that have meaning for today's children. For example, the story of Abraham and the sacrifice of his son had justification then, but not now. The stories of Joseph and King David are meaningful to today's children, and each offers elements for exciting and fascinating dramas. Materials may be drawn, also, from other sources including stories from literature, incidents from the lives of persons the children are interested in, mean-ings of biblical verse, and character traits of people in Bible lessons brought alive by likening them to people and happenings today. A favorite story for both children and adults is Shel Silverstein's *The Giving Tree*. Working in pairs, each person responds with his or her individual interpretation by improvising action (not words) as the story is read by the teacher or a member of the group.

DRAMA WITH PHYSICALLY LIMITED CHILDREN

Jeff Brewster[7]

One of the most significant truths to be aware of is that handicapped children have many more likenesses with normal children than differ-ences. All children have feelings, bodies, minds, and needs for com-munication, affection, acceptance, learning, and success. Some needs in some children are greater than others. Some abilities and potentials are different. It is the teacher's responsibility to assist each child, enabling the child to express and to want to realize his or her own potential.

[7] Jeff Brewster, Special Education Teacher, Lowell Elementary School, Seattle Public Schools, has worked with physically and mentally handicapped children for six years; graduate of University of Washington, School of Drama.

Rationale and Objectives

My underlying reason for "doing drama," particularly drama with children, is that it is so *alive,* and so are they. Drama gives children and teacher opportunities to laugh together, to be scared together, to think together, to sing together, to be trains or cats or animated refrigerators together. In drama *we are doing together* and something good is happening inside our selves. Needs are expressed, clarified, and sometimes met. Abilities and disabilities are discovered and explored. Each child is provided with an opportunity to know a little more about self and to feel exhilarated by the creative and communal spirit. Drama becomes for us an attitude that says, "Yes! Yes! Let's *do it* again!"

The impact of a physical disability is on the total child, not just on the child's motor development. Whether the disability be cerebral palsy resulting in a muscle coordination problem, rheumatoid arthritis resulting in painful movements, or spinal cord injuries resulting in loss of sensation, the disability affects the child's total personality. The disability may be focused on one aspect of development (motor, intellectual, speech, sight) but there are ramifications in all areas. It is primarily for developmental reasons that children need drama experience. By doing drama, they become involved in impersonating, role-playing, getting outside of themselves and their problems, gaining perspective, interacting in new kinds of ways, imagining, pretending, and in believing in belief by suspending disbelief.

Stated more specifically, these are the reasons *why* I do drama often with physically disabled children:

1. To encourage the children to question possibilities.
2. To have the children experience enjoyable, positive interactions between themselves and others, particularly other children, because the world of the handicapped child is largely an adult world peopled with a conglomeration of doctors, nurses, therapists, social workers, and teachers.
3. To encourage the children's independence in terms of thinking, speaking, acting, and feeling—whatever is within the limitations and scope of each child's disability.
4. To foster the development of sensory awareness, body image, positive concept of self, speech and language, and specific concept acquisition by having the whole child experience concepts in concrete ways through drama (e.g., spatial relationships, as in "Everyone get *under* the sheet, now on *top,* now stand *beside* the door").
5. To develop thinking—problem solving, reasoning, divergent thinking—to get the children excited about the possibilities not only for what they as individuals do immediately in terms of characters in group action experiences, but for what they can do independently at later times (the potential of a sand box, of water play, of a costume box, of a puppet chest).

6. To develop the children's abilities to play with ideas—to try them out, to see how they feel, to change them, try them again and again to develop the habit of exploring, exploring, exploring.
7. To assist individuals in realizing their potential,.by causing them through successful and enjoyable, imaginative drama experiences to concentrate on what they have rather than what they have not.
8. To stimulate the children's desire to use their minds and imaginations in their leisure time, for handicapped children have many hours of leisure, and when they are adolescents and adults, most likely they will have much more; to help them establish the habit of using their time creatively while they are children—from writing poems and short plays to listening to symphonies, to collecting stamps, to looking at the stars so they can appreciate living more fully all their lives.

Drama Procedures with Physically Handicapped Children

MATERIAL FOR DRAMA

My thoughts return again and again to this sound principle: If a teacher knows something about his or her children—their individual abilities and disabilities, individual needs and wants, and if the teacher knows something about the art of drama—its dynamics, creative processes, basic elements, and ancestral roots, that is all that is essentially needed to bring the two together. The children will, in their own ways, provide you as their teacher with the "material" of drama. The content of drama lies within the children's capacities for using their eyes and ears and minds to symbolize through words and actions what is going on in their worlds of meaning. If the children supply the content, all the teacher has to do is to help them give it dramatic form. Of course, it is also wonderful if the teacher introduces children to simple and existing dramas through story and poetry selections that otherwise they would not discover. I often tell my colleagues that there is no such thing as "drama with special education children," there is only drama with children. So then the question is posed as to how a teacher does drama with children.

STIMULATING THE DRAMATIC IMAGE

An important procedure in stimulating the dramatic image is the selection of sensory stimuli that start the creative process that leads to dramatic action. Imaginations need to be sparked and focused on dramatic action. This may be done in several ways. For example, by focusing children's attention on watching spiders as they crawl and spin webs to determine "spider action" if the subject of spiders has arisen; or, watching the shape and qualities of soap bubbles after children have had fun making bubbles; or, listening to the story of Hansel and Gretel, and waiting for the children to identify dramatic images that have been triggered. Stimuli must be novel, specific, and limited to one or two concrete actions at the beginning. Limitation frees the child to sense and explore a wide range of possibilities within the focus.

If the material is powerful and charged with physical and emotional action, such as that of the goats in "The Three Billy Goats Gruff," the teacher directs the children's energies by providing problems for them to solve. For example, "The goats are eating the last grass on this side of the bridge. Now they must cross the bridge that the Troll lives under. Can you show how the first billy goat crosses the bridge? He is little and scared, walks lightly, and must think quickly to talk the Troll out of eating him. . . . Now can you show how the middle-sized billy goat and, finally, how the biggest of the three goats approaches the bridge, crosses over, and deals with the Troll?" A procedure of this kind frees the teacher from the "pulling in the reins" role, and provides children with an imaginative problem that gives physical and emotional energy release. The teacher aims primarily to get the material to work by having the children identify clear dramatic action possibilities; and by structuring these possibilities in the form of problems to meet children's particular needs.

GUIDING IN ROLE

In my view, methods to guide children to experience the forming of drama are different for each teacher. Personally, I am excited by opportunities to play a role, both for the enjoyment of the experience and for its remarkable tendency to heighten and deepen dramatic action. Most often, my role within the playing context is closely related to the circumstances of the evolving drama. In recent classroom dramas the children have chosen my roles for me and, in each instance, they have been roles of "authority." For example, I have guided the children to satisfying original dramas by playing a Police Officer, Grandfather, King, and Mother. It is from within the playing of a dramatic incident that I can help children to be ever aware of the two "wants" fundamental to dramatic action: the "want" of the character whose problem it is, and the "want" of the opposing character or characters. My chief technique in role is to guide through questions that ask the players *what* shall we do, *why*, and *how*. In role, I aim to make clear to the players the *wants* underlying the conflict of interests, and to seek their help in finding a solution to the leading character's problem.

EMPHASIS ON MAKE-BELIEVE

The reminder that drama is a *show* time, *not a show-and-tell* time, has helped my children grasp the realization that drama is making believe. It is necessary for children to understand that in forming drama they imagine and act "as if" what they do is real, but they know that it is a play. This realization has helped the children focus on communicating to their peers through the use of their bodies or of speech appropriate to particular character roles.

USING PUPPETS

Puppets are of tremendous value for encouraging language development and social interaction, for children find delight in bringing a puppet to life and in speaking for it. Puppets are effective in fostering specific conceptual developments. For example, when each child is working with a hand puppet, the children enjoy responding as the teacher suggests such actions as: "Have your puppet scratch your nose, your chin, your tummy, your hair. Have your puppet wave just one of its hands, nod its head, turn around, lie down. Have your puppet sing, dance, look out the window, and now go to sleep. Have your puppet count to ten, now count the number of tables, plants, girls, boys, guinea pigs, and the number of smiles."

Puppets have been used to provide language models by involving children in such experiences as making introductions and using the telephone. For example, the teacher using a puppet approaches several children with puppets, and says, "Good morning. My name is Ezra. What is your name? Can you tell me where you live? I'd like to know your telephone number so that I can call you later. Do you know it?"

Puppets are especially well suited for involving children in the healthy experience of "getting outside of themselves." This experience occurs when two or three puppets join together to discuss topics of interest to the puppets and children; for example, favorite foods, jokes, riddles, dreams, news, wishes, gossip, and secrets. Puppets are encouraged to plan programs to share with the other puppets and children, and occasionally a puppet announces that he and his friends are ready to "put on a show for everybody."

USING DRAMA TO TEACH ACADEMIC SKILLS

There are many ways in which drama can be used to foster the development of reading, language, and mathematical skills. An example presented here illustrates how drama succeeded in involving children in an enjoyable whole-self experience of learning letter sounds. A story was introduced as a "sound story," made from the sounds of "b" and "a" as used in the words "calf" and "applesauce." The "aa-bb" story was in the form of a symphony that needed a sound orchestra to play it. The children were asked to organize themselves to become sound instruments, either an "a" or "b" instrument. Previously, the children had enjoyed the experience of being flutes (long, thin body shapes that made pleasant *ooooo* sounds), cymbals (flat, broad shapes with arms and hands clapping together accompanying *boom* sounds), and bells (small round body shapes with light *ding* sounds). In this instance the "a" instruments solved the problem of becoming instruments, with the round body shapes working on a low space level. They were to play (make the phonetic sound of "a") whenever the teacher, cast in the role of symphony conductor, pointed an

imaginary baton to indicate whose turn it was to sound. The same procedure was used for the "b" instruments, who finally decided to become
two-people instruments; one child standing tall and straight and the
other crouching low and small and attached to the tall one's leg, roughly
forming the shape of the letter "b." The sound orchestra had great fun
playing the symphony story: aa-bb-aaa-bbb-a-b-a-b-baa-abb-baa-abb.

After the children enjoyed the sensible symphony's other nonsensical
stories, two new instruments were introduced to play the sounds of "m"
and "o" as in "overalls." A similar procedure was used, with some of the
children volunteering to become the new instruments. The children
advanced to such symphony stories as: oom-oom-baa-bo-bo-moob-boom-
bamo-bamo. At this point the symphony conductor switched from using
the baton to using large cards to guide the playing. When a large printed
"a" card was held up, the "a" instruments sounded, and the symphony
continued with cards designating "o," "m," and "b." The idea came from
the children to add new sound instruments to the orchestra until all vowel
sounds and several other consonant sounds were included in the playing.

DRAMA AND THE DEAF CHILD

Taras B. Denis[8]

In this country especially, where sound and stage have become hopelessly
mixed in the minds of the cultured majority, drama as a medium of expression for the deaf minority has been largely ignored. Likewise, drama
as a participating art has for the most part been disregarded as a source
of character growth and other personal plusses.

Even in their own schools, stage performances by deaf pupils have
been mostly relegated to robot-like participation, imitations of what
these children are not. These performances are usually sympathetic
sideshows rather than the creative outlets that true drama provides.
Indeed, if any onstage learning is actually absorbed by such children, it
is bound to be drilled repetitions of a vowel or two. What the audience
seldom sees, however, are the sacrifices on the part of the young performers in terms of time away from classroom activities. Briefly, in the
typical stage production rendered at most schools for the deaf, not the
actor but the act itself receives priority, and generally with public rela-
tions undertones lurking in the wings.

However unintentional, this utter disregard for the handicapped
youngster's ego development and his or her precious time is sad enough.
But the antispontaneity accompanying such an attitude may adversely
affect the use of drama as an educational tool, which it is, especially as

[8] Taras B. Denis, Guidance Director, New York School of the Deaf, White Plains,
NY, affiliated with the National Theatre of the Deaf, and author, director, and drama
critic of theatre productions for the deaf.

grade levels rise. As is true of every other learning process, it is the beginning that counts, and deaf children are no exception. At an early age the privilege of being their natural selves in as many drama experiences and shared presentations as possible is worth whatever mistakes and losses, including missed cues, falling scenery and, least of all, an adult's prestige.

Paradoxically, the deaf child's privilege of being his or her self before an audience is full of contradictions. For example, should a particular school be oral-only in philosophy? It is obvious that communication in sign language will then be forbidden and that the performance will therefore amount to nothing more than a public demonstration of speech. Likewise, few in an audience of peers will be able to understand what the performers are saying, and if it is not for peers, what then is the purpose of the play?

For the hearing handicapped, the stage is more a place of light, sight, and movement. For them it is where actions always speak louder than words, and direct participation loudest. Sound has little meaning except in the form of vibrations, which the deaf performers can feel feet first or through some other bodily contact. (In fact, there is definite therapeutic value in employing vibrations for these youngsters onstage since they can never get enough rhythm exercise. Incorporating a drum into the play's script is an excellent way of heightening this important sense. Other musical sounds can be added as experience warrants.)

Pantomime has its moments, but sooner or later communication must make its entrance. Language problems, especially the limited vocabulary of the young deaf child, necessitate either shortened dialogue or adaptations designed according to group or individual ability. Such allowances not only permit confidence to take hold, but in their own small way aid in the development of language concepts. Gradually, and again according to ability, the speaking parts can be lengthened—the main point being that what is "spoken" should always be understood by the performer and not just the audience.

Overprotection of deaf children early in life and even thereafter fathers a type of dependency that can cripple their schooling and adult careers later on. Since this negative influence tends to flatten their imagination, improvisational skills can be utilized to offset some of the damage. Because of drama's techniques and anytime-anywhere adaptability, its practice need not be confined to a stage environment. Actually, improvisations offer release as well as reinforcement in all kinds of learning situations. There is thus much to recommend improvisations to preprimary and elementary teachers as part of the regular schedule. within their respective classrooms.

The last scene remains for the teacher, whose objectives become evident as soon as the curtain goes up. Entertainment aside, are the values as expressed by the acting of the deaf children mostly their own and identical to those of the peer members in the audience? Does the performance reflect learning experiences or even small examples of creativity for and by its pupil players? Finally, back in the classroom, is the teacher enthusiastic that a new stage presentation will complement another important lesson in the near future?

If not, why not?

TO A YOUNG DEAF CHILD
TARAS B. DENIS[9]

Listen
with your eyes
and
to your own surprise
life
is all about:
rivers run,
insects crawl,
flowers climb,
snowflakes fall—
each
without a shout.
Yes, listen with your eyes,
And your heart will hear.

SUGGESTED ACTIVITIES FOR ADULT STUDENTS

1. With a small group of peers, discuss each of the following to arrive at conclusions to be exchanged in a larger group discussion:
   a. Hughes Mearns' quote that opens this chapter.
   b. *All* children enjoy imagining and pretending in their own particular ways.
   c. Chief requirements for adults who want to involve children in drama experiences are that they understand the developmental needs of the children and individuals within the group, and that they understand drama as an art.
   d. "One of the most significant truths to be aware of is that handicapped children have more likenesses with normal children than differences."
2. Read Sarahjane Hidell's essay. Compare the procedures she uses with children of four and five years of age with those used with children of different age levels by referring to the workshops in Chapters 1 through 4.
3. Read the essay written by Sister Peggy O'Connell. Identify specific ways in which the procedures she suggests for the use of drama in religious education are similar and different from those used in the children's workshops described in Chapters 1 through 4.
4. Read Jeff Brewster's essay and reflect on his statement: "The children will,

[9] By permission of Taras B. Denis.

in their own ways, provide you as their teacher with the 'material' of drama."
Observe a group of children at different intervals during a four-week period
to test his assumption. List or describe briefly the "material" you find.

5. Read the essay written by Taras B. Denis. Reflect on and identify ways in
which drama experience for all children contributes to his conviction,
poetically stated: *"Yes, listen with your eyes, / And your heart will hear."*

Appendixes

Appendixes

❧ A
Bibliography

This is a selective rather than comprehensive bibliography. It is arranged to closely parallel the subject matter of the chapters. The books selected for playmaking with children include plays, play anthologies, children's literature, and books to stimulate the imagination. The books in puppetry, the related arts, and special education represent a highly selected and recommended list.

PHILOSOPHY AND BACKGROUND

Baker, Paul, *Integration of Abilities: Exercises for Creative Growth,* San Antonio, TX: Trinity University Press, 1972.

Broudy, Harry S., *Enlightened Cherishing: An Essay on Aesthetic Education,* Urbana: University of Illinois Press, 1972.

Bruner, Jerome S., *The Process of Education,* Cambridge, MA: Harvard University Press, 1960.

Courtney, Richard, *Play, Drama & Thought,* London: Cassell, 1968.

Dewey, John, *Art as Experience,* New York: Putnam, 1958.

Jones, Robert Edmond, *The Dramatic Imagination,* New York: Theatre Arts Books, 1941.

Laban, Rudolf, *The Mastery of Movement,* 2nd ed., rev. by Lisa Ullmann, London: MacDonald & Evans, 1960.

Langer, Susanne K., *Philosophy in a New Key,* Cambridge, MA: Harvard University Press, 1942.

Mearns, Hughes, *Creative Power: The Education of Youth in the Creative Arts,* 2nd rev. ed., New York: Dover, 1958.

Read, Herbert, *The Grass Roots of Art,* New York: Wittenborn, 1955.

Read, Herbert, *Education Through Art,* 3rd rev. ed., London: Faber and Faber, 1958.

Schwartz, Fred. R., *Structure and Potential in Art Education,* Waltham, MA: Ginn-Blaisdell, 1970.

CHILD DEVELOPMENT: LEARNING
AND TEACHING

Ashton-Warner, Sylvia, *Teacher,* New York: Simon & Schuster, 1963.
Bee, Helen, *The Developing Child,* New York: Harper & Row, 1975.
Erikson, Erik H., *Childhood and Society,* 2nd ed., New York: Norton, 1963.
Fraiberg, Selma H., *The Magic Years,* New York: Scribner's, 1959.
Ginsburg, Herbert, and Sylvia Opper, *Piaget's Theory of Intellectual Develop-
ment: An Introduction,* Englewood Cliffs, NJ: Prentice-Hall, 1969.
Maier, Henry W., *Three Theories of Child Development,* rev. ed., New York:
Harper & Row, 1969.
Moffett, James, *A Student-Centered Language Arts Curriculum, Grades K-13:
A Handbook for Teachers,* Boston: Houghton Mifflin, 1968.
Moffett, James, *Teaching the Universe of Discourse,* Boston: Houghton Mifflin,
1968.
Mussen, Paul Henry, John J. Conger, and Jerome Kagan, *Child Development
and Personality,* 4th ed., New York: Harper & Row, 1974.
Piaget, Jean, *The Language and Thought of the Child,* New York: Harcourt
Brace Jovanovich, 1926.
Schurr, Evelyn L., *Movement Experiences for Children,* Englewood Cliffs,
NJ: Prentice-Hall, 1967.
Stone, L. Joseph, and Joseph Church, *Childhood and Adolescence: A Psy-
chology of the Growing Person,* 3rd ed., New York: Random House, 1973.
Van Riper, Charles, and Katharine G. Butler, *Speech in the Elementary
Classroom,* New York: Harper & Row, 1955.

ART OF DRAMA

Boleslavsky, Richard, *Acting: The First Six Lessons,* New York: Theatre Arts
Books, 1956.
Brockett, Oscar G., *History of the Theatre,* Boston: Allyn & Bacon, 1968.
Corson, Richard, *Stage Makeup,* 4th ed., New York: Appleton-Century-Crofts,
1967.
Dean, Alexander, and L. Carra, *Fundamentals of Play Directing,* rev. ed.,
New York: Holt, Rinehart & Winston, 1965.
Dietrich, John E., *Play Direction,* Englewood Cliffs, NJ: Prentice-Hall, 1953.
Gassner, John, *Masters of the Drama,* 3rd rev. ed., New York: Dover, 1953.
Guthrie, Tyrone, *Tyrone Guthrie on Acting,* New York: Viking, 1971.
McGaw, Charles, *Acting is Believing,* 2nd ed., New York: Holt, Rinehart &
Winston, 1966.
Moore, Sonia, *The Stanislavski System,* rev. ed., New York: Viking, 1974.
Parker, Oren W., and Harvey K. Smith, *Scene Design and Stage Lighting,*
2nd ed., New York: Holt, Rinehart & Winston, 1968.
Payne, Blanche, *History of Costume,* New York: Harper & Row, 1965.
Prisk, Berneice, *Stage Costume Handbook,* New York: Harper & Row, 1966.
Roberts, Vera Mowry, *The Nature of Theatre,* New York: Harper & Row, 1971.
Smiley, Sam, *Playwriting: The Structure of Action* (Series in Theatre and
Drama), Englewood Cliffs, NJ: Prentice-Hall, 1971.

Spolin, Viola, *Improvisation for the Theater,* Evanston, IL: Northwestern University Press, 1963.

Stanislavski, Constantin, *An Actor Prepares,* trans. Elizabeth Reynolds Hapgood, New York: Theatre Arts Books, 1948.

DRAMA WITH AND FOR CHILDREN

Burger, Isabel B., *Creative Play Acting,* 2nd ed., New York: Ronald Press, 1966.

Byers, Ruth, *Creating Theater,* San Antonio, TX: Principia Press of Trinity University, 1968.

Davis, Jed H. and Mary Jane Watkins, *Children's Theatre: Play Production for the Child Audience,* New York: Harper & Row, 1960.

Drama Theatre Framework for California Public Schools, Sacramento, CA: ed. and prepared by Bureau of Publications, California State Department of Education, 1974.

Fry, Emma Sheridan, *Educational Dramatics,* New York: Moffat, Yard, 1913.

Gallagher, Kent G., ed., *Drama Education Guidelines,* Olympia, WA: Superintendent of Public Instruction Office, 1972.

Goldberg, Moses, *Children's Theatre: A Philosophy and a Method* (Series in Theatre and Drama), Englewood Cliffs, NJ: Prentice-Hall, 1974.

Kelly, Elizabeth Y., *the magic if,* Baltimore: National Education Press, 1973.

McCaslin, Nellie, ed., *Children and Drama,* New York: McKay, 1975.

Siks, Geraldine Brain, and Hazel Brain Dunnington eds., *Children's Theatre and Creative Dramatics,* Seattle: University of Washington Press, 1961.

Slade, Peter, *An Introduction to Child Drama,* London: University of London Press, 1958.

Wagner, Jearnine and Kitty Baker, *A Place for Ideas—Our Theater,* San Antonio, TX: Principia Press of Trinity University, 1965.

Way, Brian, *Development Through Drama* (Education Today Series), London: Longman, 1967.

CREATIVE DRAMATICS

Barnfield, Gabriel, *Creative Drama in Schools,* London: Macmillan, 1968.

Cheifetz, Dan, *Theatre in My Head,* Boston: Little, Brown, 1971.

Cullum, Albert, *Push Back the Desks,* New York: Citation Press, 1967.

Heinig, Ruth Beall, and Lyda Stillwell, *Creative Dramatics for the Classroom Teacher* (Series in Theatre and Drama), Englewood Cliffs, NJ: Prentice-Hall, 1974.

McCaslin, Nellie, *Creative Dramatics in the Classroom,* 2nd ed., New York: McKay, 1974.

McIntyre, Barbara M., *Creative Drama in the Elementary School* (Language Arts for Children Series), Itasca, IL: Peacock, 1974.

Pierini, Mary Paul Frances, *Creative Dramatics: Guide for Educators,* New York: Herder and Herder, 1971.

Schwartz, Dorothy Thames, and Dorothy Aldrich, eds., *Give Them Roots and*

Wings, A Guide to Drama in the Elementary Grades, Washington, DC: American Theatre Association, 1972.

Siks, Geraldine Brain, *Creative Dramatics: An Art for Children,* New York: Harper & Row, 1958.

Stewig, John W., *Spontaneous Drama: A Language Art,* Columbus: Merrill, 1973.

Tyas, Billi, *Child Drama in Action,* Toronto: Gage Educational Publishing, 1971.

Ward, Winifred, *Playmaking with Children,* 2nd ed., New York: Appleton-Century -Crofts, 1957.

SELECTED MATERIALS FOR USE IN PLAYING AND PLAYMAKING WITH CHILDREN: STORIES, ANTHOLOGIES, INSPIRATIONS

Arbuthnot, May Hill, ed., *The Arbuthnot Anthology of Children's Literature,* 4th ed., revised by Zena Sutherland, Chicago: Scott, Foresman, 1976.

Atwood, Ann, *My Own Rhythm: An Approach to Haiku,* New York: Scribner's, 1973.

Charlip, Remy, *Arm in Arm,* New York: Parent's Magazine Press, 1969.

Charlip, Remy, *Fortunately,* New York: Scholastic, 1966.

Charlip, Remy, Mary Beth, and George Ancona, *Handtalk: An ABC of Finger Spelling and Sign Language,* New York: Parent's Magazine Press, 1974.

Dunning, Stephen, Edward Lueders, and Hugh Smith, eds., *Reflections on a Gift of Watermelon Pickle,* New York: Lothrop, Lee and Shepard, 1966.

Dunning, Stephen, Edward Lueders, and Hugh Smith, eds., *Some Haystacks Don't Even Have Any Needle,* New York: Lothrop, Lee and Shepard, 1969.

Johnson, Edna, E. R. Sickels, and F. C. Sayers, eds., *Anthology of Children's Literature,* 4th rev. ed., Boston: Houghton Mifflin, 1970.

Saroyan, William, *Papa You're Crazy,* Boston: Little, Brown, 1956.

Schenck de Regniers, Beatrice, Eva Moore, and M. M. White, comp., *Poems Children Will Sit Still For: A Selection for the Primary Grades,* New York: Citation Press, 1969.

Sendak, Maurice, *Where the Wild Things Are,* New York: Harper & Row, 1963.

Dr. Seuss (Theodore Geisel), *The Foot Book* (A Bright and Early Book), New York: Random House, 1968.

Dr. Seuss (Theodore Geisel), *My Book About Me* (Beginner Books), New York: Random House, 1969.

Dr. Seuss (Theodore Geisel), *The Sneetches and Other Stories,* New York: Random House, 1953.

Siks, Geraldine B., *Children's Literature for Dramatization: An Anthology,* New York: Harper & Row, 1964.

Silverstein, Shel, *The Giving Tree,* New York: Harper & Row, 1964.

Steichen, Edward, created by, *The Family of Man,* New York: Maco Magazine Corp., 1955.

Ward, Winifred, ed., *Stories to Dramatize,* Anchorage, KY: Children's Theatre Press, 1952.

PLAYS FOR USE IN PLAYMAKING WITH CHILDREN

Cullum, Albert, *AESOP In the Afternoon,* New York: Citation Press, 1972.
Cullum, Albert, *Greek Tears and Roman Laughter: Ten Tragedies and Five Comedies for Schools,* New York: Citation Press, 1970.
Cullum, Albert, *Shake Hands with Shakespeare: Eight Plays for Elementary Schools,* New York: Citation Press, 1968.
A Dozen Little Plays: Selected from Little Plays for Little People, New York: Scholastic, 1971.
Kraus, Joanna Halpert, *Seven Sound and Motion Stories and The Tale of Oniroku,* New York: New Plays for Children, 1971.
McCaslin, Nellie, *Tall Tales and Tall Men,* Philadelphia: Macrae Smith, 1956.
Martin, Judith, and Remy Charlip, *Jumping Beans,* New York: Scholastic, 1969.
Martin, Judith, and Remy Charlip, *The Tree Angel,* New York: Scholastic, 1968.
Paper Bag Players, *Paper Bag Plays* ("Bow Wow," "The Chicken and the Egg," "Hands Off! Don't Touch," "Ma and the Kids"), New York: Paper Bag Players, 1969.
Sanders, Sandra, *Creating Plays with Children,* New York: Citation Press, 1970.
Smith, Moyne Rice, *Plays and How to Put Them On,* New York: Walck, 1961.

RELATED ARTS

ART

Lansing, Kenneth L., *Art, Artists, and Art Education,* New York: MacGraw-Hill, 1969.
Wachowiak, Frank, and Theodore Ramsey, *Emphasis: Art,* 2nd ed., Scranton, PA: Intext, 1971.

DANCE

Diamondstein, Geraldine, *Children Dance in the Classroom,* New York: Macmillan, 1971.
Exiner, Johanna, with Phyllis Lloyd, *Teaching Creative Movement,* Boston: Plays, Inc., 1974.
Hawkins, Alma, *Creating Through Dance,* Englewood Cliffs, NJ: Prentice-Hall, 1964.

INTEGRATING ART FORMS

Cole, Natalie Robinson, *Children's Arts from Deep Down Inside,* New York: John Day, 1966.
Diamondstein, Geraldine, *Exploring the Arts with Children,* New York: Macmillan, 1974.

MUSIC

Marsh, Mary Val, *Explore and Discover Music,* New York: Macmillan, 1970.
Runkle, Aleta, and Mary Le Bow Eriksen, *Music for Today's Boys and Girls,* 2nd ed., Boston: Allyn and Bacon, 1970.

POETRY

Koch, Kenneth, *Wishes, Lies, and Dreams: Teaching Children to Write Poetry*, New York: Random House, 1970.

Livingston, Myra Cohn, *When You Are Alone, It keeps You Capone: An Approach to Creative Writing with Children*, New York: Atheneum, 1973.

PUPPETRY

Baird, Bil, *The Art of the Puppet*, New York: Macmillan, 1965.

Batchelder, Marjorie, *The Puppet Theatre Handbook*, New York: Harper & Row, 1947.

Binyon, Helen, *Puppetry Today*, New York: Watson-Guptill, 1966.

Blackham, Olive, *Shadow Puppets*, New York: Harper & Row, 1960.

McPharlin, Paul, and Marjorie Batchelder McPharlin, *The Puppet Theatre in America—A History 1524 to 1948: With Supplement Puppets in America Since 1948*, Boston: Plays, Inc., 1969.

Niculescu, Margarete, ed., *The Puppet Theatre of the Modern World*, Boston: Plays, Inc., 1967.

SPECIAL EDUCATION

Gillies, Emily, *Creative Dramatics for All Children*, Washington, DC: Association for Childhood Education International, 1973.

Jennings, Sue, *Remedial Drama: A Handbook for Teachers and Therapists*, New York: Theatre Arts Books, 1974.

Lefco, Helene, *Dance Therapy: Narrative Case Histories of Therapy Sessions with Six Patients*, Chicago: Nelson-Hall, 1974.

McIntyre, Barbara, *Informal Dramatics: A Language Arts Activity for the Special Pupil*, Pittsburgh: Stanwix House, 1963.

Shaftel, Fannie R., and George Shaftel, *Roleplaying for Social Values: Decision-making in the Social Studies*, Englewood Cliffs, NJ: Prentice-Hall, 1967.

Smilansky, Sara, *The Effects of Sociodramatic Play on Disadvantaged Pre-School Children*, New York: Wiley, 1968.

❦ B
Plays for Use in Playmaking with Children

Three nonroyalty one-act plays and a scenario are included here to correspond with the discussion of playmaking in Chapter 11. (The bibliography in Appendix A contains a list of plays and play anthologies for use with children.)

A MAGIC HOOD

An Original Play by Masayuki Sano[1]
Based on a Japanese folk tale

CHARACTERS

Stage Manager (S. Manager)	Villager Master (Master)
Lighting Man (L. Man)	Villager 1
Candy Vendor (Vendor)	Villager 2
Haru, a little girl	Tokio (Daughter)
Girl 1	Monkey
Boy 1	Bird Voice 1 (Voice 1)
Boy 2	Bird Voice 2 (Voice 2)
Boy 3	

TIME   Today, perhaps, or yesterday.

SETTING   A village square in Japan with a cherry tree in full bloom.

---

[1] Masayuki Sano, Assistant Professor of English, Nagaoka Technical College, and Visiting Lecturer of English, Nügata University, Japan; master's degree from University of Washington, School of Drama. Fulbright Exchange Student at Yale University, 1965–1966.

STAGE ENVIRONMENT   The stage has two levels. The higher one, upstage, is a road which leads to the village on the right and to the Village Master's house on the left. The road slopes down to the lower level which is the village square. In the center of the square stands a cherry tree in full bloom.

(When the curtain opens the stage is dimly lighted. Stage Manager entering down left and Lighting Man entering down right stand at opposite sides. Stage Manager signals to Lighting Man.)

S. MANAGER   Give me light, will you?

(A strong glaring light fills the stage.)

S. MANAGER   No! No! This is the light of the African desert. Give me soft light, as soft as Japanese cherry blossoms.

(Light becomes softer.)

S. MANAGER   Good! That is exactly what I want. Hello, everyone. I'm glad to see everyone of you. I am the Stage Manager, and he is the Lighting Man. Our play today is called A Magic Hood. It is written by a Japanese playwright from an ancient Japanese folk tale. This is why you see a cherry tree here. It makes a Japanese village square when you bring your imagination to the play with you.

(Moving about to show the places)

Over the cherry tree you see the western mountains. Here is the road leading to the village in this direction, and to the Village Master's house in this direction. See it right off there—next to this square.

(Signaling to the Lighting Man)

Now we need the soft light to help our imaginations. We need a dreaming light. There, that is exactly right.

(To audience)

The reason we need such a dreaming light is that, just as in our dreams, anything may easily happen in it.

(Merry rhythmic sounds of a drum are heard off right. Candy Vendor enters on the higher level from right. He wears a green hood and a brightly colored Japanese costume. He carries a tray of candies balanced on his chest by a string fastened around his neck. He carries the drum and beats it merrily as he almost dances in to his own music. Suddenly he notices the cherry tree and shows great joy.)

VENDOR   Why here stands a cherry tree in full bloom! This must be the village square I saw in my dreams.

(He chants to the music of his drum.)

Hear! Hear! Hear!
Candy Vendor's here.
First time of the year.
Come children, come.
Children, children, come.   .
Candy, candy, dandy,
Sweet drops—sour drops
Cherry, lemon, rice
To bring smiles on lips
Sweet happiness in hearts.
Hear! Hear! Hear!
Candy Vendor's here.

(He starts to repeat the chant as children hurry in from left with much merriment. Each one buys candy except Haru, who stands apart from the others. Vendor notices her.)

VENDOR   Don't you want one of my fine candies too?

HARU   But I have no coins.

VENDOR   Well, let's see! Here, you take this candy because I am very, very happy to be here in your village. I know something wonderful will happen to me today, and I want everyone to be happy.

(Vendor and children, looking at the array of candies, talk happily and softly as children point to the various kinds.)

S. MANAGER   A friendly fellow, isn't he? The Candy Vendor is the hero of this play. It isn't because he's handsome or smart. It's because he has something which the others do not have. The play will show you the difference between him and the others.

(Village Master enters from up left. Villagers enter behind him. Master is angry.)

S. MANAGER   Here they come! The fat old man is the Village Master. *You* might call him the mayor. The others are villagers who work for him.

(Master shaking fist at children and Candy Vendor)

MASTER   You rascals! You *must* not make noise near my house! Do you forget? My daughter is very sick! You selfish children! Go away from this square at once.

(Shaking finger at Vendor)

And you, Candy Vendor, why do you beat your drum and shout and sing? You drive me to madness! Go away! No stranger is allowed in my village without permission. You shall never have it!

VENDOR   (Kindly) I'm sorry, indeed, to hear that your daughter is sick.

Believe me, I did not know. I will not make any more noise, but I beg of you, please let me stay here just for today.

MASTER   No! You must leave the village this very hour.

VENDOR   Please listen Master, sir. I had a dream last night. In the dream a mountain god spoke. He said I should find a village in which a cherry tree in full bloom stands in the village square. See, it is. Here I am sure I shall meet something wonderful. Please let me stay just for today.

MASTER   I said, no. You have heard. If I see your face or hear that drum once again, you shall pay for it dearly. Go away, *all* of you!

(Noticing children, shouts to Villagers.)

Chase them away!

VENDOR   Master, please show me this favor.

MASTER   ‾You shall have this! And this!

(Master thumps Candy Vendor sharply on head. Vendor cries out. Master chases him out up right. Villagers chase the children off left.)

MASTER   I cannot have any merriment while my daughter suffers. Oh, my poor young Tokio. She is as lovely as these cherry blossoms. But I fear that she may pass away just as these flowers—beautiful but alive for so short a time.

(Master and villagers leave left. Manager, who has watched down stage right, comes to the center to speak to the audience.)

S. MANAGER   The Village Master is greatly worried about his daughter. But this play is not about her. It is about the young Candy Vendor— and this!

(He takes a red hood from his pocket.)

Do you know what this is? It looks like the same sort of hood that all the men characters wear in this play. But this is not a common hood. It is magic!

(He shows the hood to audience as a small monkey peeps from behind the cherry tree to watch. Manager doesn't notice the monkey.)

I'm not going to show you any magic with it. That is what a stage magician would do. All a Stage Manager has to do is to toss it up in the air and leave it where it falls. Just like this!

(He does so, and exits down stage right. As the hood lands on the tree, the chirping of birds is heard. The monkey comes out behind the tree and makes sure that the Manager has gone. The monkey jumps, trying to get the hood and, finally, he does. Imitating the Manager, he throws it into the air. It lands on his head. He falls on his hip in a comical way. He pulls the hood down. Suddenly the chirping of birds become much louder. Monkey is

surprised and runs about. He takes off the hood in panic. The chirpings become soft. Monkey puts the hood on again. The chirpings become louder. Monkey takes the hood off and chirpings become softer again. Now he understands the magic of the hood and enjoys it. The chirpings become a lovely, rhythmic music. Monkey moves his body to the music in a funny way. He even starts to step to the rhythm.

As he enjoys it, the children sneak back to the square from stage left. They are delighted as they watch the monkey. Although Haru objects to the idea, the children decide to catch the monkey. They make a circle around him. The bird chirpings suddenly stop. The monkey sees the children and tries to run away. Much bustling and chasing follows, until the monkey is finally caught by the children in the downstage center area. As monkey is caught he chatters and cries out and tries to free himself.)

HARU   Wait! We shouldn't treat him so cruelly. He's done nothing wrong to us.

BOY 1   What do you mean? He scratched my face!

BOY 2   He bit my finger.

BOY 3   He spit at me!

BOY 2   Let's give him a good beating!

HARU   Please stop! Listen to him crying. How can you be so cruel?

GIRL 1   Oh Haru, don't be so upset. After all, he's just a monkey.

BOY 1   Look at his dirty hood. How funny he looks. Here, monkey, let me have your hood!

(The boy and other children try to take the hood, but the monkey will not give it up.)

BOY 2   How foolish this monkey is. He thinks this hood is a treasure or something. He must have stolen it somewhere.

BOY 3   He is a *bad* monkey. He deserves a *good* beating. Come, let's tie him up.

HARU   Don't do that. Don't hurt him. Please, stop!

GIRL 1   Oh, Haru, don't worry. We're just going to have some fun. We probably won't kill him.

(The children tie the monkey up to the tree. Haru runs to the right and shouts.)

HARU   Mr. Candy Vendor! Mr. Candy Vendor! They're hurting the monkey. I think they'll kill him.

(Haru runs off, up right.)

BOY 1   Funny girl, isn't she?

BOY 2   She can't take a little joke. She's a coward, that's all.

GIRL 1   I never could understand Haru.

BOY 3   I have a good idea. Let's sell this monkey at the market to get some coins.

BOY 2   Aha! That's a good idea. I'll untie this knot. Why did you make it so tight?

GIRL 1   We'll divide the coins. How many do you think we can sell him for?

(While the children gather around the monkey to untie him, the Candy Vendor is pulled in by Haru.)

VENDOR   I hope the Village Master doesn't hear us. I don't want to get involved with him again.

(The monkey, though his arms are still tied together, escapes through the legs of the children. But the boys, seeing this, yell and catch the end of the rope. They pull the monkey back as he clings to the Candy Vendor.)

(Vendor, defending the monkey, almost forgetting himself)

VENDOR   It's not very kind, children, to treat a harmless animal like this. If you put yourself in his place, you will see how bad it is to hurt him just for fun, or even to scare him. Please let him go.

BOY 2   We're not doing it *just for fun*. We're going to sell him at the market.

VENDOR   You know what will happen to him if you sell him to a merchant? He will kill him—and make a fur out of him. Do you want to see the monkey end his life like that?

(The monkey shows fear.)

GIRL 1   No, I don't want that to happen to the monkey.

BOY 1   But we can buy a lot of things with our coins, and maybe the merchant won't kill the monkey after all.

BOY 3   We know what we want to do. You're not going to stand in our way. Come on, let's go.

(The children start pulling the monkey with a rope.)

HARU   Please! Stop hurting the monkey.

VENDOR   Wait! How much do you want for him?

BOY 3   We want 10 *ryous* (coins). Look, he has good fur.

VENDOR   That is big money. And it is all I have.

(He counts his money, looks at it, and hesitates.)

Still, if it is the only way to save the monkey, here you are. Take the money, and let the monkey go.

BOY 2   Here's your monkey. Now, let's go to the market and have some fun. Come on.

(The children run off down left except for Haru, but Girl 1 comes back and pulls Haru with her hand.)

GIRL 1   Come with me. Let's go see what the boys will buy.

VENDOR   Go along and have fun.

(Haru goes with Girl 1. Candy Vendor begins to untie the rope from the monkey.)

It was told in my dream that I would meet something wonderful today. Well, maybe it's this monkey, although I must confess I had expected something quite different. You know, little monkey, I hoped I would find a pot of gold or a bag of coins. But look—I lost all the coins I had saved. I know it is the weakness of my character but I simply cannot stand by and do *nothing* at all when you or anyone else is in trouble.

(He thinks for a moment.)

Well, now that my coins are gone, my dream seems to be going as well. But you, little monkey, are still alive. I must say it was not a bad bargain after all.

(He finishes untying the monkey.)

There you are. I'm glad you're saved. Next time be careful and don't get caught.

(The monkey bows to the Candy Vendor repeatedly. Then the monkey gives the Vendor the red hood.)

No, I don't need it. You see, I've already got one, here on my head.

(But monkey persists.)

Well, if you insist, I will accept your hood.

(He takes off his own hood and puts on the red one.)

How does it fit? It's bright, isn't it?

(Vendor likes the hood and walks around laughingly. The monkey bows to the Candy Vendor and starts to run off.)

Are you going away? Well, thank you for your hood. Take care of yourself now.

(The monkey runs off over the road.)

The monkey goes back to his home, but I have no home. Ah, well, I like this bright hood very much. I will pull it down—lest I lose it.

(When the Vendor pulls it down, suddenly he hears voices of birds talking above his head.)

VOICE 1   Do you know, my dear, Mrs. Nightingale hatched seven children yesterday?

(Vendor is surprised and looks around to see who is talking.)

VOICE 2   Seven children! My, she must be very busy. Shall we go and see if we can help her?

VENDOR   (puzzled) Who speaks? Is there someone there in the cherry branches?

(Vendor looks but finds no one.)

VOICE 1   I'm afraid she will be too busy today to even think of what *we* might do to help. Let's go tomorrow.

VENDOR   I hear voices, but I see no one. Probably I must be dreaming. I will see.

(He pinches himself to make sure.)

Ouch! Ouch! I am not asleep. What is happening?

VOICE 2   Do you know, my dear, the young monkey was caught by the village children?

(Vendor takes off hood. Now, only chirpings are heard. He is surprised and looks around.)

This is very strange. Now the birds only sing. No one talks. What a puzzle! I—I must have been mistaken.

(Vendor shakes his head and puts on the hood again. Once more he hears the human voices.)

VOICE 1   Do you know, my dear, the Master's daughter is very ill?

VENDOR   Now, I *do hear someone talking.*

VOICE 2   Yes, but how foolish the Master is. He has done nothing to help her get better.

(Vendor takes off hood. The voices stop now.)

VENDOR   I see! I think I see . . . When I put on this hood, I hear speaking voices. When I take it off, I hear only singing birds.

(Vendor thinks.)

Hmmm. Now I remember, from my ancestors, the old folk tale of the magic hood. The story says that the one who wears the magic hood can understand all the languages spoken by every kind of creature. Could this be a magic hood? If so, something wonderful has happened to me. I have a *real treasure* from the mountain god.

(Vendor puts the hood on carefully. Magic music is heard.)

How does the story go?

(Slowly, as he thinks)

Once in this very village there lived a wood cutter named Gosaku.

(He sings or chants, drumming softly.)

An evening late in mountain country
Gosaku found a fox fallen into a deep pit
And saved it out of compassion.

The fox gave him an old hood in reward;
Though it looked common and useless
It was a treasure of the mountain god.

Not knowing its power, Gosaku put on the hood.
And lo! he perfectly understood
The language spoken by robins.

"Dig under the cedar tree," said the birds.
Gosaku did as he was told
And lo! he held a pot of gold.

So, Gosaku became the richest in the village,
And a happy life he led,
Thanks to the magic hood.

Might my dream be coming true? I'll keep the hood and, perhaps, find a pot of gold. No more, the Candy Vendor's life. Perhaps, I'll soon be rich as Gosaku.

(*Music stops suddenly, and light grows brighter as before. Vendor is perplexed and wonders. He takes off the hood. Crows cry ominously.*)

What's the matter with these crows? Why do they cry?

(*Vendor puts on hood.*)

VOICE 1   Beware! Beware! A fire approaches.
VOICE 2   Trees in the western mountains have caught fire.
VOICE 1   It is a small fire, but 'tis spreading, spreading . . .
VOICE 2   Fly away quickly, over the mountains, over the village.
VOICE 1   Fly away, run away! Fire now comes this way.
VENDOR   (surprised) A fire is coming—this way?

(*Vendor runs up to the road and looks anxiously about.*)

Don't see any fire—yet. The crows say it spreads. They say it will reach this village. I had better leave here. If the Village Master sees me, he will surely punish me. He may even suspect me of starting the fire. Besides, if he learns that I have a magic hood he would probably take it away. And my dream to be rich will be *gone* too. I will never meet such fortune again. Well, I must leave at once.

(*Vendor picks up his candy tray and starts to leave.*)

Wait! But if I leave, the fire will come. It will destroy the village—and maybe even the kill the children, and perhaps the monkey also.

(Vendor thinks.)

No, no more pitying others. That is my weakness. I'll lose my fortune if I stay. I must go!

(He pulls off the red hood from his head. He tries to walk, but cannot.)

Ah, but my feet stay! I must warn others of the fire. If not, they will all suffer. I cannot build my fortune on the misfortune of others.

(He shouts, in various directions, hitting the drum loudly.)

Fire! Fire! A fire is coming. Everyone, come quickly! Fire comes this way! A fire! A fire approaches!

(First the children, then the villagers come out, wondering and confused.)

CHILDREN and VILLAGERS   What's the matter? What has happened? Fire? Where is the fire? Where?

(Haru runs up to the Candy Vendor.)

HARU   Why didn't you run away? If the master finds you, he will punish you.

VENDOR   Don't worry, little one, do not worry.

(Master enters from up left.)

MASTER   Fire? Who yells "fire"? Is that you, Candy Vendor, who shouts again?

VENDOR   Master, the western mountain has caught fire. It comes this way.

(All the people try to see the western mountain. Some stand on the road, others on the shoulders of another. But none can see a fire.)

BOY 1   I see no fire. Not a sign of fire.

VILLAGER 2   Not a bit of smoke either. There can be no fire without some smoke.

MASTER   (angrily) Candy Vendor, did I not tell you to leave this village this morning? You are still here, telling lies and causing trouble. What do you mean by this?

VENDOR   Master, I'm not lying. We can't see the fire because it is now small and crawling close to the ground. But I know it is coming this way. Listen! The crows cry warnings to each other now.

BOY 3   Crows? Crows are talking?

VILLAGER 1   How can you know what crows are saying?

MASTER   I cannot believe you. You are a liar.

(Contemptuously, he adds.)

Or, you are a crow because only a crow understands what a crow speaks.

(All except Haru laugh at the Candy Vendor.)

VENDOR   You may well wonder. But I do understand what the crows say when I put on my red hood.

BOY 2   That is the monkey's hood!

GIRL 1   You mean it is the magic hood of the folk tale?

VENDOR   Perhaps . . .

(Villagers and Master laugh.)

VENDOR   If you wish, try this hood for yourselves. Then you will understand what I say is true.

VILLAGER 1   Let me try it.

(Villager 1 puts the hood on his head. Everyone is very curious, but nothing happens.)

I can't hear anything.

VENDOR   That is strange. Perhaps you must pull it down a little more. How about this?

(Villager 1 shakes his head.)

VILLAGER 1   No—I don't hear a thing. This is just a common hood.

VILLAGER 2   Of course it is. Who can believe in the *magic* hood? It's magic only in the story. What a fool!

(Everyone laughs at the Candy Vendor.)

VENDOR   I'm sorry, but you may be hard of hearing. Let's try it on another person.

MASTER   I will try it this time. Since I am the Village Master, it must be on me that a miracle should happen in this village. I say, give me the hood!

(Master puts it on his head, pulling it down so that his whole face is covered with it. Suddenly a maddening crackling noise comes up. Master screams, pulls the hood off in panic, and throws it to the ground.)

(Master to his villagers)

MASTER   Arrest him. He is an evil spirit trying to destroy me. Hold him! Don't let him go!

(Children are frightened and retreat. Villagers come up to the Candy Vendor from both sides and hold him by the arms. Vendor tries to pull himself free.)

VENDOR   The fire comes this way. Believe me, or soon you will be caught in fire trouble.

MASTER   Who can believe what a crow like you says? Tie him up, I say, and bring him to my house.

VENDOR   Please wait! Let me try the hood once more. If it should fail again, I won't complain however hard you may punish me.

(Haru runs up to him.)

HARU   Yes, Mr. Candy Vendor, yes, you must try again.

MASTER   Very well, you shall have this last chance. Let him free.

(The villagers free him from their grip.)

(Vendor to Haru)

VENDOR   Don't worry, my child. I've come to realize this hood helps only those who will listen to others. That is why these villagers, who should see the danger first, still fail to do so.

(Vendor to villagers)

Villagers, you are blind and deaf. I thought it was my weakness to listen to others so easily, but now, seeing your deafness, I wonder if my listening is really a weakness. Perhaps it is a power. My child, I think you have the same power. So, will you try the hood this time? Perhaps you will be able to hear what the birds say.

(Villagers whisper among themselves, doubting the Vendor.)

HARU   Yes, I will see if I can hear.

(Haru puts the hood on and listens. Then, she smiles.)

HARU   I do hear the talking!

(Everyone is surprised. Vendor is relieved.)

BOY 3   How do we know she isn't just pretending to hear?

VILLAGER 1   He's right. Prove to us that you hear.

VENDOR   Ask her any question. She will answer you with the help of the birds.

VILLAGER 2   I lost my purse this morning. Do you know where it is?

(Haru listens to what the birds say. She nods.)

HARU   The birds say it is under this cherry tree.

VILLAGER 2   Under the cherry tree? Where is it?

(Everyone hurries over to look for it.)

BOY 2   Here, look! I have found a purse!

VILLAGER 2   (surprised) Hum! And this is really mine!

MASTER   If the hood has magic power, tell me what is wrong with my daughter. I have been looking everywhere for good doctors and medicine, but they have all turned out to be useless.

VENDOR   Let me try this time.

(Vendor takes the hood from Haru and puts it on.)

VENDOR   Birds, please answer my question. Is there anyone who knows the cause of the illness of Tokio, the Village Master's daughter?

VOICE 1   Ten days ago, she picked a wild flower in the mountain. The flower was poisonous.

VENDOR   I see. Can you tell me how to cure her illness?

VOICE 1   I don't know.

VOICES   (echoing) I don't know! don't know; don't know. Know. Know.

(Vendor shows he is quite worried.)

VOICE 2   I don't know either. But I hear that the young monkey says he knows.

VENDOR   Oh, it is the monkey that knows.

(Vendor to children)

Will you go and find him? Perhaps he *can* cure her illness.

VOICE 2   I will go and find him.

MASTER   What has happened? Did the birds answer you?

VENDOR   Yes, they did, Master. Your daughter became ill because she breathed the poison from a wild flower. But be assured, we hope to find a way to help her very soon.

MASTER   Very soon? How soon? Are you in your right senses?

HARU   Look! Here comes the monkey with a flower in his hand.

(The monkey enters from the road.)

VENDOR   Thank you, good monkey. Perhaps the girl who is ill is to breathe the scent from this flower? Is that right?

(The monkey chatters and nods and stays close by the Vendor.)

VENDOR   Master, let someone go at once and have your daughter take a deep breath of the flower's fragrance. It is promised to cure her illness instantly.

MASTER   If it works as you say, I will give you much. But if it fails, you shall be punished.

(He turns to Villager 1.)

Come, let us go to my daughter's bedside.

(Master and Villager exit.)

VENDOR   Be assured, his daughter will be well. But do not forget that the village will soon be afire. Someone must look to see where the fire is now approaching.

(Children and villagers run up to the road.)

BOY 2   I see a small smoke rising up near the western mountain.

VENDOR   Can't you see a fire?

BOY 3   I can't see fire but the smoke is rising.

VILLAGER 2   It smells like the smoke of burning charcoal.

VENDOR   We must do something to save the village.

(Master and Villager enter.)

MASTER   I cannot believe what I saw.

VILLAGER 1   It is wondrously strange.

VENDOR   Is your daughter cured from her illness now?

MASTER   It is a miracle. As she smelled the flower, her pale cheeks grew pink and became as beautiful as the cherry blossoms. Then she sat up and has now walked out of the bed.

(Villagers are amazed and respond with joy.)

(Vendor to Villager 1)

VENDOR   Did she recover instantly?

VILLAGER 2   I can't believe this has happened . . .

VILLAGER 1   But I have seen it with my eyes.

MASTER   (surprised) Look, here she comes to thank the Candy Vendor.

(Tokio, dressed in a beautiful kimono, enters radiantly happy and as beautiful as the cherry blossoms.)

DAUGHTER   Oh father, at last I feel very well. How wonderful it is to be healthy once again. I come to thank the young Candy Vendor. Where is he, father? I see no one with the candy tray.

MASTER   (amazed) You are my daughter, my Tokio, are you not? I cannot believe what I see. But I know I am not dreaming. Here, here is the Candy Vendor.

(Tokio nods to him graciously to express her appreciation.)

Candy Vendor, we shall be grateful to you forever. Being thankful, I must give you a purse of gold. How much do you ask for your services?

(Vendor to Daughter)

VENDOR   I am glad that you are well. Master, this is not the time to speak of gold. The fire approaches. We will perish under it if we do not prepare against it at once.

(Boy 2 calls from the road.)

BOY 2   Master! A big fire is raging under the smoke. It comes this way. It spreads with the speed of an impatient wind. It approaches our village..

VILLAGER 2   We can't stop it now. It's too late. Let's hurry away. Tell the villagers to run away, too.

(There is a great commotion. People run and call to each other about the fire. Each one shouts that the fire grows near. Vendor sizes up the situation.)

VENDOR   Stop! Don't run away. We still have time before the fire gets here. Master, we must fight the fire. We must defend the village.

MASTER   You have saved my daughter. Perhaps you know truly about the fire. We may be able to save our village. All right, tell us what to do, now that you are one of us.

VENDOR   (shouting) Very well, Master. Ring the fire bells! Call out all the men, women, and children. Cut the trees around the village. Stop the fire before it reaches here. Hurry, get shovels and axes. We must save the village.

(All cheer and hurry off. Fire bells ring. Some hurry in with shovels and axes. The stage becomes dark except for the backdrop, which is lighted red as a fire. All the characters are busy fighting against the fire. They shovel and chop, and shout, but fire and winds drown out the shouting. The dark figures cut wood, dig soil, carry water, help each other and gradually win the ground. The fire mounts; the characters are in silhouette; and gradually the fire dies down. The Stage Manager comes out from down right. A spotlight is on him.)

S. MANAGER   They did a fine deed. They put out the great raging fire. Men cut trees, women shoveled the earth, and children carried water. After their desperate struggle for a time, they, at last, succeeded in saving their village from fire.

(The stage begins to be lighted with the dreaming light. All the characters have gone.)

This is why you see the cherry tree standing in the village square as beautiful as ever. After all, everything turned out as lovely and fine as the Candy Vendor's dream.

(He walks a few steps toward the center of the stage.)

But just think! Had it not been for the magic red hood, or if it had not been for the young Candy Vendor, then what would have happened? The village might have been destroyed, and many children might have perished in the fire. Fortunately, there the *hood* was, and there *he* was. He could save the village because he was willing to listen to others, and to do things that other would not do. It was his magic power.

(Merry music is heard from off left.)

Naturally, all the villagers were thankful for him. Even the Village Master was glad when he had him for his son-in-law. You see? The Candy Vendor married the beautiful daughter. You will see how happy everyone is now. Here comes the procession to honor the happy wedding of the Candy Vendor and Tokio.

(The procession comes in, up left, with music, laughter, and merriment. They greet the Stage Manager and begin a festive dance in the square. After that, they start to go. A boy takes off the red hood from the Candy Vendor's head. The Candy Vendor has been hoisted to the shoulders of the

villagers. The boy throws the magic hood into the air. Everyone shouts as the Stage Manager catches it in the air. Everyone except the Stage Manager exits up left.)

(Stage Manager to audience)

S. MANAGER Don't worry about the Candy Vendor. He really doesn't need this hood on his head. You see he already has one in his heart.

(Showing the hood to the audience)

Here is the red hood in my hand. I fold it in this way . . .

(He folds it into a small triangle.)

and put it in my pocket. But I may leave it somewhere again. So, if you find something like this, please keep it on your head or in your heart. It is a splendid treasure to be able to understand what others are saying. It is essential for your true happiness. Now I bow to you as politely as any Japanese will do and thank you for your kind audience. *Sayounara* (Good-bye).

(He bows deeply as the curtain closes.)

NOTES TO DIRECTORS

THEME OF PLAY It is true that those who are willing to listen sometimes appear to be weak in character. But, in fact, it is only they who can save the world from destruction, because happiness depends, essentially, on true communication with or correct understanding of others.

CHARACTERS Stage Manager's purpose is to set the mood and explain the meaning of the play.

Candy Vendor is the hero, a young man with a lively and sensitive heart. At first he thinks himself a coward because he never refuses to listen to others, but later he learns it is not weakness but strength.

Village Master is the opposing character. He is not really a bad man but quite short-tempered; especially so now, because his daughter is very sick. He lacks the ability to listen.

Children are merry and eager to have fun.

Villagers work for the Master and are always obedient to him. They never try to think for themselves.

Daughter is graceful and sensitive.

STAGE SETTING The setting should be simple and suggestive rather than realistic. The only requirement is a cherry tree. Distant western mountains may be painted on the backdrop.

COSTUMES Characters may wear kimonos, kabuki aprons, or their regular clothes, but each with an identifying fabric and arranged according to the character and the character's relationships. Candy Vendor and

Children wear bright colors. Village Master and Villagers wear dark colors. Daughter wears a beautiful array of colors. Monkey wears tan or brown color.

SOUND   Bird sounds, fire sounds and bells, music for the wedding festival.

LIGHTING   Bright glaring light, dreaming light, fire light, festival lights.

PROPERTIES   A red hood, Vendor's drum, flower to cure Tokio.

THE WIND AND THE SUN

Adapted from Aesop's fable
by Geraldine B. Siks

CHARACTERS

Wind, a bold giant	Singing Bird
Sun, a merry giant	Snow-capped Mountain
Woman, a human being	Tall Tree
Faithful Dog	

TIME   In the afternoon, thousands of years ago.

SETTING   A rocky hillside in a far country. The hill slopes downward on the right to an open field and on toward a distant sea. Up from the hill stands a tall snow-capped mountain and upward on the right stands a tall tree.

STAGE ENVIRONMENT   A large open space. If available a wide ramp upstage is used to heighten the visibility of the action. Several scenic blocks are arranged upstage in an irregular, broken diagonal line to represent rocks and boulders.

(The sound of the Wind opens the action. Wind enters upstage at the top of the hill. He moves and blows down the hillside and into the field using his strength to blow against the trunk of the Tree. Not succeeding, Wind whirls around and rushing through the field he blasts again upward aiming to break the Tree's branches. Sun enters up on the hill, watches Wind, and then sits on a huge rock and laughs kindly. The stage brightens slightly with the arrival of Sun.)

SUN   Wind, Wind—my good friend. Do not destroy that mighty tree. I know your strength lies in force—in blowing and . . .

WIND   Aha! At last you admit that I am stronger than you!

SUN   No, no, no! Every day we have this same argument it seems. It gets us nowhere—but look, you destroy fields and trees. To me this is destructive and needless.

WIND   But you do not believe me. You do not believe that I am stronger than you.

SUN   I will show you how much stronger I am than you. Look! I will beam my rays *gently* on the snow-capped mountain.

(The stage brightens as the Sun sends his rays to the Mountain and the snow melts slowly before their eyes. Sun is greatly pleased.)

SUN   See! The snow melts. I cause this to happen by sending my rays gently.

WIND   Come, come! You do not understand what I mean by being *stronger*.

(Wind whirls around in anger. The stage grows darker.)

SUN   Look then, Wind.

(Sun stands on one of the boulders and beams his rays downward toward the distant sea.)

SUN   I beam my rays to the bottom of the sea yonder. Look; they light up the dark ocean floor. See I am more powerful than you—no ranting, no raging about.

(Wind grows angry and impatient. He blows downward toward the sea, then turns and blows upward using all of his strength against the tall tree. The sound of his blast is more frightening than before. The stage grows darker.)

WIND   Look! It rains on the nearby hills! Aha! I blew in the clouds.

(The sound of a sudden rain is music to Wind's ears even though the rain lasts for only a few seconds.)

WIND   Sun—look! You could never do this in a thousand years.

(The Wind stops to get his breath and rests on a large rock.)

SUN   Why should I try? If I wanted to I could burn the grasses and trees and turn them brown and destroy the fields and flowers. But that is not my way, Oh bold Brother.

(Suddenly a barking is heard. Faithful Dog enters from the top of the hill and barks at the two giants. Singing Bird flies in singing and makes a complete circle as she peers curiously at the two. The Woman enters on the hilltop. Her companions quiet down and join her. She wears a long cloak and walks with a walking stick. The Woman shakes her walking stick at the two giants as they greet her by rising and offering her a place to sit upon the rocks.)

WOMAN   Listen—listen, you foolish ones. You fight and argue day after day. You tear at the trees and the growing things. You send the creatures searching for hiding places. Why . . . why . . . why?

SUN   O Wise Woman, welcome! Welcome! This is what I tell Wind day after day and still he does not believe me.

(The Wind grows angry again.)

WIND   Strange woman, why should I listen to you or to him?

WOMAN   Quiet, now. Listen to me. Your fighting has gained nothing for thousands of years. There is a wiser way.

WIND   A wiser way, a wiser way, what is it?

WOMAN   A contest!

SUN   A contest?

WOMAN   I shall arrange a contest between you to settle your argument forever.

SUN   Fair enough, Old Wise One.

WIND   I shall not agree until I hear what the contest is.

WOMAN   Look, I wear my treasured cloak about my shoulders. See my Faithful Dog. He too wears his coat upon his shoulders—and my Singing Bird—she wears her cloak of feathers.

(Dog and Bird respond with pleasurable sounds as the Woman touches each one's cloak.)

WOMAN   To show that the contest is fair, I will not ask you to try to remove the cloaks of my companions but see how my cloak is fastened. Whichever one of you cause me to remove my cloak, *he* will be the stronger.

WIND   Fair enough! Fair enough! I will join the contest, and I shall be first. There will be no need for you to try, O Gentle Brother.

SUN   Very well, you shall have first chance.

(Woman moves out on the hill. Dog and Bird follow her. Woman waves her walking stick.)

WOMAN   Let the contest begin. Come my companions.

(Woman, Dog, and Bird start to walk slowly down the hillside. The Wind whirls and blows down the mountainside stronger than before. The sound is more fearful and the stage grows darker. Wind sends a furious blast that tears at Woman's cloak. Dog howls at the Wind and Bird chirps anxiously. The Wind tries a second time. Woman holds her cloak close against her and her companions come close to her for safekeeping. Wind tries a third time using more force than before. He tries blowing downward, then upward, then whirls to tear the cloak loose but his force causes the Woman to hold the cloak more tightly. Wind stops out of breath and rests on a huge rock.)

(Woman and her companions are relieved that the Wind has stopped. They turn and start toward the tree.)

WIND   Sun, you try. I think neither of us can win this contest.

(Sun smiles and stands on a large stone. He beams his rays gently against the Woman's cloak. The stage grows brighter.)

SUN   I shall do it my way, O Brother Wind.

(As the Sun continues to beam his rays, Bird flys and sings. Dog barks and follows after Woman. Sun laughs aloud as he watches the Woman seek the shelter of the Tree. The Tree's branches droop slightly.)

SUN   A few more gentle rays, O Wise Mother.

(The Dog and Bird find shelter under the Tree. The snow on the Mountain melts again. The Woman fans herself with her hand. The Wind is pleased.)

SUN   One more ray!

(Sun sends a sharp beam toward the Woman. The stage brightens. The Woman's cloak falls from her shoulders to the ground. She lifts her walking stick in tribute to the Sun.)

WOMAN   You win, O Sun! Your gentle way is powerful. What do you say now, Bold Wind?

(Wind speaks kindly at last.)

WIND   Sun wins *this* contest. But Wise Woman, I see you need a cool breeze. So I blow a kiss to you and your companions.

(Wind sends a gentle breeze across the valley. The sound is a pleasant whistling sound. The Woman and her companions are grateful. The Tree and the Sun are pleased.)

WOMAN   Thank you my Brothers. We on the earth have need for both of you.

(The Dog barks and the Bird sings as if in agreement. The Wind and the Sun stand on the rocks and wave in a friendly gesture to the Old Woman and her companions as they leave to go on down the hillside on their way.)

HENNY-PENNY

Adapted by Geraldine B. Siks
from the old folk tale that moves
quickly and merrily up to a point.

CHARACTERS

Henny-Penny	(Henny-P)	Goosey-Poosey	(Goosey-P)
Cocky-Locky	(Cocky-L)	Turkey-Lurkey	(Turkey-L)
Ducky-Daddles	(Ducky-D)	Foxy-Woxy	(Foxy-W)

TIME   In the fall, in late afternoon in fantasy land.

SETTING   A corn field with a large tree, a winding path, and a doorway leading to Foxy-Woxy's cave at one end of the path.

STAGE ENVIRONMENT   A large open space with appropriate scenic objects to represent the tree and the entrance to the cave.

(Henny-Penny, the most intelligent and industrious of her relatives, is in the harvested cornfield. She scratches in the earth and eats any kernels of corn she finds. Foxy-Woxy watches Henny-Penny from the doorway of the cave. All the other characters are resting or sleeping in the field or on the path with their backs to Henny-Penny, except Turkey-Lurkey who is off somewhere in the barnyard.)
(The stage is brightly lighted with sunshine.)

HENNY-P   Cluck . . . cluck! This is fine corn. The best feast I've had since last year at this time.

(Foxy-Woxy steals foxily out of his cave to watch her. A sudden wacking sound is heard. Apparently something hits Henny-Penny on the head for she jumps and clucks in surprise. Her jumping sends Foxy-Woxy back to his cave where he continues to watch. Henny-Penny looks around in surprise. She looks upward.)

Goodness, gracious me! What is it? The sky! The sky's falling in. I must go to tell the king at once.

(Henny-Penny, cackling in panic, hurries across the field and heads toward the path. Cocky-Locky hears her and runs to meet her. Foxy-Woxy steals out of his cave and hides behind the tree.)

COCKY-L   Where are you going, Henny-Penny?
HENNY-P   I'm going to tell the king that the sky's a falling!

(Cocky-Locky crows in surprise.)

COCKY-L   The sky's a falling? The sky! May I come with you?
HENNY-P   Certainly, Cocky-Locky!

(Together they go down the winding path clucking and crowing. They go in the direction opposite from the cave. Ducky-Daddles sees them. She quacks and waddles to meet them.)

DUCKY-D   Where are you going, Henny-Penny and Cocky-Locky?

HENNY-P AND COCKY-L   We're going to tell the king that the sky's a falling in!

DUCKY-D   (Alarmed) The sky—falling in? May I come with you?

HENNY-P AND COCKY-L   Why, certainly!

(The three hurry down the path cackling, crowing, and quacking. Goosey-Poosey hurries to meet them.)

GOOSEY-P   Where are you going Henny-Penny and Cocky-Locky and Ducky-Daddles?

OTHERS   We're going to tell the king that the sky's a falling in!

(Goosey-Poosey honks and hisses in panic.)

GOOSEY-P   May I come with you?

OTHERS   Why, certainly!

(The four hurry down the path. They are more excited than before. Turkey-Lurkey enters. She runs and gobbles as she meets them.)

TURKEY-L   Where are you going Henny-Penny, Cocky-Locky, Ducky-Daddles, and Goosey-Poosey?

OTHERS   We're going to tell the king that the sky's a falling in!

(Turkey-Lurkey looks at the sky, struts about gobbling in panic.)

TURKEY-L   May I come with you?

OTHERS   Why, certainly!

(The five hurry down the path. Each speaks to the others in greater alarm than before. Foxy-Woxy comes out quite casually from behind the tree and greets them in a most friendly manner.)

(The sun goes behind a cloud. The stage light very slowly becomes less bright.)

FOXY-W   Where are you going Henny-Penny, Cocky-Locky, Ducky-Daddles, Goosey-Poosey, and Turkey-Lurkey?

OTHERS   (alarmed) Oh, we're going to tell the king that the sky's a falling in!

FOXY-W   (slyly) The sky? The king? Oh this is not the way to the king, Henny-Penny, Cocky-Locky, Ducky-Daddles, Goosey-Poosey, and Turkey-Lurkey.

OTHERS   Not the way?

FOXY-W   Oh, it's a way all right, but I know the proper way—a much shorter way. Shall I show it to you?

OTHERS   Why, certainly, Foxy-Woxy!

FOXY-W   Come along! Come along with me!

(Foxy-Woxy turns and leads them down the path toward his cave. Each one follows and speaks to the others in poultry fashion about the way and about the calamity of the sky falling in. They are all in a state of panic except for Foxy-Woxy.)

(The light dims slightly.)

FOXY-W   Here we are! This is the *short way* to the king's palace. You'll get there soon if you follow me. I will go first and you come after Henny-Penny, Cocky-Locky, Ducky-Daddles, Goosey-Poosey, and Turkey-Lurkey.

OTHERS   Why, certainly! Of course! Without doubt, why not?

(Foxy-Woxy goes into his cave and turns around to wait for the others.)

FOXY-W   (slyly) Come on—this is the short way—the short way to the king's palace. Come along dear Turkey-Lurkey.

(Turkey-Lurkey is pleased to be asked first. She goes in. The others continue to talk of the calamity. A sound comes from within the cave: "Hrumph!" Turkey-Lurkey, inside the cave, calls sharply.)

TURKEY-L   Gobble! Gobb . . . .

FOXY-W   Come along, dear Goosey-Poosey.

(Goosey-Poosey is pleased to be asked next. She enters the cave. A sound comes from within the cave: "Hrumph!" Goosey-Poosey, inside the cave, calls sharply.)

GOOSEY-P   Honk! Hon . . . .

(Henny-Penny cocks her head and listens. She clucks to herself but the others are talking among themselves, and have not listened to the sounds from within the cave.)

FOXY-W   Come along, dear Ducky-Daddles!

(Ducky-Daddles is pleased to be invited to enter. He goes in. A sound comes from within the cave: "Hrumph!" Ducky-Daddles, inside the cave, calls sharply.)

DUCKY-D   Quack! Qua . . . . . .

(Henny-Penny listens, cocks her head, and moves away from the cave wondering.)

FOXY-W   Now, come along, dear Cocky-Locky!

(Cocky-Locky struts into the cave. A sound comes from within the cave: "Hrumph!" Cocky-Locky, inside the cave, calls sharply to warn Henny-Penny.)

COCKY-L   Cock-a-doodle-dooo! Run, Henny-Penny! Cock-a- . . . . .

(Henny-Penny cackles loudly and knowingly. She turns her tail and runs off home cackling triumphantly, even though she didn't get to tell the king that the sky was a falling in. Foxy-Woxy leaps into the doorway of the cave. He looks first to the left and then to the right wondering which way she went. He leaps upward with a sharp bark. Apparently he loosens a stone from the top of the cave for suddenly there is a LOUD WHACK SOUND. The sound is ten times louder than the sound that set the play in action. The sun comes out and the stage light brightens. The stone apparently hits Foxy-Woxy on the head in just the right place, for at the moment of the SOUND he is outfoxed. He falls to the ground stretched out like a fox rug. He is ended in one blow without a struggle. Henny-Penny, seeing this from a distance, cackles even more triumphantly as she returns to the cornfield. The stage is brightly lighted.)

THE WISE ONES

A scenario in one act adapted
by Geraldine B. Siks
from an old tale

CHARACTERS

Four Wise Travelers—men and women
Boatman's Daughter
Two Heralds

TIME   At dawn, long ago.

SETTING   A boatlanding on the river bank with the river running by. On
the other side of the river is a meeting place.

The Boatman's Daughter sleeps in the boat on the landing. Across the
river the Heralds sound trumpets and call loudly to announce that the
first meeting of the Wisest People in the World is about to begin. The
Boatman's Daughter, awakened by the trumpets, gets out of the boat
and is startled to hear the voices of the Wise Travelers calling for the
Boatman, her father.

The Travelers hurry down the path to the river. The Daughter greets
them and they impatiently ask where the Boatman is. She tells them that
the Boatman is her father who is so ill that she cannot disturb him. The
Travelers explain their need to cross the river. She tells them she will
take them, explaining that she can handle the boat with almost the same
skill as her father. She has learned from her father the ways of the river
and the boat.

The Travelers get into the boat and ask her to hurry to take them
across the river. She refuses to take them all at once. She asks three of
the Travelers to get out. She explains that the river is too high and that
the boat carrying so many will be too heavy. She will take them one at a
time for she must obey the law of the river.

The Travelers insist, however, that they must all go to the meeting at
once. They have traveled for many months. They must all go together.
She refuses to take them. The Oldest Traveler hands her a bag of gold
and asks to rent the boat. She looks at the gold longingly. She admits that
her father is a poor man who earns his living from the boat. She will rent
it to them but warns that they must travel with no more than two in the
boat at a time.

The Travelers, determined to get to the meeting without delay, decide to leave their luggage and risk the dangers of four going in the
boat. They will return for their luggage in the evening if she will guard
it for them. The Boatman's Daughter gets the boat ready for them. They
get into the boat with the Oldest Traveler at the oars.

The Boatman's Daughter shoves the boat off from the shore. The boat moves slowly out into the stream. Suddenly it sinks and the Travelers scream, struggle, and swim for their lives back to the shore. The Boatman's Daughter hurries into the water, swims for the oars, rights the boat, and rows it back to shore.

The Travelers, frightened by their experience, believe that one of them is drowned. The Oldest Traveler lines them up to count them. He asks each one to put out both hands. The Travelers, dripping with water and still fearful, keep brushing off their clothes; and the Oldest Traveler finds it difficult to count. He counts six hands. He is alarmed for he knows six is not the correct number. A second Traveler says he will count, and asks them to turn around so he may count their backs. He counts three. He is fearful for he knows one of them is missing. A third Traveler decides to count. She asks the others to turn around and bow their heads so she may count their heads. She counts three heads.

The fourth Traveler, alarmed that one is missing, asks the Boatman's Daughter to go in the boat and search at once for the missing Traveler.

The Boatman's Daughter, who has been watching, asks if she may count. She asks them to line up and asks each to extend his right hand. This they do. She counts four Wise Travelers. The Travelers rejoice that all are safe. They are amazed at the child's wisdom. They agree that she is wise and knows more than the laws of the river. They ask her now to take them across the river one at a time on her terms.

The Oldest Traveler gets into the boat. The Boatman's Daughter shoves the boat from shore, and rows steadily into the stream. While she takes the boat safely across, the other Travelers watch. They decide that the Boatman's Daughter must be invited to the meeting of the Wise People for she is indeed a wise young one when it comes to rivers, boats, careful counting, and using her senses.

The Heralds sound the trumpets and, calling loudly, announce that the meeting is ready to begin. The Travelers rejoice for they know they will soon be there to introduce a newcomer to the delegation of the wise.

✦ C
Audiovisual
and Instructional
Materials

"Animate Your Curriculum" (Sue Lerner, Fairwood Elementary School, 16600 148th Ave. S.E., Renton, WA 98055).

Audiovisual Instruction (Association for Educational Communications and Technology, Publications Department VLF, 1201 16th St. N.W., Washington, DC 20036).

Audiovisual Notes (Eastman Kodak Company, Motion Picture and Education Markets Division, 343 State St., Rochester, NY 14650).

Film Teacher's Idea Book (Alpha Cine Education Service, 2601 121st Ave. S.E., Bellevue, WA 98004).

FILMS FOR TEACHERS

Basic Movement Education in England (University of Michigan, Audio-Visual Education Center, Ann Arbor, MI 48103), 19 min, black and white, sound. A problem-solving approach to the study and refinement of movement through space, this film stresses individual development with examples from various age levels.

Building Children's Personality with Creative Dancing (Bailey Films, 6509 Delongpre Ave., Hollywood, CA 90028), 30 min, color, sound. The teaching skills in this film guide each child toward uniquely personal and improvised creative movement/expression.

Creative Dramatics: The First Steps (Northwestern University Film Library, P.O. Box 1665, Evanston, IL 60204), 29 min, color, sound. Demonstrates the teaching of creative dramatics to a group of fourth-grade students from their first experience into playmaking.

Dorothy Heathcote Talks to Teachers. Parts I and II (Northwestern University Film Library, P. O. Box 1665, Evanston, IL 60204), Pt. I – 30 min, Pt. II – 32 min, color, sound. Films of the lectures given by Mrs. Heathcote during a teaching series at Northwestern University, Summer 1972.

Ideas and Me (Dallas Theatre Center, 3636 Turtle Creek Blvd., Dallas, TX 75200), 17 min, color. Children are shown participating in all aspects of creative theatre. Emphasis is on personal growth and development.

"Movement in Time and Space," Segment 6 in *Discovery and Experience* (Time-Life Films, 43 W. 16th St., New York, NY 10011), 30 min, black and white, sound. Originally produced for BBC-TV, this segment deals with drama and dance as bodily movement to stimulate expression of what is within a child's mind.

People Soup (Learning Corporation of America, 711 Fifth Ave., New York, NY 10022), 14 min, color, sound. A fantasy story in which two young brothers, using household ingredients, mix magic potions which turn one into a chicken and the other into a sheep dog.

Rhinoceros (Contemporary/McGraw-Hill Films, 1221 Avenue of the Americas, New York, NY 10020), 11 min, color, sound. Ionesco's satire on mass conformity; animated.

Why Man Creates (Pyramid Films, P.O. Box 1048, Santa Monica, CA 90406), 25 min, color, sound. Film of unusual design inquiring into the wellsprings of the creative person. Combines humor, satire, and irony with serious questions.

A Windy Day (Grove Press Film Division, 53 E. 11th St., New York, NY 10003), 12 min, sound. The creative fantasy world of children is depicted.

SOURCES FOR FILMS

American Educational Films, 132 Lasky Drive, P.O. Box 5001, Beverly Hills, CA 90210.

Contemporary/McGraw-Hill Films, 1221 Avenue of the Americas, New York, NY 10020.

Index to Sixteen-Millimeter Educational Films, New York: R. R. Bowker Company, 1969.

International Film Bureau, 332 South Michigan Ave., Chicago, IL 60604.

King Screen Productions, available from Holt, Rinehart and Winston, Inc., 383 Madison Ave., New York, NY 10017.

Learning Corporation of America, 711 Fifth Ave., New York, NY 10022.

RESOURCE MATERIAL FOR TECHNICAL ASPECTS OF PLAYMAKING

Hunt, Kari, and B. W. Carlson, *Masks and Mask Makers*, New York: Abingdon Press, 1961.

Lighting Services, Inc., 77 Park Ave., New York, NY 10016.

Mole-Richardson Co. (lighting equipment), 937 N. Sycamore Ave., Hollywood, CA 91605.

Simon, Bernard, ed., and Avieah Simon, assoc. ed., *Simon's Directory of Theatrical Materials, Services & Information*, 5th ed., New York: Package Publicity Service, 1975.

SELECTED LIST OF MUSICAL RECORDINGS

Excerpts from the recordings listed here have stimulated the imagination of children in the process of plot construction.

To use music for this purpose a teacher needs to listen to several recordings to find an excerpt that is appropriate both for a particular group of children and for plot construction. From the latter point of view music needs to invite imaginative participation. It needs to be clearly structured to evoke "dramatic action" with beginning, middle, and ending action that occurs within a one- or two-minute period of time. Employing rhythm, mood, and melody, the music should begin at a comparatively high level of tension and rise in intensity as it moves toward a climax and resolution.

Adventures in Music (A New Record Library for Elementary Schools), produced by Peter Dellheim, National Symphony Orchestra, Howard Mitchell, Conductor; *Teacher's Guide* prepared by Gladys Tipton and Eleanor Tipton, RCA Corp, 1961.

Dukas, *Sorcerer's Apprentice.*

Grieg, *Peer Gynt Suite,* No. 1, "In the Hall of the Mountain King," "Morning."

Grofé, *Grand Canyon Suite,* "Cloudburst," "Sunrise."

Herbert, *Natoma,* "Dagger Dance."

Kabalevsky, *The Comedians,* "March and Comedians' Gallop," "Pantomime."

Kodaly, *Hary Janos Suite,* "Viennese Musical Clock."

Listen, Move and Dance, vol. 1, arranged and directed by Vera Gray, Electronic Sound Pictures; "A Wish and A Magic Journey," "Witches, Wizards, Alchemists, Sorcerers," "Journey Into Space," "Underwater Adventure," "Dreams."

Listen, Move and Dance, vol. 2, Electronic Sound Patterns.

Moussorgsky, *Night on Bald Mountain.*

Moussorgsky, *Pictures at an Exhibition,* "Ballet of the Unhatched Chicks," "Bydlo."

Popcorn, recorded by Hot Butter, "Popcorn" by Kingsley.

Saint-Saens, *Danse Macabre.*

Strauss, Richard, *Also Sprach Zarathustra,* opening theme.

Stravinsky, *The Firebird Suite,* "Infernal Dance of King Kastchei."

Vaughan Williams, *The Wasps,* "March Past of the Kitchen Utensils."

Wagner, *The Ring of the Nibelung,* "Magic Fire Music," "Ride of the Valkyries."

Index